COREL® PAINT SHOP PRO® X
REVEALED

Sonja Shea
with contributions by Peter Mayer

THOMSON

COURSE TECHNOLOGY

Professional ■ Technical ■ Reference

**Publisher and General Manager,
Thomson Course Technology PTR:**
Stacy L. Hiquet

Associate Director of Marketing:
Sarah O'Donnell

Manager of Editorial Services:
Heather Talbot

Marketing Manager:
Heather Hurley

Acquisitions Editor:
Megan Belanger

Marketing Coordinator:
Jordan Casey

Project Editor:
Tonya Cupp

Technical Reviewer:
Peter Mayer

PTR Editorial Services Coordinator:
Elizabeth Furbish

Interior Layout Tech:
Marian Hartsough

Cover Designer:
Steve Deschene

Cover Art:
Ron Lacey

Indexer:
Katherine Stimson

Proofreader:
Anne Smith

THOMSON

COURSE TECHNOLOGY

Professional ■ Technical ■ Reference

Thomson Course Technology PTR, a division of Thomson Course Technology 25 Thomson Place Boston, MA 02210 http://www.courseptr.com

Corel and Paint Shop Pro are registered trademarks of Corel Corporation. All other trademarks are the property of their respective owners.

Important: Thomson Course Technology PTR cannot provide software support. Please contact the appropriate software manufacturer's technical support line or Web site for assistance.

Thomson Course Technology PTR and the authors have attempted throughout this book to distinguish proprietary trademarks from descriptive terms by following the capitalization style used by the manufacturer.

Information contained in this book has been obtained by Thomson Course Technology PTR from sources believed to be reliable. However, because of the possibility of human or mechanical error by our sources, Thomson Course Technology PTR, or others, the Publisher does not guarantee the accuracy, adequacy, or completeness of any information and is not responsible for any errors or omissions or the results obtained from use of such information. Readers should be particularly aware of the fact that the Internet is an ever-changing entity. Some facts may have changed since this book went to press.

Educational facilities, companies, and organizations interested in multiple copies or licensing of this book should contact the publisher for quantity discount information. Training manuals, CD-ROMs, and portions of this book are also available individually or can be tailored for specific needs.

ISBN: 1-59863-010-5

Library of Congress Catalog Card Number: 2005927426

Printed in the United States of America

06 07 08 09 10 PH 10 9 8 7 6 5 4 3 2 1

This book is dedicated to the creators and programmers (both past and present) who have spent untold hours developing such a great program! Thanks for always looking to improve the software! And a very special thanks goes to the original creators for having the talents and creativity to make PSP such a popular software. The program has brought my friends and me countless hours of graphics pleasure. Thanks for all of your dedication and hard work. I hope you have moved on to even bigger and better things. I sincerely wish you the best of luck in all of your future endeavors. The software world needs more creative minds like yours!

Revealed Series Vision

The *Revealed* series is your guide to today's hottest multimedia applications. These comprehensive books teach the skills behind the application, showing you how to apply smart design principles to multimedia products, such as dynamic graphics, animation, Web sites, and video.

A team of design professionals, including multimedia instructors, students, authors, and editors worked together to create this series. We recognized the unique needs of the multimedia market and created a series that gives you comprehensive step-by-step instructions and offers an in-depth explanation of the "why" behind a skill, all in a clear, visually-based layout.

It was our goal to create books that speak directly to the multimedia and design community—one of the most rapidly growing computer fields today. We feel that the *Revealed* series does just that—with sophisticated content and an instructive book design.

—The *Revealed* Team

Author's Vision

The target audience for this book is the new user who is dying to get his or her feet wet and wants to learn important new information. If you have a sense of adventure, an interest in graphic arts, an interest in home photography, or just a healthy artistry, then this is the book for you! The focus is hands-on and the style is informal and to-the-point. My goal is not only to teach you, but also to encourage you to explore your creative side. I hope the book inspires you to further explore PSP and opens a whole new world of creativity for you.

Sonja Shea has been a private beta tester for Paint Shop Pro for the past five versions of the program and is currently a C-Tech Volunteer for PSP. She is also an instructor for the Leader in Virtual Studies Online Classes (LVS Online), which is a Corel Training Partner. Sonja has worked as a technical editor on a number of beginner-level Paint Shop Pro and photography titles by Thomson Course Technology PTR. Sonja is also an active moderator on several graphic filter lists. Even with her busy schedule, she finds time to help newbies become successful with their new software purchases.

Special Thanks and Acknowledgments

This book would never have been a reality if it weren't for the help of so many others! I want to thank:

- Megan B. for allowing me the opportunity to explore my writing skills.

- Tonya Cupp and Megan B. again for their patience and faith in me.

- The PSP Development Team for all of their help and support, both past and present.

- Nancy P. for allowing me to use her wonderful images.

- Julie for the use of her incredible mime images.

- Zoe and Susan for keeping me sane and standing behind me through all the crises in my life. I couldn't have gotten anywhere if it weren't for all of the guidance and help from my buddies in the LB. Most of all, thanks for your friendship.

- Peter, for your contributions and editing advice—much appreciated.

- Ann for her contributions.

- Vikki for her unconditional friendship and support. I would not have gotten this far without you!

- Sally B. for her support, guidance, friendship, and reality checks (all of those much-needed "smacks" on my head!). I sincerely thank you from the bottom of my heart.

- Ron (aka "Toonman" and "Bug Boy") for all of his encouragement, words of wisdom, and magnificent photos he used in designing the cover. All of the PSP community will feel a great loss not having you around!

- My biggest thanks, though, goes to my family—especially to my wonderful Brian! You have put up with so much while I have put in so many long hours working on this book. I was truly blessed the day we met! I know I could never have seen this through to completion without your patience, your support, and especially your love! Thanks from the bottom of my heart!

Introduction to Corel Paint Shop Pro

Welcome to *Corel Paint Shop Pro X Revealed*. This book offers creative projects, concise instructions, and complete coverage of the basic skills for Paint Shop Pro X, helping you create your own unique Paint Shop Pro works of art and edit your own photographs. You can use this book now as a learning tool for Paint Shop Pro basics, and later as a reference guide while your skills advance.

The text is organized into easy-to-read chapters with exercises that follow along with the reading. All of the bonus content is available online at the Course Web site. In these chapters, you will first learn your way around the interface, how to customize to best suit your workflow needs, and then move on to basic tools of the trade. You'll learn many skills in addition to those already mentioned: how to work with layers and filters, how to create and use selections most effectively, and how to edit some of the most common photograph problems. The online content is available for downloading at www.courseptr.com/downloads. The downloadable content contains each file you need to work along with the exercises in the book. There are also free trial offers for filters so that you can experiment and explore in Chapter 6, "Adding Effects with Filters, Plug-Ins, and Deformation." In addition, there are discounts for readers who might wish to purchase any of these filters.

What You'll Do

A "What You'll Do" figure is shown at the beginning of each lesson. This figure gives you an at-a-glance look at the skills covered in the chapter and shows you the completed data file for the lesson.

Comprehensive Conceptual Lessons

Before jumping into instructions, in-depth conceptual information tells you what skills are applied. This book provides the "how " and "why" through the use of professional examples. Also included in the text are helpful tips and sidebars to help you work more efficiently and creatively or to guide you toward more information about a skill you are currently using.

Step-by-Step Instructions

This book provides information with concise steps to help you learn Paint Shop Pro. Each set of steps guides you through a lesson where you apply Paint Shop Pro techniques to a project file. References to images and summaries of steps round out the lessons. You can download the files for the steps at the following URL: www.courseptr.com/downloads. The figures in this book are provided to help follow the steps, and the callouts help you locate onscreen icons, buttons, and commands.

Chapter Summaries

This book contains chapter summaries that highlight the key tasks and terms you learn in each chapter. You can use these summaries as a quick refresher anytime.

Patches

This book was written for version X. Since the writing of this book, several patches have been released. I recommend that you periodically check for updates to correct any problems that you might be experiencing with your program.

CONTENTS

PAINT SHOP PRO X
REVEALED

1

GETTING STARTED WITH
PAINT SHOP PRO X

1. Start Paint Shop Pro.

2. Explore the workspace, part I.

3. Explore the workspace, part II.

4. Work with files.

5. Get help within Paint Shop Pro.

GETTING STARTED WITH
PAINT SHOP PRO X

Using Paint Shop Pro

Corel Paint Shop Pro is one of the fastest growing image-editing programs on the market today. An image-editing program allows you to manipulate digital images, which are pictures in electronic form. Using Paint Shop Pro, you can create your own original artwork, make color adjustments, and retouch all your treasured family photos with just a few mouse clicks. Using a toolbar, various tools, menus, and a variety of techniques, you can modify an image by resizing, rotating, changing colors, or adding text. Paint Shop Pro also helps you create and open different file formats, which enables you to create your own unique images, import them from a digital camera or scanner, or use files from outside sources.

QUICKTIP   You can learn more about the history of Paint Shop Pro by visiting the manufacturer's web site at www.corel.com.

Considering the source

Because Paint Shop Pro offers you a multitude of options to manipulate images, you should consider the legal and moral implications of altering images from outside sources. Is it proper to alter an image just because you have the technical know-how to do so? In today's fast-paced technoworld, intellectual property (which includes ideas) has become more prominent. You should make sure you have the legal right to alter an image, especially if you plan to display it on the web or share it with friends. When using images from an outside source, know who retains the rights to that image, and if necessary, obtain written permission before you use it. Not doing so could be costly. To learn more, visit www.copyright.gov.

Differentiating Between Flavors

Basically, computer graphics come in two flavors: vector and bitmap. Bitmap (or raster) images are the most commonly used. Don't confuse these flavors with file formats. File formats, simply speaking, are the extensions after the file name that determine how the image information is stored. I cover file formats later in this chapter.

Bitmap graphics are made up of little dots called pixels. Two things determine the number of pixels in a bitmap image: resolution, or pixels per inch (ppi). An image that is 72 pixels and has a resolution of 72 ppi and 1" × 1" contains 72 rows with 72 pixels each; it's 72 × 72. Using all your fingers and toes, that comes out to 5,184. That is a lot of pixels for such a small image, not to mention that the pixels contain information about each color. Vector graphics do not contain all this extra bulk, making your image file sizes much smaller.

Another problem you will run into with bitmap images is resampling. (Take an in-depth look at resampling and resizing in Chapter 9.) Consider the 1 × 1 image: a one-inch square. If you resize it to 2 inches, you are still limited to the original pixel information, even with the multitude of resizing dialog box options, which smooth out the jaggies, a staircasing effect of lines that do not fit perfectly in the pixel grid. You just can't create information that was not there in the first place. Figure 1 shows an example of the jaggies. The inset is the original file at 100 percent. To the right is the same image zoomed at 300 percent to show the jaggies.

Vector images handle the information a little differently, giving you more sizing flexibility because it contains no pixel information whatsoever! A vector file contains a set of mathematical instructions telling the computer how to assemble the image. On the most basic level, the instructions contain the description of a path. The path is defined as the distance between two nodes, nodes being the starting and ending points of a line.

Consider a simple vector file like a stroked (outlined) rectangle in a 1-inch-square image. The file tells the computer to start at a given coordinate and draw a straight line to another point, turn right, carry on to another coordinate, and so on until the four sides are complete. Add a fill, the contents of the center of the image within the stroke, and you have your completed image. It's much more compact than the 5,184 pixels the bitmap file has to track. If you decide you want a really big rectangle, you simply change the instructions for how long the four lines should be. With no pesky pixels to get all jaggy, your image remains crisp and clear.

FIGURE 1

Example of jaggies

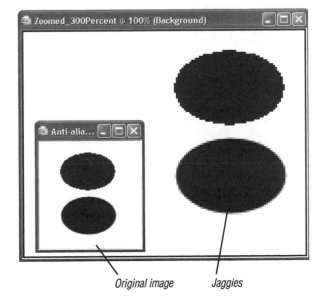

Original image   *Jaggies*

Tools You'll Use

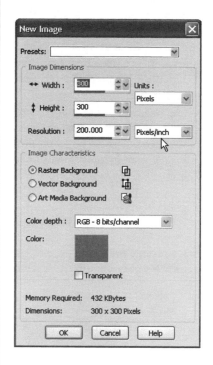

Tools You'll Use

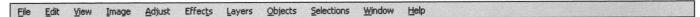

File   Edit   View   Image   Adjust   Effects   Layers   Objects   Selections   Window   Help

Learning Center

◀ ⌂ **Get Photos**

▶ **Get Photos**
Get photos from your camera, PC, or scanner.

▶ **Adjust**
Make your photos look their best.

▶ **Retouch and Restore**
Remove flaws from your photos.

▶ **Collage**
Combine multiple photos.

▶ **Text and Graphics**
Turn your photo into something more.

▶ **Effects**
Add artistic effects to your photos.

▶ **Print and Share**
Print, e-mail, and share photos.

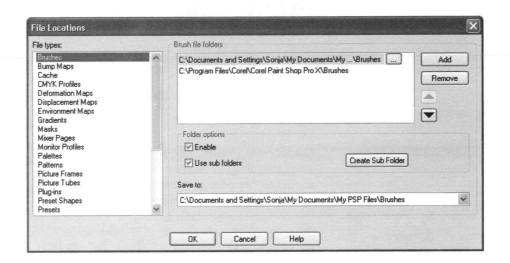

File Locations

File types:
- Brushes
- Bump Maps
- Cache
- CMYK Profiles
- Deformation Maps
- Displacement Maps
- Environment Maps
- Gradients
- Masks
- Mixer Pages
- Monitor Profiles
- Palettes
- Patterns
- Picture Frames
- Picture Tubes
- Plug-ins
- Preset Shapes
- Presets

Brush file folders

C:\Documents and Settings\Sonja\My Documents\My ...\Brushes   [...]
C:\Program Files\Corel\Corel Paint Shop Pro X\Brushes

Add
Remove
▲
▼

Folder options
☑ Enable
☑ Use sub folders

Create Sub Folder

Save to:
C:\Documents and Settings\Sonja\My Documents\My PSP Files\Brushes

OK   Cancel   Help

START PAINT
SHOP PRO

What You'll Do

 In this lesson, you'll launch Paint Shop Pro X, set up file associations and file locations, then close Paint Shop Pro X.

Starting Paint Shop Pro

You can start Paint Shop Pro with any of several methods. Most common is the shortcut that you can place on the desktop when installing the program. You can also start Paint Shop Pro from the Start menu or use a shortcut that you can place during the installation. Starting the program from the Start menu is shown in Figure 2.

Setting File Format Associations

File format associations control how Paint Shop Pro interacts with many different types of file formats, the structure of a file that defines how it is stored. For example, Paint Shop Pro's native format is .PSPImage, which retains all your editing information so that it can be accessed again. A JPEG image flattens out the

file and you lose any editing information. You can have certain file formats open automatically in Paint Shop Pro from anywhere on your computer when you double-click files with those formats. The associated files also display the Corel Paint Shop Pro icons. During installation, Paint

FIGURE 2
Starting Paint Shop Pro

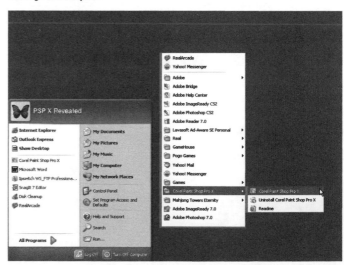

Shop Pro automatically selects five file formats to associate for you:

- **JPEG**, *Joint Photographic Experts Group*, supports 24-bit (or 16,777,216) color but no transparency.
- **BMP**, *Bitmapped*, is an image composed of pixels, which are arranged in columns and rows. Each pixel is assigned a specific color and location.
- **GIF**, *Graphics Interchange Format*, supports transparency, but only 8-bit (256) color. Commonly used in web graphics.
- **PNG**, *Portable Network Graphics*, is designed for web graphics and supports both transparency and 24-bit color.•
TIFF, *Tagged Image File Format*. Format commonly used to exchange images between different user platforms.

You can change the selections at any time by accessing the file format associations through your preferences. From the context menu, click File, Preferences, then click File Format Associations.

QUICKTIP To explore almost every possible file format in the world, visit the Programmers Resource at www.wotsit.org.

Setting File Locations

Paint Shop Pro resources include items such as **workspaces**, the customizable area in which you work. A complete list of other resources displays along the left side of the File Locations dialog box shown in Figure 3. Paint Shop Pro saves and searches for resources in several default folders on your computer. Changing **file locations** preferences alters where the program looks for and saves these resources. You can also control how it uses **plug-ins** (programs that enhance Paint Shop Pro's performance) and which web browsers preview your images. Straight out of the box, otherwise

called **default**, all new files you create are saved in the appropriate subfolder in My Documents\My PSP Files. Most default program resources are stored in the appropriate folder in Y:\Program Files\Corel\Corel Paint Shop Pro X, where *Y* indicates the specific letter on your hard drive where Paint Shop Pro is installed.

QUICKTIP You can add or remove folders in which Paint Shop Pro can store and retrieve the various resources. Removing a folder means that Paint Shop Pro no longer looks in the folder for any items. The folder, however, is not deleted from your computer.

FIGURE 3
Complete list of Paint Shop Pro X resources

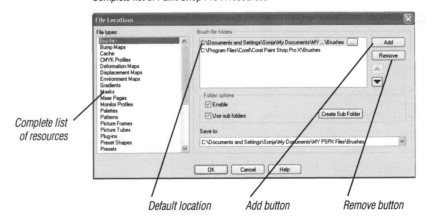

Complete list of resources

Default location   Add button   Remove button

Start Paint Shop Pro

1. Click the **Start button** ⓘ start on the taskbar. Click **All Programs**, **Corel Paint Shop Pro X**, then click **Corel Paint Shop Pro X**.

   Paint Shop Pro X starts and displays the default workspace, as shown in Figure 4.

2. Click **File** on the menu bar; click **Preferences**, then click **File Format Associations**.

   The File Format Associations dialog box opens.

3. Place a check in any file formats you want associated with Paint Shop Pro. Remove a check from any file format you don't want associated with Paint Shop Pro.

4. Click **OK** to close the File Format Associations dialog box.

5. Click **File** on the menu bar; click **Preferences**, then click **File Locations**.

   The File Locations dialog box opens.

6. Click a category in the **File Types**, then click either the **Add** or **Remove button**.

7. Click **OK** to apply the changes and to return to the Paint Shop Pro workspace.

8. Click **File**, then click **Exit**.

   Paint Shop Pro prompts you to save any open files (if necessary), then closes.

You opened Paint Shop Pro, set file associations and file locations to enable more options, then closed Paint Shop Pro.

FIGURE 4

Paint Shop Pro's default workspace

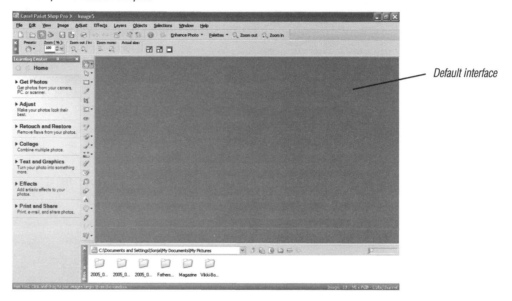

Default interface

EXPLORE THE
WORKSPACE, PART I

What You'll Do

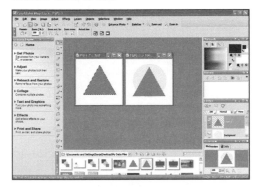

 In this lesson, you'll familiarize yourself with the various toolbars and palettes, as well as with the workspace.

Defining the Workspace

Your **workspace**, the area where you do your image editing, contains Paint Shop Pro's most common palettes and toolbars. A **palette** is a collection of tools providing quick access to selected elements. Toolbars display tools for managing files and commonly used menu functions. By default, most of the palettes and toolbars are **docked**, or stuck to the outer edges of the interface. You will learn how to dock your palettes and toolbars in Chapter 2.

Going through the Context Menu Bar

The menu bar is located at the very top of the workspace. Each command on this menu lets you perform a task. File, New opens the New Image dialog box and lets you select your **image dimensions** (size), **image characteristics** (various components, such as the type of background), **color depth** (number of colors), and **background color** (color your background layer is when the new image is opened). You can access any other menu by clicking its name or using the appropriate shortcut. For example, to access the Open dialog box, press [CTRL+O], which is displayed beside each command in the menu.

Looking at the Status Bar

At the very bottom of the Paint Shop Pro workspace is the status bar, which displays a variety of information. When you hover the mouse pointer over an icon on any toolbar, the status bar displays a description of the relevant Paint Shop Pro command. When you move the mouse pointer on the image, the status bar displays information about the active tool. On its right, the status bar shows the cursor coordinates and the image dimensions and color depth, as seen in Figure 5.

Going through the Main Tools Toolbar

The Tools toolbar, which by default is on the left side of your workspace, contains most of Paint Shop Pro's image-editing and selecting tools. Next to the Materials palette, the Tools toolbar is one of the most important features and one you'll use often. Some icons on the Tools toolbar are for single tools only and some are for groups of tools. For example, the selection tools include Selection, Magic Wand Selection, and the Freehand Lasso tools. Any icon with a group of tools has a small arrow to the right of the active tool. To open and see the hidden group, click the arrow for that tool group.

FIGURE 5

The status bar shows cursor coordinates, image dimensions, and image color depth

Hoover cursor

Cursor coordinates

Image dimensions

Color depth

Choosing Options with the Tool Options Palette

Below the standard toolbar is the **tool options palette**. Figure 6 shows the tool options bar for the Selection tool. The Selection tool options allow selection type, meaning the **shape** (rectangle, circle, ellipse, and so on), **mode** (replacing, adding to, or subtracting from the selection), Feather (does what its name implies), and Anti-alias (softens the outer edges of your

selected area to avoid jaggies). The palette's first icon allows for a custom selection, bringing up a dialog box where you enter the exact spot on the image to apply the selection size.

If you switch to the Paint Brush tool, you will notice that its options differ greatly from the Selection tool. Figure 7 shows the options for the **Brush tool**. The Brush tool reveals many more options. From the tool options palette, you can control the shape

and size of the brush tip, in addition to any other personal preferences you might have. Each tool's options are covered more in depth as you progress through this book.

QUICKTIP You can toggle the tool options palette on and off by pressing the [F4] key or by choosing View > Palettes > Tool Options.

FIGURE 6

Selection tool options differ dramatically from other tool options

Icon for Tool options

FIGURE 7

The Brush tool options contains more complex options than the Selection tool

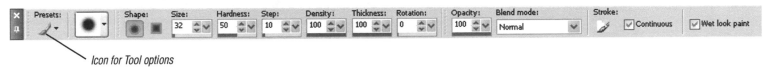

Icon for Tool options

Work with files

1. Open the **PSP1-1.PSPImage** from the drive and folder where your data files are stored.

   Your image opens and the Materials palette opens in your workspace.

2. Click **File, Save Copy As**.

   The Save Copy As dialog box opens as seen in Figure 8.

   > TIP   Saving a copy of the original PSP1-1.PSPImage file retains your original image untouched. Should you make any errors, you would be working on the copy and can always reopen the original file.

3. In the File name box, type **bluejay** for the name of your image, then click the **Save button**.

   The Save Copy As dialog box closes and returns you to your workspace.

4. Click the **Close** button in the image window.

   You opened your data file, then resaved the file with a new name, keeping the original image intact.

FIGURE 8

Rename your image using the Save As dialog box

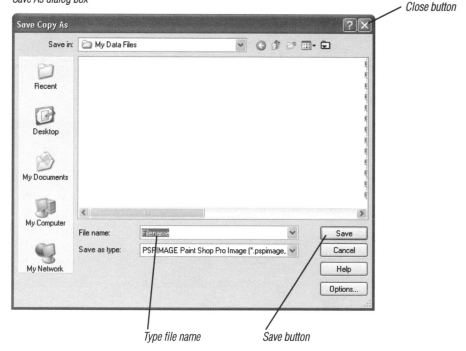

Close button

Type file name

Save button

FIGURE 9
Hidden tools are revealed

Shape Selection tool

Freehand Selection tool

Magic Wand tool

Flyout/Submenu

Selection   S
Freehand Selection
Magic Wand

bluejay @ 60% (Background)

photo by Ron Lacey

1. Open the **bluejay.PSPImage** from the drive and folder where your data files are stored, then save the file with a new name.

2. Click the **Selection tool** on the main toolbar. Hold down the mouse button until the menu reveals the hidden tools, as shown in Figure 9.

3. Click the **Magic Wand tool**.

   The icon in the main toolbar changes from the Shape Selection tool to the Magic Wand Selection tool.

4. Click the **Magic Wand tool** on the main toolbar and hold down the mouse button to reveal the hidden tools.

5. Click the **Freehand Selection tool**.

   The icon changes from the Magic Wand Selection tool to the Freehand Selection tool.

6. Close your image.

You opened your renamed image, selected the Shape Selection tool, revealed and then selected hidden tools, letting you choose the best tool for the task.

EXPLORE THE
WORKSPACE, PART II

What You'll Do

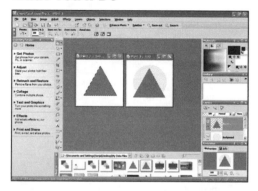

In this lesson, you'll discover how to show all toolbars and palettes. In addition, you'll copy one image onto another using your selection tools.

Assessing Other Toolbars and Palettes

Not every person will use all the powerful features within Paint Shop Pro. Some only use photo tools to touch up or repair family pictures. Graphic enthusiasts and online designers might only use a fraction of the tools available to make simple web components. To keep the workspace uncluttered and organized, Paint Shop Pro does not reveal all of the available toolbars and palettes (which are listed in Table 1). In addition to those that are displayed by default, you can create and show hidden toolbars and palettes. Figure 10 shows an opened image (maximized) in the Paint Shop Pro workspace with some of the most commonly used palettes and toolbars.

QUICKTIP You can access any hidden toolbar or palette by clicking View, Toolbars (or clicking View, Palettes), then selecting the appropriate toolbar or palette.

QUICKTIP Most toolbars and palettes are customizable so you can change them to suit your needs. This is covered more in Chapter 2.

Looking at the Layers Palette

The Layers palette provides you with a powerful tool. Layers provide flexibility so you can separate your image into different pieces for editing. This way, you can edit only portions of your image, leaving the rest untouched (for instance, changing the color of an article of clothing or removing that former significant other from a group photo). Think of layers as a clear plastic sheet on which you can paint and draw. Like pieces of plastic, layers can be stacked, one on top of another, allowing any solid color (**nontransparent** or **opaque**) to show through.

TABLE 1: Toolbars and Palettes

Toolbars		Palettes	
Browser	Includes commands for navigation and display on how the browser works. It is attached to the top of the browser when opened.	Brush Variance	Specifies the behavior of brushes and supported tools. Especially useful in combination with a graphic tablet and pen.
Effects	Includes commonly used effects such as drop shadows, bevel, hot wax, and many others.	Histogram	Displays the histogram values of an image in graph form.
Photo	Includes common photo enhancements and corrections such as red eye removal.	History	Keeps track of steps used and allows for selective undo and redo.
Script	Includes sets of instructions that produce a series of actions or effects. Buttons include run, stop, edit, record, and save.	Layers	Displays the layers in the active image. Here you can also add, delete, and move layers.
Web	Includes web function tools such as image slicing, optimizing, and seamless tiling.	Learning Center	Displays helpful tooltips and tutorials.
		Materials	The main control for selecting colors, textures, gradients, strokes, and fills.
Status	Displays text about the selected tool or menu command, as well as image information including the dimensions, color depth, and cursor position.	Mixer	Is Art-Media specific and allows for realistic paint mixing. Settings can be saved and reloaded.
		Overview	Displays a thumbnail of the image with the displayed area highlighted and allows for pan and zoom on the image.
Standard	Includes common file functions such as new, open, print, and save.	Browser	Displays folder content on your computer and lets you manage image files.
Tools	Includes basic drawing and editing tools such as zoom, straighten, crop, and brushes and selection tools.	Script Output	Records steps and appears automatically if there is an error while running scripts. Useful for troubleshooting scripts.
		Tool Options	Contains the settings for the currently selected tool.

Tool options palette

Learning Center

Context menu

Standard toolbar

FIGURE 10
Commonly used palettes

Materials palette

History palette

Layers palette

Overview palette

Tools toolbar   Browser   Status bar

photo by Ron Lacey

Getting into the Materials Palette

The Materials palette, which by default is docked on the right edge of the workspace, enables you to select the active materials and colors for drawing or painting. From here, you can set your **foreground/stroke** (an object's outline color) and **background/fill** (color that makes up the area within the stroke) colors for various tools. In addition to solid colors, you can use **gradients** (a gradual blending of colors), **textures** (fill with high and low surface spots to achieve depth), and patterns (like plaids, polka dots, and stripes). The Materials palette will become your best friend as you learn to work with Paint Shop Pro.

Paint Shop Pro's general program preferences offer a multitude of preferences for how the program operates in conjunction to your workflow. You can personalize to suit your needs by changing the way files display to changing the way units of measure display. You can access these options at any time by clicking File > Preferences > General Program Preferences, or right-clicking anywhere in your workspace, then selecting the General Program Preferences option. Be advised that not all changes will be permanent until you have closed and then restarted Paint Shop Pro.

Going Back with the History Palette

The History palette lists each command you've applied to the active image. The most recent action appears at the top of the list and you can quickly undo or redo any actions applied to the current image. In addition to its basic functions, the History palette also offers several other powerful and time-saving functions, like selective undo. This feature allows you to undo any listed action; they don't necessarily need to be undone or redone in the order presented in the History palette. By default, the palette stores up to 250 actions, but you can change this at any time through the general program preferences.

QUICKTIP The Undo controls cannot undo the following actions: renaming files; saving, opening, or closing files; emptying the Clipboard; making program-wide changes (such as changes to color settings and preferences); or using commands that do not change the pixels (such as zooming and scrolling).

QUICKTIP You can drag and drop any History palette actions onto another image.

Looking over the Overview Palette

The Overview palette is a handy way to get a broad look at your image while you are working on zoomed areas. The Overview window allows you to preview the entire image, regardless of any zoom ratio. The zoom ratio is the percentage of magnification; 100 percent is full size. You can set the zoom ratio directly in the numerical textbox or you can use the icons to zoom in or out. If you can't see the area of the image you want to edit, click and drag the rectangle around the portion you want to see in the Overview palette. Once complete (or for a spot check), you can click the Actual Size icon to see your image.

QUICKTIP You can toggle the Overview palette off and on by pressing the [F9] key.

Look at the Layers palette

1. Open **PSP1-2.PSPImage** and **PSP1-3.PSPImage** from the drive and folder where your data files are stored.

2. Click the **title bar** of PSP1-2.PSPImage to make it the active image.

   > TIP To make any image active, click its title bar, as shown in Figure 11.

3. Click the **Selection tool** on the main toolbar. Holding down the mouse button, click the **Magic Wand tool** (if necessary).

   The tool options palette changes to reflect the Selection tool options.

4. Click the **red triangle**.

   The red triangle is selected and surrounded by dashed lines as shown in Figure 11.

5. Click **Edit**, then **Copy**.

   Your image is copied to your Windows Clipboard, but you will not see anything happen. Rest assured, it is there.

6. Click the **title bar** of PSP1-3.PSPImage to make it the active image.

   The title bar darkens to show it is the active image.

7. Click **Edit**, then click **Paste as New Layer**.

   The Layers palette opens and your red triangle is pasted, as a new layer, on top of the original image as shown in Figure 11.

8. Save your image.

You copied one image file and pasted it onto another image, automatically opening the Layers palette.

FIGURE 11

One file pasted on another, revealing the Layers palette

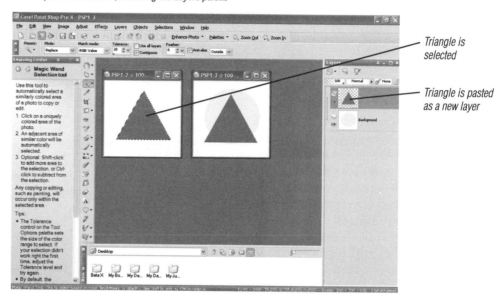

Triangle is selected

Triangle is pasted as a new layer

Identifying a selection

A selection is an area of the image surrounded by a marquee, a dashed line that surrounds the area you want to edit or move to another document. The dashed line is more commonly known as "marching ants."

FIGURE 12

Materials palette displays

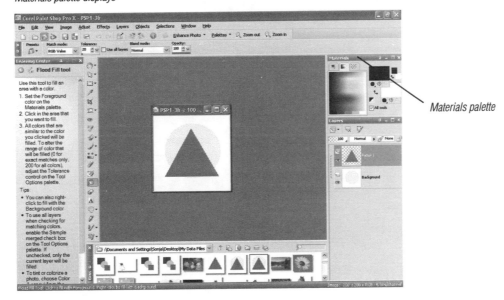

Materials palette

1. Open **PSP1-3b.PSPImage** from the drive and folder where your data files are stored.

2. Click the **Flood Fill tool** .

   The Flood Fill tool becomes active, the tool options palette changes to reflect the Flood Fill tool options, and the Materials palette appears on the right side of your workspace. See Figure 12.

3. Click the **Close button** on the Materials palette.

   The Materials palette closes and the Layers palette expands to compensate for the space.

4. Click **View**, **Palettes**, then click **Materials palette**.

   The Materials palette reappears.

You displayed the Materials palette via the Smart Interface feature. Paint Shop Pro opened the Materials palette when you chose Flood Fill. You closed the palette and re-opened, learning an additional method for revealing the Materials palette.

Go back with the History palette

1. Open **PSP1-3c.PSPImage** from the drive and folder where your data files are stored (if necessary).

2. Click **View**, **Palettes**, then click **History Palette**.

   The History palette opens with no history showing, as you can see in Figure 13.

3. In the Layers palette, click the **Delete Layers icon** 🗙.

   A dialog box asks if you are sure you want to delete this layer.

   TIP   Place a check in the box next to Don't Show This Anymore if you do not want to be asked this each time you delete a layer.

4. Click **Yes**.

   The dialog box closes. The topmost layer (blue rectangle) is removed from the image and the Layers palette. The History palette displays the delete layer action, as shown in Figure 14.

   You revealed the empty History palette, then deleted a layer to add your very first action.

FIGURE 13

History palette displays with no history

History palette

FIGURE 14

History palette actions

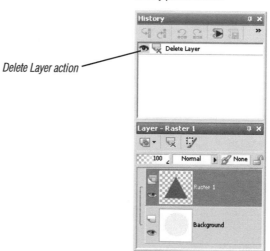

Delete Layer action

FIGURE 15

Numerical entry box reflects change

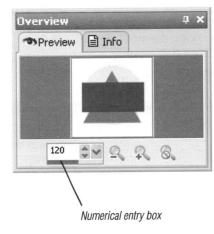

Numerical entry box

FIGURE 16

Visible areas not shaded

Look over the Overview palette and zoom

1. Open **PSP1-3c.PSPImage** from the drive and folder where your data files are stored.

2. Click **View**, **Palettes**, then click **Overview Palette**.

   The Overview palette displays.

   TIP Because your palettes are docked, you might find that your them scrunched together after opening the Overview palette. Use the History palette's shortcut key [F3] to toggle it on and off as necessary. This allows your Overview palette to expand, giving you a better look at the overall image.

3. Click the **Zoom In icon** .

   The image in your workspace zooms in 20 percent. The number in the textbox changes from 100 to 120, as shown in Figure 15.

4. Enter **300** in the textbox.

   The image in your workspace zooms in 300 percent. The Overview palette preview area changes. The area that is not displayed in the workspace is now shaded. The unshaded rectangular area reflects what is showing in your workspace, like you see in Figure 16.

   QUICKTIP To quickly return the image to normal size, click the Normal Size icon at the far right.

5. Click and drag the **rectangle** around the image to see another area of your image.

You used the Overview palette to view your image, which enabled you to zoom in for careful edits and zoom back out to see how your edits look.

WORK WITH
FILES

What You'll Do

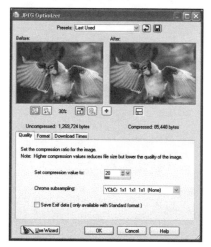

 In this lesson, you'll take a closer look at opening and saving files in different formats.

Opening and Saving an Image File

Paint Shop Pro enables you to edit existing images or create your own images from scratch. You can retouch a photograph, modify clip art, and draw or paint an image by hand and much more. In many programs, starting the software creates a new, blank file. Not in Paint Shop Pro. You have to open an existing file or create a new, blank file to work from. Often, the project you are working on determines the techniques you use for opening and saving files. For instance, you might want to work on a copy of a file while leaving the original intact. You can open the file, then immediately save it with a different name or in a different file format.

QUICKTIP Autosave automatically saves your files at specific intervals. This can prevent you from losing work (or much work) if your computer shuts down unexpectedly.

Creating and Saving a New, Blank Canvas

In most instances, you already have an image you want to edit when you open Paint Shop Pro. What if you want to display those images on your web site? Or create a unique logo to put on all your images (so when you become famous everyone you know can say, "We knew you when…")? Before you create a new image, determine how and for what you will be using the image. For example, will you display the image on the web, send it as an email attachment, or print it? How you use the image helps determine its size, resolution, and color depth, all of which contribute to the file size.

Choosing color depth

Color depth is the number of bits of color information available for each pixel. Each pixel's color information is stored in a certain number of computer bits, from 1 to 48 bits. In a 1-bit image, a pixel can only display one of two colors, black or white. In a 48-bit image, each pixel can display one of 16 million colors. 48-bit offers the best quality (with a few exceptions, such as solid blocks of one color; those save best in GIF format) because they contain the most color options. However, they also require more memory to edit and store. Select the color depth, which can be any of the following:

- RGB: 8 bits/channel
- RGB: 16 bits/channel
- Grey: 8 bits/channel
- Grey: 16 bits/channel
- Index: 2-color palette
- Index: 16-color palette
- Index: 256-color palette

Saving a New File

The PSPImage file format supports image-creation features. I recommend saving and editing your images as PSPImage files. You can then save a copy to a standard file format if you want to e-mail the image, use it on a web page, or send it to a printing service. You can save a PSPImage file with or without **compression**, a process that reduces the file size by compressing data. Both Paint Shop Pro compression methods are **lossless**, reducing the file size without losing any image information. Keep in mind that uncompressed files require more

disk space. You might want to use compression if you have a small hard drive.

Paint Shop Pro uses the following compression methods:

- Run length encoding (RLE) is fast, compressing most multilayered images to about 75 percent of their original size. It works well with images that contain large areas of the same color.
- LZ77 compression is slower. However, it compresses most images to smaller sizes than RLE. It works well with photorealistic images.

QUICKTIP When you save a new image, you select its location, name, and file format. When you save an image and then edit it, the title bar displays an asterisk after the filename to indicate that the file has been changed but not saved. To keep the changes, save lots and save often. The asterisk disappears once the edited image has been saved.

If you do not change the format of the file you open and want to preserve the original image, you must use the Save As command, rather than the Save command, to avoid overwriting the original file.

Using Exporters to Save Files

The majority of web browsers recognize GIF and JPEG images, so these two formats are used most often for saving web images. Newer browser versions also recognize the more recent PNG format, and many also support Windows Wireless Bitmap (WBMP) and iMode formats, which are popular for wireless devices.

When saving files for the web, size is one of the most important factors and it affects users trying to access your site. A larger file takes more time to download. You should use a file format that reduces the image size while keeping the quality as high as possible. The export wizards and optimizers help you do this. The export wizards guide you through step by step, whereas the optimizers leave you with most of the control. Choose from the file formats shown in Table 2 when saving images for use on the web.

TABLE 2: File Formats for the Web

Format	Supports	Lossy or Lossless
GIF	Compresses line art and images with similar colors or solid blocks of one color. Supports 8-bit (256) color. Has two versions: 89a, which supports transparency and information, and 87a, which cannot. Both are recognized by most browsers.	Lossless
JPEG	Compresses photographic images efficiently. It supports 24-bit (16.7 million) color and most web browsers recognize it.	Lossy
PNG	Supports up to 24-bit (16.7 million) color. It is not as widely used as JPEG nor is it recognized by all browsers.	Lossless
WBMP	Used in conjunction with many wireless devices (such as Bluetooth and PDAs). The images are displayed in black and white only.	Lossless
TIFF	Standard file format for printing and sharing images between programs. The file size is less suitable for e-mailing and the web.	Lossless
RAW	Different formats: RAW graphic (preferred by 3D graphic artists) and camera RAW (unaltered digital camera data). Either is suitable for storage, but not for email or the web.	Lossless

Opening a File Using the Browser

You can view, open, sort, and organize your files from within the Paint Shop Pro Browser. When you open the Browser, you see image thumbnails (small preview), the path to the file folder you are viewing on your hard drive, and icons to help customize and best utilize the Browser.

QUICKTIP Paint Shop Pro can show you a thumbnail of your image in the Open dialog box. Place a mark in the checkbox beside Show Preview to turn this option on. Remove the mark to turn it off.

FIGURE 17

*New Image dialog box offers
many options*

1. Click **File**, then click **New**.

The New Image dialog box opens, as shown in Figure 17.

2. Enter the width and height dimensions for your new canvas.

When setting dimensions, use pixels, inches, or centimeters for your measurements. Pixels are most common, but if printing often, consider inches.

3. Set your resolution.

If you are displaying the images only on your computer monitor, 96 is fine. For printing, go between 150–200, depending on your printer's dpi (dots per inch) setting.

4. Click the Color Depth **down arrow**, then choose **RGB - 8 bits/channel** (if necessary).

5. Click the color swatch to bring up the Color Picker; select **white**, then click **OK**.

The Color Picker dialog box closes and returns you to the New Image dialog box.

6. Click **OK** to open the blank canvas, then click **File, Save As**.

The Save As dialog box opens, as shown in Figure 18.

7. Browse to the folder on your hard drive where you store your data files, then click the **Options button** in the dialog box.

8. Choose the **PSP 9 compatible option** (if necessary), then click **OK**.

The Options dialog box closes and returns you to the Save As dialog box.

9. Type in the name for your file, then click **Save**.

The dialog box closes and your image is now saved to the appropriate folder on your hard drive, in the format you specified.

You created a new, custom, blank canvas with a white background, then saved the file with a unique name in a previous version format so you can share the file with a friend who uses Paint Shop Pro 9.

QUICKTIP You can create a new, blank canvas by using shortcut keys, too. Press Ctrl+N to bring up the New Image dialog box.

FIGURE 18

Save for different versions of Paint Shop Pro

FIGURE 19

JPEG Optimizer reduces file size

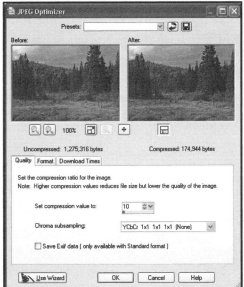

photo by Ron Lacey

1. Open the **PSP1-4.PSPImage file** from the drive and folder where your data files are stored.

2. Click **File**, **Export**, then click **JPEG Optimizer**.

   The JPEG Optimizer dialog box opens. The "before" compression is shown on the left pane and the "after" is on the right pane, as shown in Figure 19.

3. Set the compression value to **10**, chroma subsampling to **None**.

4. Click the **Format tab**.

5. Click the **Standard option**, then click the **Download Times tab**.

   The Standard option shows the picture line by line as it loads, whereas Progressive shows pixel by pixel. The Download Times tab shows the time it will take the image to load on various speeds, including 56k dial-up. Times can vary depending on hour of the day, and so on.

6. Click **OK**.

   The Optimizer closes and the Save As dialog box prompts for a name.

7. Type a name for your file and save to the folder in which your data files are stored.

8. Click the **Close button** to close the image.

You opened an existing data file, used the JPEG Optimizer to manually control the image's compression, how it views, and how it downloads on a web page.

Open a file using the Browser

1. Click the **Browser palette icon** [icon] to open the Browser, if necessary.

   The Browser opens.

2. Click the **Folders List icon** to view a hierarchical tree of your hard drive files.

   The Browser displays the tree, as shown in Figure 20.

3. Navigate through the hierarchical tree to where you keep your data files.

4. Double-click the **PSP1-4.PSPImage file**.

   The data file opens in the Paint Shop Pro workspace.

You used the Browser to easily, visually locate an image, then opened the image in Paint Shop Pro.

FIGURE 20

Browser displays hierarchical tree of files

GET HELP WITHIN
PAINT SHOP PRO

What You'll Do

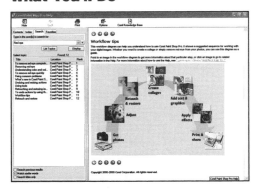

 In this lesson, you'll display and use various forms of help offered in Paint Shop Pro X.

Viewing Help Files

Paint Shop Pro X offers a wealth of features—so many that it can take some time to master them all. When you can't remember what command or tool you need or require instruction using a specific feature, you can consult the Help files included with the program or use the new and improved
Learning Center.

When you start the Help system (by choosing Help > Help Topics), it will open to the Workflow Tips page shown in Figure 21. The diagram on the right side is designed to help you understand how to use Paint Shop Pro. A suggested sequence for working with digital images is displayed. Whether you want to print your images or simply remove red eye, you can use the diagram as a guide. Place your cursor over any of the workflow suggestions to see a more detailed listing of what each task includes. Click to view the complete list of options available for that task.

The Help topics dialog box provides three ways to find information. You can choose a topic from the Contents page, use the Index page to search for a specific topic, or use the Search page to look for specific words and phrases. You can also print topics from Help. The Favorites tab lets you create a list of Help topics for easy access at anytime. Not sure what you are looking for exactly? Browse through all of the Help files by clicking the Contents tab (if necessary), clicking the (+) beside the book (category) icon, then clicking the topic you want to see.

Accessing Help from Tooltips

Paint Shop Pro includes mouseover tooltips to help you identify the purpose of a toolbar button or control in a palette or dialog box. To display a tooltip, move the mouse pointer over the item in question and hold it in place until the tooltip appears—no need to click.

FIGURE 21

Workflow Tips page

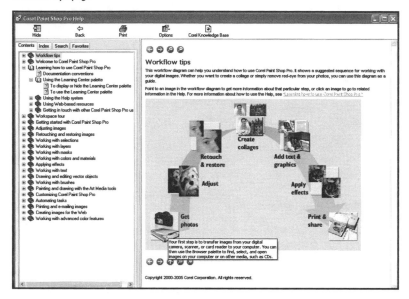

FIGURE 22

Learning Center home page

Using the Learning Center

The Learning Center palette contains helpful information about tasks, commands, and tools to help first-time users, as well as people with more experience, work more efficiently. The Learning Center palette's home page provides workflow based on a task. The tutoring begins by teaching you how to get your photos into Paint Shop Pro. From there, the workflow takes you through tasks such as adjusting and retouching photos, creating collages, adding text, graphics, and effects, and printing and sharing.

QUICKTIP   If you still can't find the topic you are searching for, check the Corel Knowledge Base online, directly from Paint Shop Pro, by clicking Help > Online Support and Resources.

Each task displayed on the home page has its own topics with instructions describing its related tools or commands. You can click a topic to access a related tool or command. This way, you can learn about a task as you perform it. Get more information about a task by clicking the More Details link (when applicable), in the Learning Center palette, under the displayed Quick Guide. Figure 22 shows another view of the Learning Center.

FIGURE 23

The tree displays Help topics relevent to a category

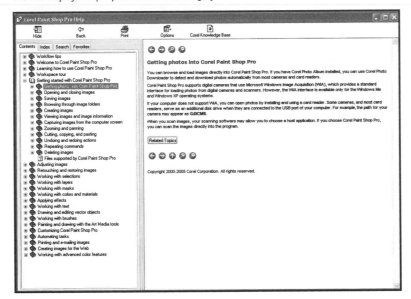

1. Click **Help**, then click **Help Topics**.

   The Paint Shop Pro Help window opens.

2. Click the **Contents tab**.

   The list of Help categories displays in the left pane of the Paint Shop Pro Help window.

3. Click the **+** next to the Getting Started with Paint Shop Pro book icon.

   The tree will expand to display the list of topics in that category, as shown in Figure 23.

4. Click **Files Supported by Corel Paint Shop Pro**.

   A list of file formats supported by Paint Shop Pro displays in the right pane.

You used the Help files to easily locate a list of file formats that can be opened with Paint Shop Pro.

Search for a Help Topic

1. Click **Help**, then click **Help Topics** (if necessary).

   The Paint Shop Pro Help window opens.

2. Click the **Search tab**.

   The Search panel appears.

3. Type **red eye** in the Type In the Keyword to Find text box.

4. Click the **List Topics button**.

   The Help topics associated with the words "red eye" display in the Select topic pane of the window, as shown in Figure 24.

5. Click **To Remove Red Eye Quickly** in the Select Topic pane, then click the **Display button**.

   The right pane changes with help instructions for quickly removing red eye via the Red Eye tool, as shown in Figure 24.

6. Click the **Close button** to close Help.

   TIP To see other Help files related to removing red eye, click the Related Topics button.

You used the Search feature in help files to quickly find an effective method for removing the red eye from your treasured photograph.

FIGURE 24

Search for red eye in the Help topics

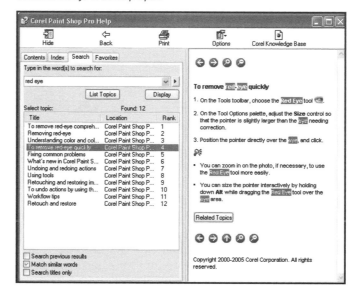

FIGURE 25

Tooltip for Browser Palette icon

photo by Ron Lacey

1. Open **PSP1-4.PSPImage** from the drive and folder where your data files are stored.

2. Place your cursor over the **Browser palette icon** in the standard toolbar, but do not click.

The Tooltip displays, showing you that it is the icon for the Browser. See Figure 25.

3. Click the **Browser palette icon**.

The Browser palette closes.

You used Tooltips to locate the Browser icon so that you can temporarily turn off the Browser palette, freeing up more workspace.

Use the Learning Center

1. Click **View**, **Palettes**, then click **Learning Center** (if necessary).

   The Learning Center displays.

2. Click **Get Photos**.

   The Learning Center displays various methods for getting your images into Paint Shop Pro, as shown in Figure 26.

3. Click **Browse: (Find photos on your PC.)**.

   The Browser that you closed in the previous exercise re-displays.

4. Navigate to the drive and folder where your image is stored, then drag the image into the workspace.

   TIP   To quickly return to the Learning Center's main menu, click the house icon.

You used the Learning Center to learn just one of the methods for getting your images into Paint Shop Pro.

Lending a helping hand

With the new, groundbreaking Learning Center you are never without a helping hand. Not only is it easy to start making your pictures look professional, but help is always just a click away! You are free to experiment with every tool in Paint Shop Pro. Selecting any tool with the Learning Center open displays a short description of how to use it.

FIGURE 26

Learning Center Browser palette

CHAPTER SUMMARY

In this chapter you started Paint Shop Pro, exploring and making changes to its workspace to get the most efficient use out of the program. You learned about different file formats and which formats best suit your workflow needs, depending on the project you are working on. You know that saving a copy of your image and working on that copy is the best technique for avoiding losing the original image. You have also taken a look at different methods of getting help and used the Learning Center as a guide to getting your images into Paint Shop Pro.

What You Have Learned:

- How to start Paint Shop Pro.
- How to work with various file types.
- How to show/hide palettes and toolbars.
- How to open and save files.
- How to use Help within Paint Shop Pro.
- How to use the Learning Center for help.

Key Terms

bitmap   Graphics made up of small colored dots called pixels.

color depth   Limit of colors allowed in an image.

compression   A process that reduces size.

digital image   A picture in its electronic form.

file formats   The structure of a file; defines how it is stored.

jaggies   A staircasing effect.

node   The starting and ending points of a line.

path   The distance between two nodes.

stroke   Outline.

vector   Graphics made up of mathematical instructions.

workspace   Customizable area where you work.

2

CONTROLLING MENUS,
TOOLBARS, AND PALETTES

1. Customize the workspace.

2. Investigate the Materials palette.

3. Use basic drawing and painting tools.

4. Explore color- and pattern-replacing tools.

2 CONTROLLING MENUS,
TOOLBARS, AND PALETTES

Examining Your Workspace

The first goodies you're likely to use in Paint Shop Pro are drawing and painting tools such as Paint Brush, Airbrush, Preset Shape, Eraser, Pen, and Text. For now, you look at the basic functions of some of these tools, but only in raster mode and raster layers. In Chapter 5, "Construct Vector Graphics and Text," you take a closer look at vector drawing.

You gain access to these tools in the toolbars, which are nested in your workspace. The **workspace** is made up of all the program's palettes and toolbars, as well as any images that you might have open. By setting up your workspace to appear and respond in ways that best suit your workflow needs, you'll not only have a better experience but will likely find yourself working faster and more efficiently, saving valuable time for those more important things, like shopping, playing, sleeping . . . and did I mention shopping?

Checking Out Tools

You may find that the way you like to arrange your workspace while editing photographs is completely different than when you are creating web elements—you'll use certain tools doing one thing, another group of tools doing another. Fortunately, Paint Shop Pro allows you to create and save any number of workspace arrangements, letting you load the workspace that best applies at the time.

While **toolbars** display the program's main tools, the **palettes** display each tool's options. For example, the Materials palette displays the available color choices for the selected tool. Like toolbars, palettes can be docked or dragged to any location over the workspace. Paint Shop Pro includes 11 different palettes to assist you when working, but only three are displayed by default: the tool options palette, Browser palette, and Learning Center.

Tools You'll Use

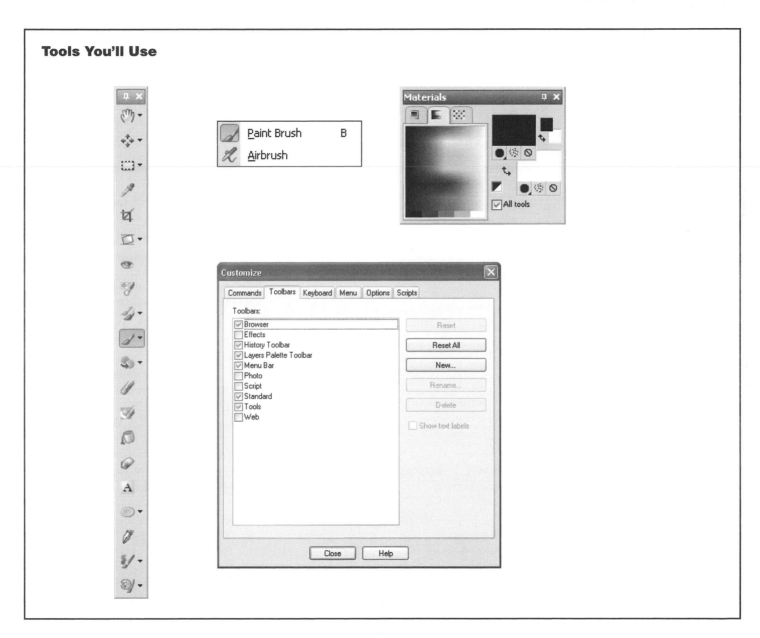

CUSTOMIZE THE WORKSPACE

What You'll Do

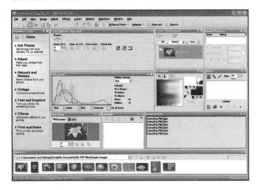

 In this lesson, you'll customize the user interface by undocking your palettes and toolbars.

Enabling and Disabling Autohide

Click the pushpin on any palette to roll it up when you're not using it. This feature, called Autohide, is in use if the palette is docked and the pushpin button is pointing down. The palette remains fully displayed in its docked position when you move the cursor away from it. If the pushpin is pointing left, the palette slides into the area on the side of the Paint Shop Pro window. With Autohide enabled, the palette just rolls up inside itself. You then see a tab with the palette name, as shown in Figure 1.

QUICKTIP To display the palette again, run your cursor over the tab.

The pushpin functionality changes somewhat if the palette is **floating** (sitting freely in the workspace), instead of **docked** (stuck to one edge of the screen). If the pushpin is pointing down, the palette remains completely open when you move your cursor away from it. If the pushpin is pointing to the left, the palette rolls up and only the palette top is visible. That portion is called the title bar.

Adding to, Removing from, or Customizing a Toolbar

Whether touching up those precious photos or building your happening web site, specific tools and commands will be more popular with you while doing one project versus another. You can easily add, remove, or create your own toolbar using the Customize dialog box. The dialog box also allows you to show or hide any of the toolbars and palettes currently not in use, leaving you as much free space to work in as possible. Don't need a specific command for your current project? You can remove (or add, for that matter) any icon from the toolbars and even have Paint Shop Pro save open images. Either drag the icons onto the toolbar or, if not wanted, drag them from the toolbar back into the Customize dialog box.

Creating Keyboard Combinations

The Customize dialog box enables you to assign key combinations to a function (like pasting, for example). A combination is a pair (or more) of keys that you type instead of clicking an icon or a menu command. Setting up a key combo for some of your most commonly used actions will save you valuable time and energy. For instance, the one I use a lot is Shift+D, the combo for duplicating the image. Any time I open an image for editing, I duplicate it and save a copy in case of any mistakes or unforeseen mishaps. To change an existing combination or to create a new one, go to the Keyboard tab in the Customize dialog box.

QUICKTIP To find out which commands are associated with which key, access the Keyboard Map available under Help.

Docking and Undocking

Paint Shop Pro preferences define the behavior of various features, and control the program overall. Through the program preferences, you can decide which palettes and toolbars you want to dock; just add or remove a mark in the appropriate checkbox. While some options in the program preferences can affect your workspace appearance, you primarily customize the workspace through the Customization dialog box. You may find that you prefer the ability to move some of your palettes around the interface as you work, thus leaving the palette or toolbar floating.

You can also tell Paint Shop Pro if you want to see the Learning Center each time you start the program. I recommend turning off this feature to allow for maximum workspace. You can always access the Learning Center again via the [F10] key or the context menu at the top of your screen.

FIGURE 1
Learning Center and Browser with Autohide enabled

Learning Center and Browser palettes with Autohide enabled

Materials and Layers palettes with Autohide not enabled

Enable and disable Autohide

1. Click **View**, **Palettes**, then click **Learning Center** (if necessary).

   The Learning Center displays.

2. Click the **pushpin icon**  so it points to the left.

3. Move the cursor away from the palette.

   The palette rolls up into itself, leaving only the title bar, which is shown in Figure 2.

4. Click the **pushpin icon**  again to restore it to a fully open position.

   The Learning Center palette reopens, as shown in Figure 3.

You enabled Autohide for the Learning Center, freeing up more space to work in, then disabled Autohide.

> TIP   You can quickly enable or disable docking features on any palette by entering your program preferences, selecting docking options, then adding or removing a mark in the appropriate checkbox.

> TIP   You can use the shortcut key **[F10]** to quickly show or hide the Learning Center.

FIGURE 2

Autohide in the on position

Autohide in on position

FIGURE 3

Autohide in the off position: Learning Center reopens

Learning Center with Autohide enabled

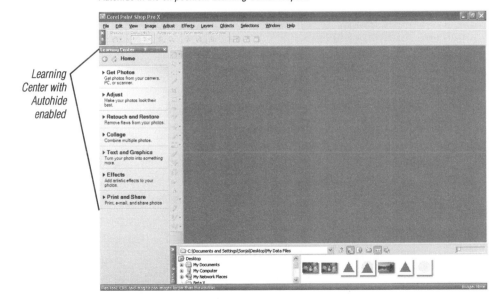

FIGURE 4
Drag and drop any icon onto toolbar

Drag and drop selected icon onto toolbar

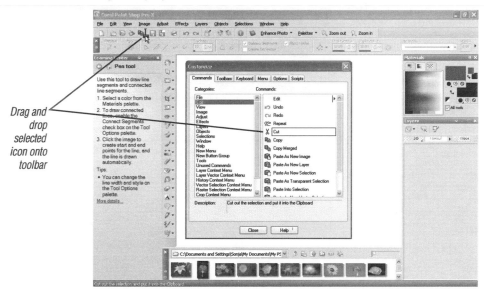

1. Right-click any empty space, then choose **Customize**.

2. Click a **category** from the left pane.

3. Click a **command** from the right pane.

4. Drag any **icon** onto the existing toolbar, then release the mouse.

The cursor changes to reflect your action, as shown in Figure 4.

> TIP To remove an unused command from the toolbar, do the reverse: Drag the icon back into the Commands pane.

You added a new command icon to an existing toolbar using the Customize dialog box, so now you have access to only the tools you need.

Customize a toolbar

1. Right-click any empty space, then choose **Customize**.

2. Click the **Toolbars tab**, then click **New**.

   A small naming dialog box opens.

3. Type a **unique name** for your toolbar, then click **OK**.

   Your new toolbar is listed in the Customize dialog box and a new, empty toolbar appears. Mine is shown in Figure 5.

   TIP   Drag the new toolbar over to the side of the Customize dialog box to avoid it jumping behind the dialog box when you select additional tabs or options.

4. Click the **Commands tab**.

5. Click **Edit** (if necessary).

6. Click **Edit**; click the **Paste as New Image icon** 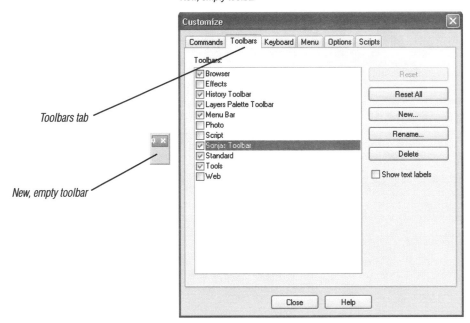, then drag it onto the new toolbar.

   The new command icon appears in the toolbar.

7. Repeat these steps to add command icons.

8. Click **Close**.

You created a new toolbar suited to meet your workflow needs and to help you work more efficiently.

FIGURE 5
New, empty toolbar

Toolbars tab

New, empty toolbar

FIGURE 6

Keys show as unassigned in the box until you click the Assign button

Assigned keys

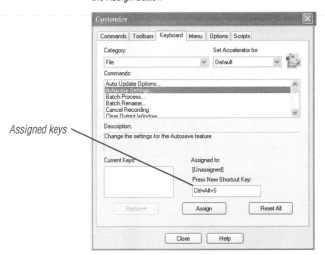

1. Right-click any empty space, then choose **Customize**.

   The Customize dialog box appears.

2. Click the **Keyboard tab**.

3. In the Category drop-down list, choose the **menu** associated with the command, script, or tool whose keyboard combination you want to modify.

   I assigned a combo to the Autosave settings.

4. Press the **keys** you want to assign to the command.

   The keystrokes appear in the Press New Shortcut Key box as you press them on the keyboard. They show up as unassigned in the Customize dialog box, shown in Figure 6.

5. Click **Assign**.

   The newly assigned keys move over to the Current Keys box, showing as the current setting.

6. Click **Close** to close the Customize dialog box.

You created a new key combination so you can access and change settings with a few simple keystrokes.

Undock a palette

1. Click **File**, **Preferences**, then click **General Program Preferences**.

   The Paint Shop Pro Preferences dialog box displays.

2. Click **Palettes**.

   The options for the selected topic display on the right.

3. In Allow docking of, mark the checkbox next to any palettes you want to be able to dock.

4. In Allow docking of, remove the mark from any checkbox next to any palettes you do not want to dock.

   The palettes with marks beside them are now dockable around the outer edges of your interface. See Figure 7.

5. Click **OK**.

   The Paint Shop Pro Preferences dialog box closes.

Through general program preferences, you selected palettes to dock and deselected those you didn't want docked, allowing for maximum workflow.

FIGURE 7

Palettes checked in this list will be made dockable

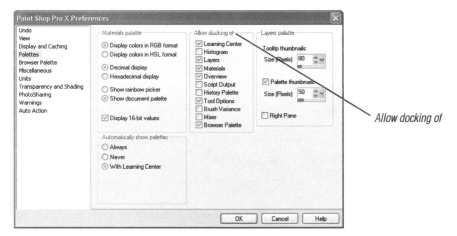

Allow docking of

INVESTIGATE THE
MATERIALS PALETTE

What You'll Do

In this lesson, you'll learn how to choose, from the Materials palette, colors for painting, drawing, or filling.

Breaking Down the Materials Palette

Whether you are applying color to an image or adjusting color in a photograph, it's important to understand how Paint Shop Pro works with color and how you select it within the program. You can draw, paint, and fill with a variety of colors, styles, and materials. A style is a color, gradient, or pattern. A material is the style plus an optional texture. The Materials palette offers a variety of ways for you to choose those things. And you get to choose both a foreground and background color. Generally speaking, you use the foreground materials for (brush) strokes and the background materials for fills. For example, when using the Paint Brush tool, clicking paints with the foreground

material. Right-clicking the brush paints with the background material. For text and vector objects, the foreground is considered the stroke (outline), and the background is considered the fill of the text or shape.

The Materials palette functions the same for raster and vector tools, which are discussed in Chapter 1, "Getting Started with Paint Shop Pro X." However, when using an advanced feature, such as the Art Media tools, you will notice that some of the palette's functions are disabled. The Materials palette contains three tabs: Frame, Rainbow, and Swatches. Table 1 gives a brief description of each component, including tabs, within the palette. Figure 8 visually breaks down the Materials palette for you.

TABLE 1: Materials Palette Contents

Element	What it does
Frame tab	This is the first tab across the top. It displays an outer hue rectangle and an inner saturation rectangle, as well as a strip containing white, black, and three shades of grey. You can drag the vertical slide to adjust lightness, and drag the horizontal slider to adjust the saturation.
Rainbow tab	This is the second tab across the top. It displays the available colors panel, where you can click to select a color. At the bottom of the tab you can select white, black, or three shades of grey.
Swatches tab	This is the third tab across the top. It displays swatches, which are materials you create on your own and save for use anytime in the future.
Foreground/background color boxes	Displays the current foreground or background color.
Foreground/background material boxes	Displays the current foreground or background material (the style—color, gradient, or pattern—plus the texture).
Style button	Specifies which style is currently being used: color, gradient, or pattern.
Texture button	Turns the current texture on or off. To choose a new texture, click the foreground or background material boxes.
Transparency button/null sign	Specifies whether the foreground or background material is transparent. Use transparent material mostly with text and vector objects. A transparent foreground in a vector object means no outline.
All Tools checkbox*	If marked, the selected foreground and background materials apply to all tools. If not, the selected materials apply only to the active tool.

*Note the All Tools command does not apply to the Edit Text command.

Choosing Colors with Material and Color Boxes

Whether editing an image or creating a new masterpiece, you often need to choose color: before you paint, when making manual color corrections, or when choosing a background for the new image. You can choose colors using one of several methods:

- For images with 16 million colors or more, choose from the color picker, shown in Figure 9.

- For images between 2–256 colors, choose from the Image palette.
- For any image, choose from an open image or any displayed color.
- Choose a color from the Frame or Rainbow tab on the Materials palette.

Since you can select colors by clicking the material boxes, you may wonder why the Materials palette includes color boxes too. With the foreground/stroke or background/fill property box, you can select a new color, even when the material box displays a gradient or pattern. The color boxes provide a quick and easy method of changing colors without changing the other parts of the material.

QUICKTIP Count colors in an image by going to the Image > Count Image Colors menu. You'll learn more about counting colors in Chapters 8 and 9.

Choosing Colors from the Image Palette

Images that have a color depth of less than 24 bit (16 million colors) are called paletted images—the available colors are a subset of all the colors your computer can display. The palette varies from 2 to 256 colors, depending on your image's color depth. With this type of image, you must choose foreground and background from the palette rather than from the color picker. (These images are also called **web safe** because they use so few colors and all monitors can display them.)

FIGURE 8
The Materials palette

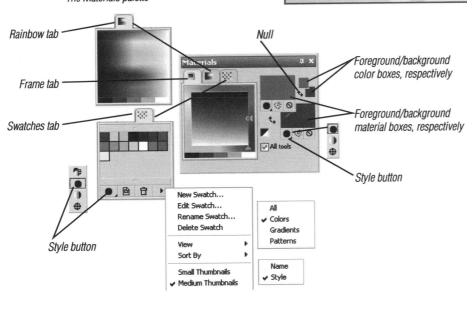

Rainbow tab

Null

Frame tab

Foreground/background color boxes, respectively

Swatches tab

Foreground/background material boxes, respectively

Style button

Style button

New Swatch...
Edit Swatch...
Rename Swatch...
Delete Swatch

All
✓ Colors
Gradients
Patterns

View
Sort By

Name
✓ Style

Small Thumbnails
✓ Medium Thumbnails

FIGURE 9
The color picker

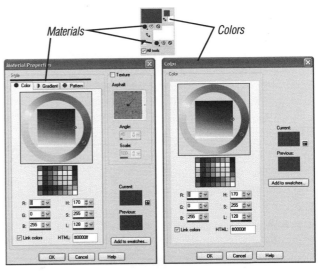

Materials

Colors

Choose colors from the Rainbow tab

1. Open **PSP2-1.PSPImage** from the drive and folder where your data files are stored, then save it as **Smiley**.

2. Click the Paint Brush tool 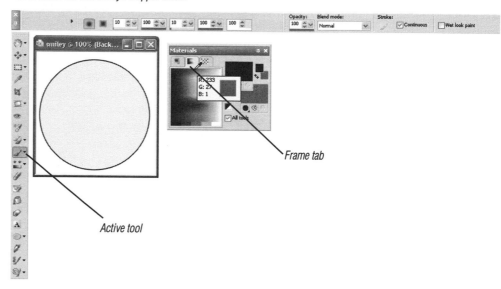.

   The Paint Brush tool becomes active and the tool options palette reflects options available for the tool.

3. Change your settings to match those seen in Figure 10.

4. Click the Frame tab in the Materials palette, then click black.

   The Frame tab becomes active and your cursor changes to an eye dropper as you move across the colors; see Figure 10. A small box attached to the cursor displays the RGB settings for the selected color; the foreground color changes to black.

5. Right-click a bright red area to set the background/fill color.

   The background/fill color changes to the selected red.

6. Click and drag to draw a curved line in the yellow circle (think smiley mouth); then click and drag to draw two small circles for eyes.

   The mouth and eyes are painted in black, as shown in Figure 11.

7. Right-click and draw a nose.

   The nose is painted in red, as shown in Figure 11.

8. Save your image.

You chose foreground/stroke and background/fill colors from the Rainbow tab, then painted a face by clicking and right-clicking.

FIGURE 10
Active Frame tab and the eye dropper cursor

Frame tab

Active tool

FIGURE 11
The mouth, eyes, and nose are painted

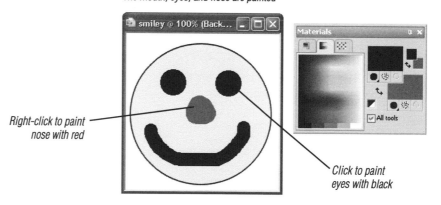

Right-click to paint nose with red

Click to paint eyes with black

FIGURE 12
The Material Properties dialog box

Foreground and stroke material swatch

Material Properties dialog box

Color wheel

Shift and click to make straight line

Start here

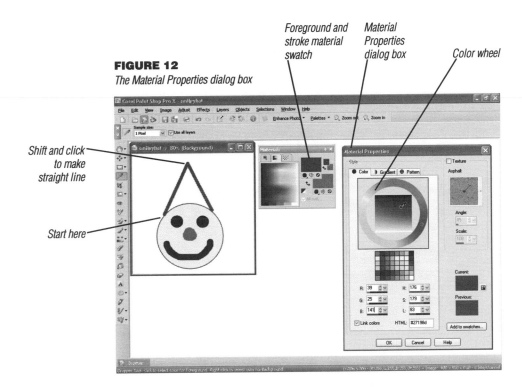

Choose a foreground/stroke color from the materials box

1. Open **PSP2-2.PSPImage** from the drive and folder where your data files are stored, then save it as **Smileyhat**.

2. Click the **Paint Brush tool**, then change your settings to match those given in the following steps.

3. Click the **foreground/stroke materials** box in the Materials palette.

   The Material Properties dialog box appears, as shown in Figure 12.

4. On the color wheel, click the approximate color or drag the **selection ring** around to choose.

   The color wheel represents the hue. The H box updates with a value between 0 and 255 as you go around the wheel.

5. On the Saturation/Lightness box, click to choose a color variation or drag the **selection ring**.

   I chose a blue with 176 for hue, then chose RGB=39/25/141, as shown in Figure 12.

6. Click **OK**.

   The material property color picker closes.

7. Click the starting point for your hat.

8. At the same time, press **Shift** and click an angle to create the point for the hat. Repeat for the other side of the hat.

9. Save your image for the next objective.

You used the foreground/fill materials box to choose a color for the hat outline, then made sure to draw straight lines with the selected color by pressing Shift and clicking.

Choose a background/fill color using the materials box

1. Open **Smileyhat.PSPImage** from the drive and folder where your data files are stored, then save it as **Coloredhat**.

2. Click the **Paint Brush tool** 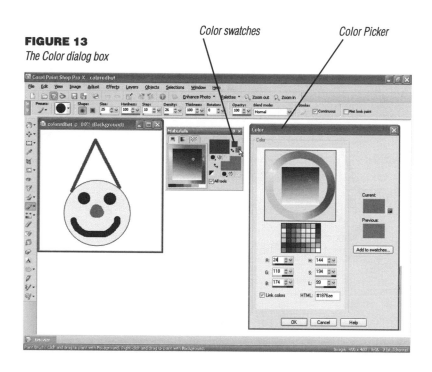.

3. Match the settings shown in Figure 13 (if necessary).

4. Click the **background/fill color** box in the Materials palette.

   The Color dialog box appears, as shown in Figure 13.

5. On the color wheel, click the approximate color or drag the **selection ring**.

6. Select a color for the hat, then click **OK**.

   The color picker closes.

7. Right-click to paint inside your hat with the background color.

8. Save your image and move to the next objective.

You used the color boxes to select a background color, then painted inside your hat.

FIGURE 13
The Color dialog box

Color swatches   Color Picker

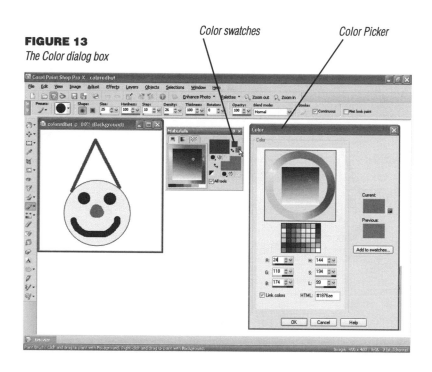

FIGURE 14

The Load Image Palette dialog box

1. Open **PSP2-3.gif**, then save it as **Palette.gif**.

2. Click the **Rainbow tab** in the Materials palette.

   The Rainbow tab becomes active.

3. Click **Image**, **Palette**, then click **Load**.

   The Load Image Palette dialog box appears, as shown in Figure 14.

4. Under Palette, click **Safety**, then click **Load**.

   The Safety palette loads in the Rainbow tab, showing only 256 available colors.

5. Select a color and decorate your hat.

6. Save your image.

You loaded a 256-color palette, ensuring that your colors are web safe and will view properly in all browsers. You then selected colors to finish painting your hat.

USE BASIC DRAWING
AND PAINTING TOOLS

What You'll Do

▶ *In this lesson, you'll use the Paint, Air-brush, and Eraser tools. You'll also look at the Background Eraser and use it remove an image background.*

Tooling with the Paint Brush and Airbrush

The Paint Brush and Airbrush are the most basic painting tools within Paint Shop Pro. They differ from each other in the way they paint the image. The Paint Brush applies in dabs. You get the same effect when you stay in one place while pressing either mouse button as when simply clicking the mouse button. The Airbrush, on the other hand, acts like a can of spray paint. If you keep the mouse in one place and press, paint is applied until you release the mouse button. In Figure 15, the top options palette displays the options available for the regular Paint Brush tool, the bottom one displays the Airbrush options. Each time you select a tool, the options bar changes to reflect that specific tool.

When using either of these tools, you can control the brush shape, size, width, rota-tion (angle), density (solidity), and hard-ness (brush edges), as well as the steps between the dabs or sprays painted when you drag the mouse. You can also control the paint's opacity (how much is applied) and how it is blended with whatever is already on the image in the tool options palette. Other controls available with the Paint Brush are Wet Look Paint (resem-bles a low hardness setting), Continuous, and Stroke.

Removing with the Eraser Tool

This is no ordinary eraser—it's much more flexible than the eraser on your pencil. The Eraser does not work on a background layer. Paint Shop Pro automatically pro-motes your background layer to a regular layer if you try to use the Eraser on the background layer. If you paint by clicking the mouse, the pixels you paint over become transparent. Those pixels are indicated by a checkerboard pattern; see Figure 16. If you paint with the right mouse button, this repaints anything you erased. The Eraser tool options are essentially the same as those for the Paint Brush tools, and you should set them according to your image. For example, if you're working on a small image, you don't want a 200-size brush.

FIGURE 15

Paint Brush and Airbrush tool options

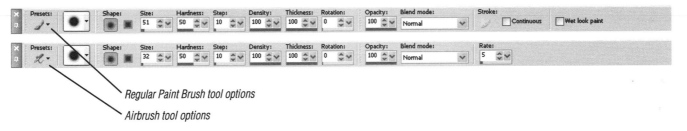

Regular Paint Brush tool options

Airbrush tool options

FIGURE 16

Erased areas represented by transparency checkerboard

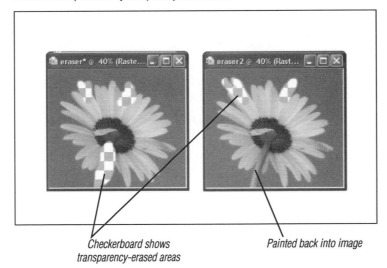

Checkerboard shows transparency-erased areas

Painted back into image

Removing with the Background Eraser

Previously, you saw how to use the Eraser tool to erase part of an image, which allowed the underlying, or background, color to show through. Paint Shop Pro has another Eraser tool, the Background Eraser, which works much like the regular Eraser tool but includes options to determine which pixels get erased. Also different than the regular Eraser tool, the Background Eraser tool works more from the center of the brush and erases around a specific area, which can give you softer edges. For example, if you have a photograph of a goose in water and just want the goose without the water (or anything else that's in the background), then the Background Eraser is the tool to use. Think of it as an eraser with a brain. When you select the Background Eraser (thirteenth down on the toolbar), the tool options palette displays the typical options, in addition to those listed in Table 2.

TABLE 2: Additional Background Eraser Tool Options

Option	What it does
Tolerance	Determines how closely pixels must match the sampled pixel. The range is 0–200. With lower settings, only pixels with very similar colors are erased. With higher settings, more pixels are erased. If the Auto Tolerance checkbox is marked, this option becomes unavailable and the Background Eraser determines the tolerance based on pixels in its path, changing as the tool moves over different parts of the image.
Sampling	Determines how the tool decides what pixels to erase. Choices are Once, Continuous, Backswatch, and Foreswatch. Once samples at the center of the brush where you first click, and it erases all matching pixels for the duration of the stroke. Continuous samples at the center of the brush at every step and erases matching pixels. Backswatch erases all pixels matching the current background color in the Materials palette. Foreswatch erases all pixels matching the current foreground color in the Materials palette.
Limits	Determines whether erased pixels must be adjacent to each other. Choices are Contiguous, Discontiguous, and Find Edges. Find Edges restricts the erasing according to the image's edge information.
Use All Layers	Samples data from all layers merged together, although only pixels in the current layer are erased.
Ignore Lightness	Mark this checkbox when the colors in the object you want to isolate are strongly saturated and the background is unsaturated.

Using pressure-sensitive tablets

A tablet is like a drawing pad that uses a special pen. Tablets are ideal if you are using brushes or simply like to draw. Wacom makes one of the least expensive and effective starter tablets and offers a variety, from beginner to professional. Not only does the tablet offer you more control and precision, but it also takes the pressure off your wrist. You can find out more by visiting www.wacom.com.

FIGURE 17
Wacom Intuos tablet

photo by Ron Lacey

Tool with the Paint Brush and Airbrush

1. Open a new, 300 × 300 raster image with a white background, then save it as **Paintbrush**.

2. Click the Paint Brush tool 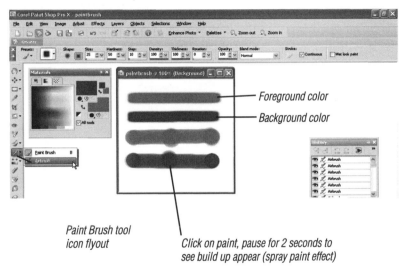.

3. Click, then drag the **brush** across the canvas, painting a line.

   The line appears with your foreground color on the canvas.

4. Right-click, then drag the **brush** across the canvas, painting a line.

   The line appears with your background color on the canvas, as shown in Figure 18.

5. Click the **Paint Brush tool**, holding down the mouse button until the flyout menu appears, then select the **Airbrush tool**.

   The flyout menu appears. Once selected, the options bar switches to the Airbrush options.

6. Click, then hold the **brush** for 2 seconds. Slowly drag the **brush** halfway across, pausing midway, then complete the line.

   The line appears with your foreground color on the canvas; paint is built up where you paused.

7. Right-click and hold the **brush** for 2 seconds. Slowly drag the **brush** halfway across, pausing midway, then complete the line.

   The line appears with your background color on the canvas; paint is built up where you paused, as shown in Figure 18.

8. Save your image.

You painted lines with the Paint Brush tool, using foreground/stroke and background/fill colors and both the left and right mouse buttons. You saved time by not having to select new colors from the Materials palette for each new stroke.

FIGURE 18
Paint Brush and Airbrush examples

Foreground color

Background color

Paint Brush tool icon flyout

Click on paint, pause for 2 seconds to see build up appear (spray paint effect)

FIGURE 19

Eraser options: Change size to 20

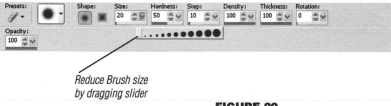

*Reduce Brush size
by dragging slider*

FIGURE 20

Erased stem and green areas

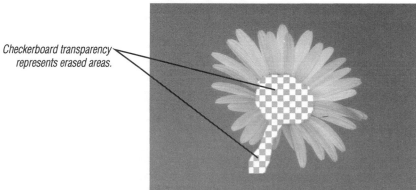

*Checkerboard transparency
represents erased areas.*

FIGURE 21

Right-click to paint an area back in

Erased areas painted back in

Remove with the Eraser tool

1. Open **PSP2-9.PSPImage** from the drive and folder where your data files are stored, then save it as **Erase**.

2. Click the **Eraser tool** .

   The Eraser tool is activated and the tool options palette changes to reflect the options shown in Figure 19.

3. Reduce your brush size by clicking the **arrow**, then dragging the **slider** to change the size to **20**.

4. Click, then drag the **Eraser tool** over the stem and center, removing only the green area of the flower.

   The stem and green areas are erased and represented by the transparency checkerboard, as shown in Figure 20.

5. Right-click, then drag the **Eraser tool** back over the stem areas you erased.

   The erased area is painted back into your image, as seen in Figure 21.

6. Save your file.

You used the Eraser tool to remove unwanted areas of an image, then put them back in using the right-click button.

Remove a background

1. Open **PSP2-7.PSPImage** from the drive and folder where your data files are stored, then save it as **Background**.

2. Click the **Background Eraser tool** 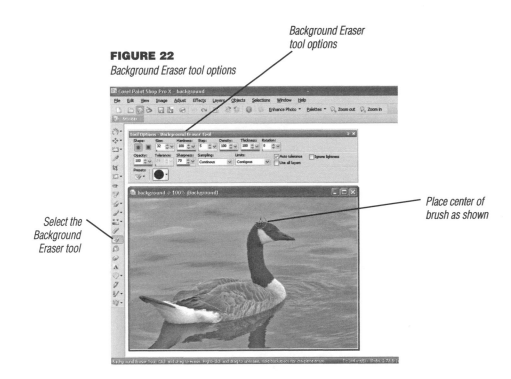.

   The Background Eraser tool becomes active and the tool options palette changes to reflect its options.

3. Enter **32** for Size, **0** for Rotation, **70** for Sharpness, then **100** for Hardness, Density, Thickness, and Opacity.

4. Continue settings, choosing **Continuous** for Sampling, **Contiguous** for Limits, then marking the **Auto Tolerance checkbox**, which matches the settings in Figure 22 (if necessary).

5. Place your cursor on the goose's head.

   Make sure that you place the center of the crosshairs of the precise cursor where you want to erase instead of the edge, like you would with the regular Eraser tool. See Figure 22 for placement.

6. Drag the **eraser** around the goose to get rid of the water.

7. Continue erasing until you have an erased outline.

8. Save your image.

You used the Background Eraser tool to isolate an object.

FIGURE 22
Background Eraser tool options

Background Eraser tool options

Place center of brush as shown

Select the Background Eraser tool

EXPLORE COLOR- AND
PATTERN-REPLACING TOOLS

What You'll Do

▶ *In this lesson, you'll learn to use the Eye Dropper tool to select specific colors for use with other tools.*

Selecting Colors with the Eye Dropper Tool

The Eye Dropper (or Dropper) isn't a painting tool. It enables you to pick up a color from any image and set the foreground/stroke or background/fill material color for use with tools like the Airbrush, Paint Brush, and Flood Fill.

Sample size can be 1 × 1, 3 × 3, 5 × 5, 7 × 7, or 11 × 11 pixels, as seen in the Dropper tool options in Figure 23. The Dropper is useful when you need to

FIGURE 23
Dropper tool options

precisely match a specific color. For instance, notice the areas where the paint is chipped on the red truck in Figure 23? You could paint with any red color—but why do that when you can become your own body shop?

Covering with the Color Replacer Tool

The Color Replacer covers all of one color with another by using the foreground or background colors, depending on whether you click the left or right mouse button. The tools options palette is like the one for Paint Brush with one important exception: the Tolerance setting. Tolerance controls how much of one color is being replaced with the new color. If you set Tolerance to 0, the replaced pixels must match the specified color exactly. Setting Tolerance higher changes colors that closely match. Figure 24 shows two floral images using the Color Replacer tool on the background of each.

The left flower uses a tolerance setting of 5; the right uses a tolerance setting of 40. The 40 setting lets all the background color be replaced.

Painting with the Clone Brush

The Clone Brush is handy when you need to modify a photo. It can apply any part of the image as if it were paint. The source can be either the image you're working on or some other. Its options are almost iden-

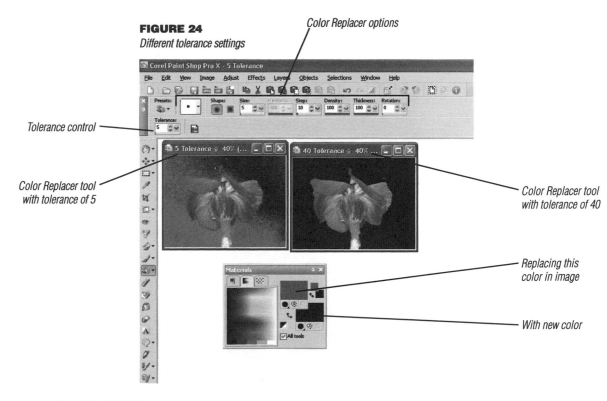

FIGURE 24
Different tolerance settings

Color Replacer options

Tolerance control

Color Replacer tool with tolerance of 5

Color Replacer tool with tolerance of 40

Replacing this color in image

With new color

tical to other brushes, with the characteristics and paint opacity as shown in Figure 25. **Aligned mode** determines the brush's behavior.

- **Aligned mode checked:** The starting point of your cloning shifts to the point at which you stopped painting.
- **Aligned mode unchecked:** The Clone Brush returns to the original source point each time that you stop painting and then starts again.

Using the Flood Fill Tool

Because the Flood Fill tool can fill pixels that match certain conditions (such as RGB value), its effect is similar to the Color Replacer tool but with the following exceptions: The Flood Fill tool fills matching pixels that are contiguous (next) to the initial pixel that you click. When the tool finds pixels that don't match, it breaks the chain,

making it discontiguous. The Color Replacer changes pixels either within the brush stroke or in the layer. The other exception is the Color Replacer tool. It changes colors based on RGB value. The Flood Fill tool changes pixels based on RGB, hue, brightness, or opacity, as shown in the tool options in Figure 26.

FIGURE 25

Using Aligned mode with the Clone brush

Aligned mode

FIGURE 26

Flood Fill tool options

Match mode options

Select colors with the Eye Dropper tool

1. Open **PSP2-4.PSPImage** from the drive and folder where your data files are stored, then save it as **Dropper**.

2. Click the **Dropper tool** [⌖].

   TIP When any tool is active, you can temporarily change it to the Dropper tool by pressing the Ctrl key. You can then click a color to set it as the foreground/stroke or right-click to set the background/fill.

3. In the Dropper tool options palette, click the **Sample Size arrow** to reveal the drop-down list, then click **3 × 3**.

4. Place your cursor over the top of the truck, then click to pick up the red.

   The cursor icon changes to a dropper. A box appears as you move the dropper, giving the RGB settings for each 3 × 3 pixel area under the cursor. The foreground/stroke color changes to reflect that color in the Materials palette, as shown in Figure 27.

5. Place the cursor over the over the scratched area (the white area), then right-click to pick up the color to be replaced.

   The cursor icon changes to a dropper. A box appears as you move the dropper, giving the RGB settings for each 3 × 3 pixel area the cursor is over. The background/fill color changes to reflect that color in the Materials palette, as shown in Figure 27.

6. Save your image and move to the next objective.

You used the Eye Dropper tool to select a precise color from your image to be used with the Color Replacer in the following objective.

FIGURE 27
Eye Dropper tool

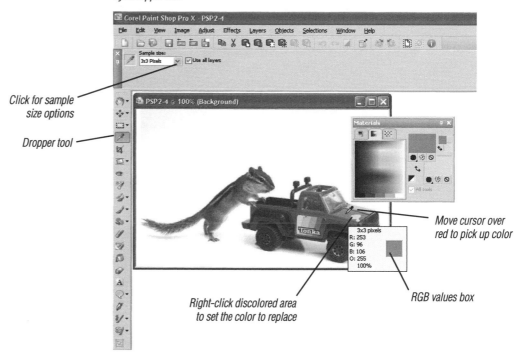

Click for sample size options

Dropper tool

Move cursor over red to pick up color

Right-click discolored area to set the color to replace

RGB values box

FIGURE 28

Discolored area repaired with the color replacer

Color replaced
and truck repairs
complete

1. Click the **Color Replacer tool** in the main toolbar.

   The Color Replacer tool options palette appears.

2. Click the **Size arrow**, then set Size to **5**.

3. Click the **Tolerance arrow**, then set Tolerance to **2**.

4. Double-click the **scratched area** on the image.

   The discolored, scratched area changes to the foreground/stroke color that you selected with the Dropper tool, as seen in Figure 28. All fixed: Mr. Chipmunk will never know.

   TIP Double-clicking allows you to replace all the color at one time. If you want to replace only small portions, click and drag like you do with the Paint Brush tool.

5. Save your image.

You used a precise color that you previously selected with the Dropper tool, then used the Color Replacer for the discolored section of your image.

Paint with the Clone Brush

1. Open **PSP2-5.PSPImage** from the drive and folder where your data files are stored, then save it as **Cloned**.

2. Click the **Clone Brush**  on the main toolbar.

   The Clone Brush tool options palette appears.

3. Click the **Size arrow** and set Size to **13**. Set Hardness to **50**, Step to **10**, Density and Thickness both to **100**, then Rotation to **0**.

4. Mark the **Aligned mode checkbox**. Set Blend mode to **Normal** (if necessary).

5. Click **View**, then click **Zoom to 100%**.

   The image zooms to full size, enabling you to better see the imperfections.

6. Right-click any area next to the blemishes on her chin.

   This sets the source so that when you next click over any blemish, the area you right-clicked is painted in its place. If you have speakers on your system, a click confirms that you have set the source.

   The imperfections disappear and the source paint replaces it, as seen in Figure 29.

   > TIP For the best results, use the Clone Brush in small sizes and reset the source often, so the spot you are replacing matches the area surrounding it.

7. Repeat until all blemishes are replaced.

8. Save your image.

You used the Clone Brush to remove unwanted items from an image.

FIGURE 29
Imperfections cloned out

Aligned mode

Clone Brush options

Source paint replaces blemish

FIGURE 30
Image filled with foreground color

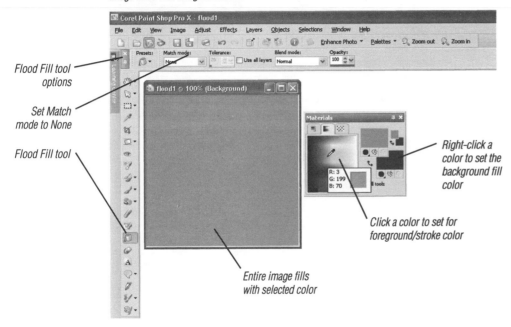

Flood Fill tool options

Set Match mode to None

Flood Fill tool

Right-click a color to set the background fill color

Click a color to set for foreground/stroke color

Entire image fills with selected color

1. Open **PSP2-10.PSPImage** from the drive and folder where your data files are stored, then save it as **Flood1**.

2. Click the **Flood Fill tool** 🖼️.

   The tool options palette changes to reflect its options.

3. Set Match mode to **None**, Blend mode to **Normal**, then Opacity to **100**.

   By selecting None for the Match mode, the entire image is filled.

4. Select a color from the Rainbow tab.

   > TIP Click to select the foreground/stroke color; right-click to select the background/fill color.

5. Click once inside your image.

   The image fills with the selected foreground/stroke color, as shown in Figure 30.

You used the Flood Fill tool with Match mode set to None, filling an entire image and changing its background color to the color of your choice.

Use Flood Fill with gradient

1. Open **PSP2-11.PSPImage** from the drive and folder where your data files are stored, then save it as **Gradientfill**.

2. Click the **Flood Fill tool** [icon].

3. Click the **Style arrow**, then select **Gradient**.

   The style changes from Solid to Gradient.

4. Click the foreground/stroke swatch in the Materials palette.

   The Material Properties dialog box appears, as shown in Figure 31.

5. Click the **Gradient tab** (if necessary).

6. Click **Sunburst** for Gradient Style, then click the preview window arrow.

   The preview window changes to reflect the Sunburst style. The Gradient options expand.

7. Select **Duotone Lavender**.

   The expanded options closes and the selected color gradient is displayed in the preview window, as shown in Figure 31.

8. Click **OK**.

   The Gradient dialog box closes.

9. Click once inside the selection.

   The image fills with the selected gradient color, as shown in Figure 32.

You used the Flood Fill tool with a gradient to give the image a 3D feel.

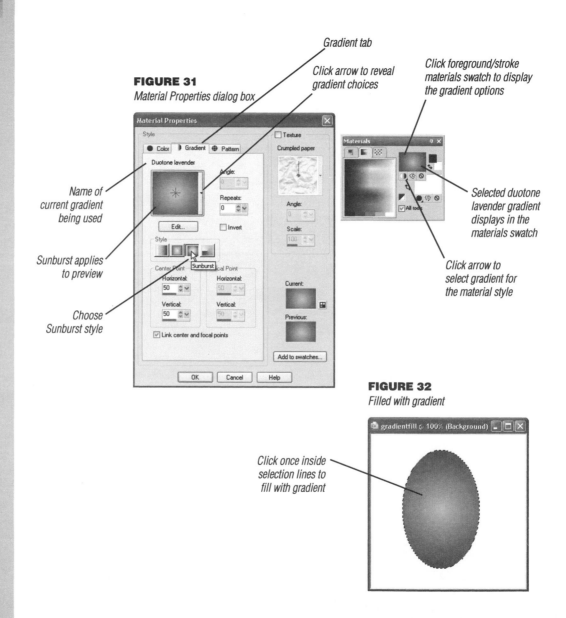

Gradient tab

Click arrow to reveal gradient choices

Click foreground/stroke materials swatch to display the gradient options

FIGURE 31
Material Properties dialog box

Name of current gradient being used

Sunburst applies to preview

Choose Sunburst style

Selected duotone lavender gradient displays in the materials swatch

Click arrow to select gradient for the material style

FIGURE 32
Filled with gradient

Click once inside selection lines to fill with gradient

CHAPTER SUMMARY

In this chapter, you took an even closer look at your interface and learned to customize it by enabling and disabling the Autohide feature. You learned how to use some of the basic painting and drawing tools, as well as how to fill an entire image with solid colors and gradients. You discovered how to use one of Paint Shop Pro's best features, the Background Eraser, to remove an unwanted background.

What You Have Learned

- How to customize your workspace.
- How to enable and disable the Autohide function.
- How to create custom keyboard combinations.
- How to select specific colors.
- How to replace specific colors.
- How to fill an entire image with color.

Key Terms

Aligned mode Determines a brush's behavior.

combination A pair (or more) of keys that you type instead of clicking an icon or a menu command.

contiguous Connecting, adjacent.

density A brush's solidity.

docked Stuck to the side of the interface.

fill Background of text or a shape.

floating Undocked and movable.

hardness A brush's edges

material The style plus an optional texture.

opacity How much color is applied.

palette Displays each tool's options.

rotation A brush's angle.

stroke Outline.

style The color, gradient, or pattern.

swatch Material you create and save.

title bar The top of a Paint Shop Pro image.

tolerance Controls the amount of range when selecting a color.

toolbar Displays the main tools.

workspace The toolbars, palettes, and open images.

chapter

3 BEING SELECTIVE

1. Select shapes easily.

2. Modify selections.

3. Use selections for special effects.

4. Save selections.

5. Paint with the Edit Selection command.

chapter 3 BEING SELECTIVE

Making a Shape Selection

Often what you want to create involves using an image or part of an image from another file. To use part of an image, you must first select that part. A **selection** is an area of an image surrounded by a **marquee**, a dashed line that surrounds the area you want to edit or move. This technique for combining images is called **compositing**. Sources for the other images can include other Paint Shop Pro images, royalty-free images, pictures taken with your digital camera, and scanned artwork or images.

You can use two basic methods to makes selections: using a tool or using color. You can use any of the 15 fixed selection tools to create shapes like rectangles or circles,

or you can use the Magic Wand tool to make selections using color. In addition, menu commands can increase or decrease the sizes of the selections you made with these tools. A freehand selection, which is made with the mouse, lets you create unique selections.

Choosing a Method

With so many tools to choose from, how do you know which one to use? After you know the different selection options, you'll learn how to look at images and determine your selection choices. After time and with some experience, you'll learn how to identify colors that can be used to isolate a specific object.

Tools You'll Use

[::]	Selection	S
⌒	Freehand Selection	
⬟	Magic Wand	

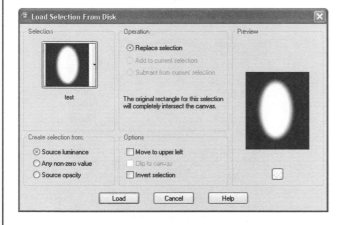

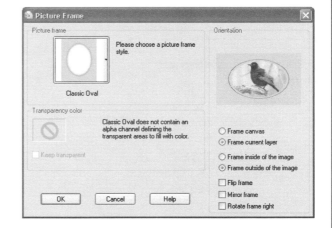

SELECT
SHAPES EASILY

What You'll Do

In this lesson, you'll make selections with different tools, edit your selections, use rulers, and access saved selections.

Using the Magic Wand or Shape Selection Tool

In a perfect world, every object you wanted to choose would be selectable with the rectangle or elliptical Selection tool, since they are the easiest to use. In a nearly perfect world, the Magic Wand tool would be the second option. Unfortunately, it's not a

perfect world. While a lot of objects are round or rectangular, many are an unusual or irregular shape. Making selections can sometimes be a nerve-racking process, because many objects don't have clearly defined or straight edges. The selection is defined by the marquee encircling the flower shown in Figure 1. You

FIGURE 1
Elliptical marquee

Selection marquee

photo by Ron Lacey

can make the marquee visible at all times so you always know where your selection is. However, often the marquee can obstruct your view of your editing—especially when zoomed in. You can hide the marquee without losing the selection: Choose Selections > Hide Marquee.

QUICKTIP A marquee is sometimes defined as marching ants because its dashed lines appear to be moving.

The Paint Shop Pro selection tools make it easy to select objects that are rectangular, circular . . . just about any shape you can imagine. Once you choose the selection tool, the tool options palette displays the settings available for that specific tool. Figure 2 shows the surplus of shapes you get to choose from in the Selection type drop-down menu.

Employing the Freehand Tool

Rectangles and elliptical shapes are going to be your closest shapely friends, and though drawing an elliptical marquee is tougher than drawing a rectangular one, with practice and time you'll be able to create both easily. When the shape tools don't cut it, move on to the Freehand tool. Figure 3 shows a marquee surrounding an irregular shape made using the Freehand

FIGURE 2
Shape Selection tool options

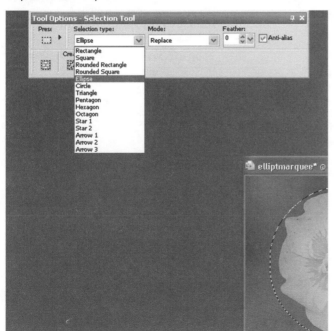

FIGURE 3
The Freehand tool in Smart Edge mode

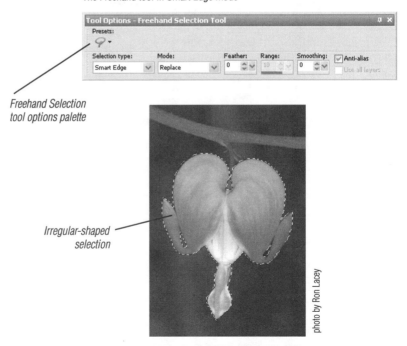

Freehand Selection tool options palette

Irregular-shaped selection

tool in Smart Edge mode. Smart Edge mode works by selecting areas of contrast in the image and is quite useful when trying to select complex shapes and objects from an image.

Selecting, Deselecting, and Reselecting

You've committed to a shape and made a selection. Now you can move, copy, or adjust it. That is, you can move it to another file, copy it if you need to choose many of the same shape, or finesse the shape if it's not to your liking. It stays selected until you deselect it. You can deselect by clicking Selections on the menu bar, then Select None. You can also click Select All from the menu; this selects the entire image.

QUICKTIP Each command in the context menu has an icon that you can place on the toolbar of your choice for easier access. Right-click any area and choose Customize. Under the categories, choose Selections. All the available icons for the selections menu are displayed. Click, drag, and drop the desired icon onto the toolbar. Chapter 2 talks more about customizing toolbars.

You also have a mode option to choose from, which determines if you want to replace, add to, or remove from a selection. Other controls for this tool include the Anti-alias, Feather, Custom selection, and Create selection from buttons. Later in this chapter, Table 1 explains these buttons.

Displaying Rulers

Vertical and horizontal rulers can help you better position your elements. The rulers can display in either pixels (the default), inches, or centimeters. Pixels will display more tick marks than inches or centimeters, making it easier to position elements precisely. To change the measurement, enter preferences by going to File > Preferences > File Format Associations. Then, under Units, select your choice by clicking the arrow in the Display Units box for rulers.

Saving and Loading Selections

When you create a selection, especially a complex one, it's often helpful to save and use it again. Selections can be saved to a file and then reloaded anytime later through Selection > Load. When you save a selection to your hard drive, Paint Shop Pro saves it as a separate file with a .PSPSelection extension. You can load the selection into the current image or any image down the road.

FIGURE 4
Rulers displayed

Title bar

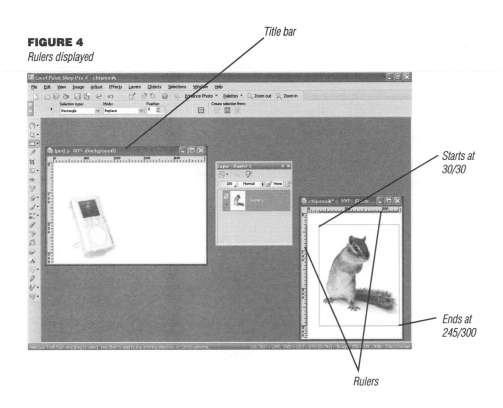

Starts at
30/30

Ends at
245/300

Rulers

1. Open **PSP3-1.PSPImage**, then save it as **Chipmunk**.

2. Click **View**, then click **Rulers**.

   The rulers display on your image, as shown in Figure 4.

   > TIP A checkmark to the left of Rulers in the View menu indicates that the rulers will be displayed.

3. Open **PSP3-2.PSPImage**, save it as **Ipod**, then click the **Chipmunk image** to make it active.

4. Click the **Shape Selection tool** 🔲.

5. Click the **Type arrow**, click **Rectangle**, set **Feather** to **0**, then select **Anti-alias**.

6. Drag the pointer from **30/30** to **245/300**, as shown in Figure 4.

   The first measurement refers to the horizontal ruler and the second refers to the vertical ruler.

7. Click **Edit**, **Copy**, then click the Ipod image's **title bar**.

   The selected area is copied to your Windows Clipboard and the Ipod image is active (indicated by highlighting, which darkens the title bar).

8. Click **Edit**, then click **Paste as New Selection**. Do *not* yet click the image again.

> TIP   When pasting a selection, your image is "stuck" to your cursor until you click the canvas to release it.

The Clipboard content (chipmunk image) appears in your Ipod image and is stuck to your cursor.

9. Move the cursor to position the chipmunk at **220/80** and **435/350**, then click to drop the image off your cursor.

The image drops from the cursor, giving you what you see in Figure 5.

Using the rectangular Shape Selection tool, you chose an element from one image. Then, using rulers, you positioned one image onto another at precise coordinates.

FIGURE 5
Pasting a selection into an image.

*Pasting coordinates
display in the status bar*

FIGURE 6

Hidden marquee

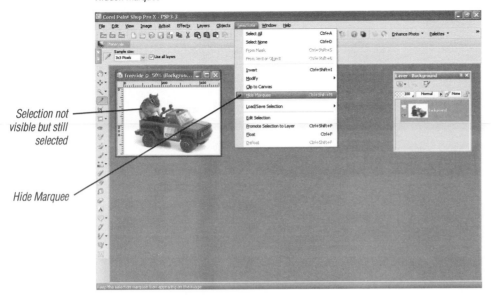

Selection not visible but still selected

Hide Marquee

FIGURE 7

Selected, removed area displays background/fill color

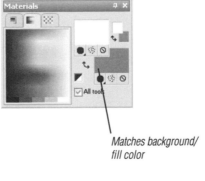

Matches background/ fill color

1. Open **PSP3-3.PSPImage**, then save it as **Freeride**.

2. Click the **Shape Selection tool**.

3. Draw out a selection around the chipmunk's head.

   The marquee appears around the chipmunk's head, indicating the selection.

4. Click **Selections**, then click **Hide Marquee**.

   The marquee disappears; see Figure 6.

   > TIP Hiding the marquee removes the distraction of movement, allowing you to see all areas of the image. This is especially handy for work on photographs, when you want to edit the fine detail but stay within the selection.

5. Click **Edit**, then **Cut**.

   The selected head disappears, leaving a blank area. The background/fill hue in the Materials palette determines the area's color; see Figure 7.

You selected a portion of your image, then hid the marquee so you could see when cutting the selected area from the image.

Lesson 1   Select Shapes Easily

Select and deselect a selection

1. Open **PSP3-4.PSPImage**, then save it as **Bear**.

2. Click the **Selection tool** ⬚▾.

3. Drag a selection around a portion of the bear.

4. Click **Selections**, then click **Select None**, like you see in Figure 8.

   The marquee disappears.

   | TIP Right-clicking deselects a selection, saving you few steps.

You chose a portion of the image, then deselected it using the Select None option. That enabled you to manipulate the entire image (instead of just the confines of your selection).

FIGURE 8
Deselect a selection using Select None

FIGURE 9
Freehand tool in Replace mode

Freehand tool

FIGURE 10
Freehand tool selection cursor

Lasso and attached box

1. Open **PSP3-5.PSPImage**, then save it as **Chippy**.

2. Click the **Freehand tool** ⏥.

   The tool options palette appears.

3. Choose **Smart Edge** for Selection type, **Replace** for Mode, **0** for Feather, **0** for Smoothing, and select **Anti-alias** to match Figure 9.

4. Click anywhere close to the edge of the chipmunk to start the selection.

   The cursor changes to a lasso with an attached box, as shown in Figure 10. Table 1 describes the Freehand tool settings.

5. Move the cursor a short distance, keeping the center of the box where you want to anchor one side of the selection, then click.

   You set the next anchor point when you click. A line appears, showing the beginning outline of your selection.

   TIP This tool works best if you work slowly and make small steps between your selection anchor points. Smart Edge mode works by selecting areas of contrast between clicks. A large space between clicks creates a large contrast in the selection, giving an excess of unwanted pixels in your selection.

6. Move slowly around the chipmunk, setting anchor points until you are at the starting point; then double-click to connect the selection.

   The start and end points connect and the solid lines turn into a marquee.

You created a selection with the Freehand tool in Smart Edge mode, so the edges were automatically detected for you, making for much quicker selections.

Create a selection with the Magic Wand tool

1. Open **PSP3-6.PSPImage**, then save it as **Flower**.

2. Click the **Magic Wand tool**.

   The Magic Wand tool becomes active and the tool options palette displays its options.

3. Choose **Replace** for Mode, **RGB Value** for Match mode, **35** for Tolerance, then **0** for Feather.

4. Click **Contiguous** and **Anti-alias**, then choose **Outside** from the drop-down menu.

   Figure 11 shows these settings. Table 1 describes the Magic Wand tool settings.

5. Click anywhere in the background area of the flower.

   The solid background color becomes selected.

6. Click **Selections**, then click **Invert**.

   The marquee inverts and the flower is selected, as seen in Figure 12.

7. Click **Edit**, **Cut**, then click **Paste as New Image**.

   The selected flower is cut from the background and is now its own, transparent image.

8. Save the image with a new name.

Using the Magic Wand tool, you selected a solid background, then inverted the selection to simplify the element's extraction.

FIGURE 11

Magic Wand tool settings

Mode: Replace | Match mode: RGB Value | Tolerance: 35 | ☐ Use all layers ☑ Contiguous | Feather: 0 ☑ Anti-alias | Outside

FIGURE 12

Inverted selection

TABLE 1 Selection Tool Settings

Freehand Tool Settings

setting	description
Feather	Determines the amount of fade between the selection and the pixels surrounding it. This setting is measured in pixels and can be a value between 0–200.
Smoothing	Lets you determine the amount of smoothing you want applied to the edges.
Anti-alias	Determines the smoothness of the selection by softening the color transition between edge and background pixels, avoiding jaggies.
Use All Layers	Searches for an edge in all layers of the selected area. This option is available only if your image has multiple layers and if you are using the Edge Seeker or Smart Edge selection type.

Magic Wand Tool Settings

setting	description
Match mode	None: Chooses all pixels. RGB Value: Chooses pixels that match the red, green, and blue values of the color selected in the image. Color: Chooses pixels that match the color selected in the image. Hue: Chooses pixels that match the position in the color wheel of the hues selected in the image. Brightness: Chooses pixels that match the brightness of the color selected in the image. All Opaque: Chooses opaque pixels and excludes transparent pixels. Opacity: Chooses pixels according to their level of opacity or transparency.
Tolerance	Controls how closely the selected pixels match the pixel you click in the image. At low settings, only similar pixels are chosen; at higher settings, a wider range of pixels are selected.
Contiguous	When checked, selects only the pixels connected to the clicking point. Unchecked, selects colors throughout entire image regardless of connection point.
Outside/Inside	Controls whether the feather is on the outside or inside of the selection.
Mode (Globally)	Add: Adds selections to any existing selection. Remove: Deletes any part of an already existing selection. Replace: The default. Creates a new selection or replaces an existing selection with a rectangle selection.

Save a selection

1. Open **Flower.PSPImage** (if necessary).

2. Click **Selections**, **Load/Save Selections**, then click **Save Selection to Disk**.

   The Save Selection to Disk dialog box appears, as shown in Figure 13.

3. Type in a name that is easy for you to remember, then click **Save**.

   Your selection is saved to your hard drive, in a folder within Paint Shop Pro; then the dialog box closes.

4. Click **Selections**, then click **Select None**.

   The selection marquee disappears.

5. Save, then close your image.

You opened an image with an existing selection, then saved the selection to your hard drive so you can use it again later.

FIGURE 13

Save Selection to Disk dialog box

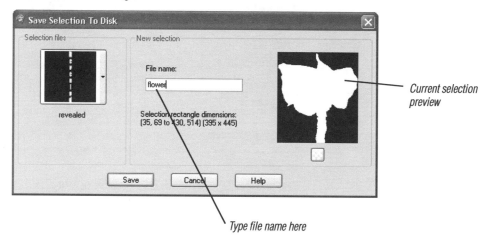

Current selection preview

Type file name here

FIGURE 14

Load your selection from this dialog box

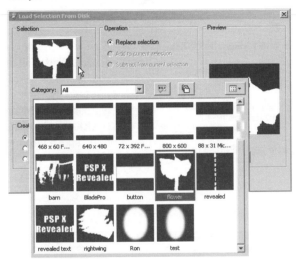

1. Open **Flower.PSPImage** (if necessary), then save it as **Load**.

2. Click **Selections**, **Load/Save Selections**, then click **Load Selection from Disk**.

   The Load Selection from Disk dialog box displays, as shown in Figure 14.

3. Click the **drop-down arrow** to display all the saved selections, then click your selection.

   In the Selection box, your selection appears with the name just below it.

4. Click **Load**.

   The Load Selection dialog box closes and your selection appears around your image just as you had originally selected it.

5. Save, then close your image.

You used a previously saved selection by using the Load Selection from Disk option, saving time since you did not need to recreate the selection.

MODIFY SELECTIONS

What You'll Do

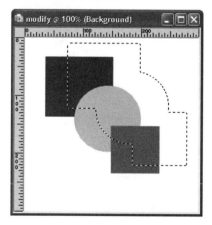

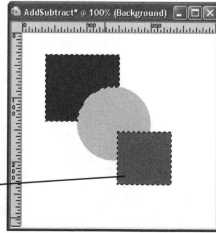

In this lesson, you'll learn how to modify your marquee, then move it where you want it.

Changing a Marquee's Size

As you saw in Lesson 1, not all objects are easy to select. Oftentimes, once a selection is made, you wish it were just a little bigger, just a little smaller, or just a little softer around the edges. Changing selections is simple and can be done different ways. Say you've chosen a nice blue square. Wait! You didn't notice that red square. Red's your favorite color. What to do? Luckily, each selection tool's option bar contains a Mode option that allows you to either add or subtract from the selection. Take a look at Figure 15. I modified the left marquee into the one on the right

FIGURE 15
Original marquee on the left, added selection on the right

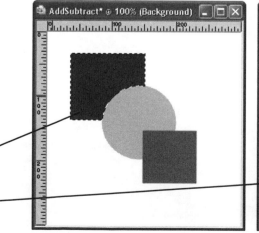

Original selection

Added selection

by using the Add to Selection option. After choosing the Add to Selection option, you can select an additional color (using the Magic Wand tool) to be added to the current marquee.

What if you marked a little too tightly and need to make the marquee bigger? The Expand command, available through the Modify menu, is one method for increasing the size. If you expand your selection and then decide it was too much, shrink the marquee using the Contract command. Check out the difference in Figure 16.

Modifying and Moving a Marquee

You can do more than change sizes. Smooth out edges using the Smooth command or select similarly colored areas of the image with the Select Similar command. After you create a marquee, you can move it without moving the elements it contains. Figure 17 shows the solid outline you see when moving the marquee but not its contents. Releasing the mouse sets the new marquee location. This comes in handy if you want to make two selected elements the same unusual shape. For instance, you could use the unusual shape shown in Figure 17 as a web page banner or navigation bar.

FIGURE 16
A selection first expanded, then contracted

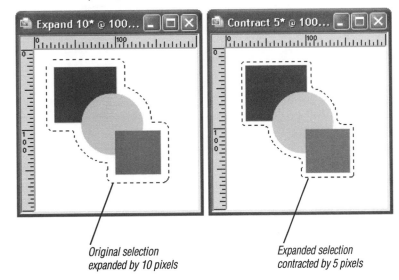

Original selection expanded by 10 pixels

Expanded selection contracted by 5 pixels

FIGURE 17
Moving a marquee

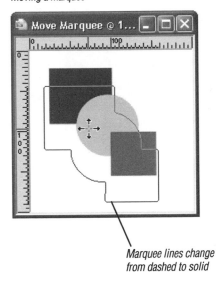

Marquee lines change from dashed to solid

Change a selection size

1. Open **PSP3-7.PSPImage**, then save it as **Expand**.

2. Click the **Magic Wand tool** 🪄.

3. Choose **Replace** for Mode, **RGB Value** for Match mode, **35** for Tolerance, then **0** for Feather.

4. Mark **Contiguous**, then **Anti-alias**.

   The settings match those shown in Figure 18.

5. Click the **blue rectangle**.

   A marquee appears around the rectangle.

6. Click **Selections**, **Add**, then click the **other square**.

   The circle and the square are selected.

   | TIP Take a shortcut to this command by pressing Shift, clicking the circle, then pressing Shift and clicking the other square.

7. Click **Selections**, **Modify**, then click **Expand**.

   The Expand Selection dialog box appears.

8. Enter a value of **5**, then click **OK**.

   The Expand Selection dialog box closes and the marquee around the selection expands by 5 pixels, as shown in Figure 19.

Using the Magic Wand tool, you selected an object and added elements to create a marquee that met your unique shape needs.

FIGURE 18
Magic Wand tool options

Mode:	Match mode:	Tolerance:		Feather:		
Replace ▾	RGB Value ▾	35 ▲▾	☐ Use all layers ☑ Contiguous	0 ▲▾	☑ Anti-alias	Outside ▾

FIGURE 19
Expanded selection

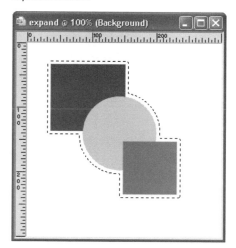

FIGURE 20

Smooth Selection dialog box

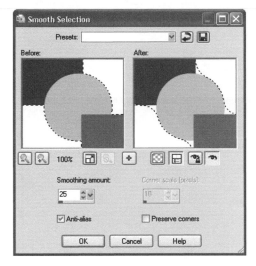

FIGURE 21

Moved selection

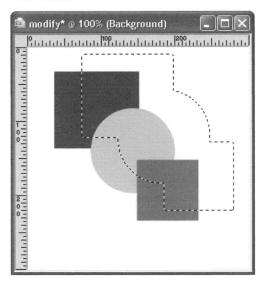

1. Open **Expand.PSPImage**, then save as **Modify**.

2. Click **Selections**, **Modify**, then click **Smooth**. The Smooth Selection dialog box displays.

3. Enter **25** for the Amount, mark the **Anti-alias checkbox**, then remove the check from the **Preserve corners checkbox**.

   Your settings should match those shown in Figure 20.

4. Click **OK**.

   The Smooth Selection dialog box closes and the modified selection appears around your image, with smooth edges—no sharp corners.

5. Right-click and hold down the mouse button within the marquee, then drag the **marquee** to a new position.

   As you drag, the marquee changes to a solid outline and moves with the cursor.

6. Release the mouse button.

   The marquee reappears in the new position shown in Figure 21.

7. Save your image.

You opened an image that had an existing selection, rounded the edges using the Smooth command, then moved the marquee to a new position without moving its elements.

USE SELECTIONS
FOR SPECIAL EFFECTS

What You'll Do

▶ *In this lesson, you'll create a vignette and apply a picture frame.*

Creating a Vignette

Typically, a **vignette** is a picture or portrait whose border fades into the surrounding color at its edges like you see in Figure 22. A vignette can be simply for effect or to tone down a loud background. It's one of the most popular effects and uses feathering to fade a selection marquee. The feather setting blurs the area between the selection and the surrounding pixels, which creates a distinctive fade.

Different methods achieve the vignette effect. One method is **masking**, which lets you protect or modify parts of an image and is created using a selection marquee. (Because masking is a more complex process, you will learn more about it in Chapter 4, "Using Layers and Masks.") The other, less complex, method simply uses the feather, copy, and paste options with a marquee. You can create the vignette

FIGURE 22
Vignette example

using any of the selection tools, including Freehand, Magic Wand, or Shape. Once the selection is made, you modify the feather setting to increase the blur effect on the outside edge of the selection. A 15–20-pixel setting usually creates a nice fading effect.

Applying Mattes and Picture Frames

Vignettes are further enhanced with frames and mattes, which can provide an eye-catching final touch to your image. A matte is a decorative border around an image that serves as a frame or provides contact between the image and frame. Choose from square or oval frames, modern or classic styles, glass or metal, and more. The Picture Frame Wizard applies the frame/matte inside or outside the existing canvas or only on the current layer. You can also flip, mirror, or rotate the frame.

Making for easier selections

When you first start making selections, you might feel like a klutz. Making selections is a skill, and like most skills, it takes lots of practice and time to become proficient. In addition to practice, make sure you are comfortable with your workspace, that your hands are steady, and that your mouse is working well. A dirty mechanical mouse (the kind with the rolling ball) can make selecting a real headache, so be sure to clean it regularly and make sure it is functioning correctly.

Create a vignette

1. Open **PSP3-8.PSPImage**, then save it as **Handsomedude**.

2. Click the **Ellipse tool** 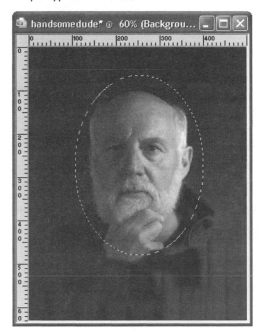. Set Type to **Ellipse**, Mode to **Replace**, Feather to **0**; then mark **Anti-alias**.

3. Place the cursor near the handsome dude's nose, then draw out an elliptical selection.

   The marquee appears around the selected area, as shown in Figure 23.

   > TIP Don't worry if a selection isn't perfect. Remember, you can move it if you need to. If your selection is not quite big enough but covers the general area you want, expand the selection by any number of pixels (up to 100 at a time) through the Selection, Modify, Expand command.

4. Click **Selections**, **Modify**, then click **Feather**.

   The Feather Selection dialog box opens, as shown in Figure 24.

5. Enter **35** in the Feather dialog box, then click **OK**.

   In the right pane of the dialog box you see a preview of the newly feathered selection, then the dialog box closes.

   > TIP You can preview the selected feather setting on the actual image instead of in the smaller preview windows without leaving the Feather dialog box. Click the Preview icon; it looks like an eyeball. The Preview icon with the padlock will lock on your preview. I don't recommend this for older computers—it tends to slow them down.

FIGURE 23
Marquee appears around selected area

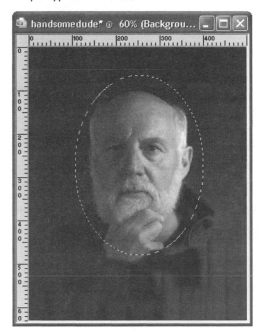

FIGURE 24
Feather Selection dialog box

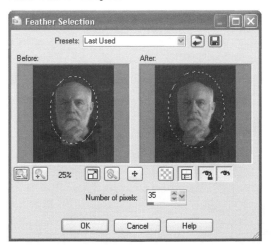

FIGURE 25

Feathered selection on vignette image

6. Click **File**, then **New**. Use the following settings: **Raster, 500w × 600h, white** background, **8-bit color**; click **OK**, then save the file as **Vignette**.

7. Click the **title bar** of the Handsomedude image to make it active, then click **Edit, Copy**.

   The selected area is copied to your Windows Clipboard.

8. Click the Vignette image **title bar** to make it active, then click **Edit, Paste as New Selection**; place the selection in the middle of the image.

   Your feathered selection appears on the new image with the marquee still showing, as you see in Figure 25.

9. Save your image in .PSPImage format to maintain the selection marquee.

You used a selection tool and the Feather command to give an image a vignette effect, then saved the image in the native Paint Shop Pro format, maintaining the selection.

Apply a matte

1. Open **Vignette.PSPImage** (if necessary), then save it as **Matte**.

2. Click **Image**, then click **Picture Frame**.

   The Picture Frame dialog box appears.

3. Click the **drop-down arrow** in the Picture Frame dialog box.

   The thumbnails dialog box appears, as shown in Figure 26.

4. Click **Classic Oval**.

5. Check the **Frame Current Layer radio button** and the **Frame Outside of the Image radio button**.

6. Click **OK**, then deselect your selection.

   The Picture Frame dialog box closes and the matte appears on your image, as shown in Figure 27.

7. Save your image.

Using the Picture Frame Wizard, you added a matte to enhance your image.

FIGURE 26
Matte options

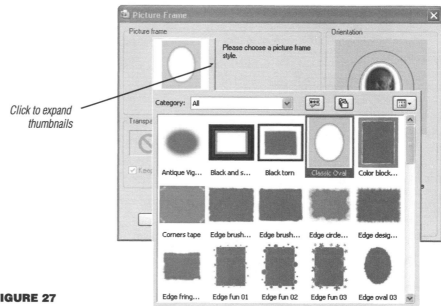

Click to expand thumbnails

FIGURE 27
Matte appears on image

FIGURE 28
Preview of picture frame

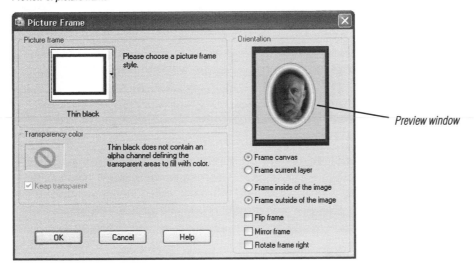

Preview window

FIGURE 29
Picture frame appears on image

Frame

photo by Ron Lacey

1. Open **Matte.PSPImage** (if necessary), then save it as **Frame**.

2. Click **Image**, then click **Picture Frame**.

   The Picture Frame Wizard opens.

3. In the Picture Frame dialog box, click the **drop-down arrow**.

   The thumbnail dialog box appears.

4. Select **Thin black**.

5. In the Orientation area, click the **Frame canvas radio button** and the **Frame outside of the image radio button**.

   The frame appears around your image in the preview window, as shown in Figure 28.

6. Click **OK**.

   The Picture Frame dialog box closes and the frame surrounds your image, as shown in Figure 29.

7. Save your image.

Using the Picture Frame Wizard, you added a frame to your matted, vignetted image, making it more visually pleasing.

> TIP If you select a rectangular frame with no transparent areas outside, click OK to apply the frame. If transparent areas surround the edges (as with any nonrectangular frame), you can check the Keep Transparent check-box. Or, uncheck this box and choose a color to replace the transparency: Click the Color dialog box, then pick the color you want.

PAINT WITH THE EDIT
SELECTION COMMAND

What You'll Do

▶ *In this lesson, you'll use the Edit Selection command and zoom into your image.*

Using the Edit Selection Command

In order to have complete control over your images, you need a good understanding of selections, **masks** (greyscale selections), and **color channels** (layers of the primary colors that compose an image). When working on a detailed image, you might find that using one of the selection tools is a cumbersome project. Paint Shop Pro's Edit Selection feature enables you to paint your selection. This is especially useful when trying to seamlessly remove elements from a photo. You can then define your selection more precisely with the Paint Brush controls (such as hardness).

For example, in Figure 30 I made the initial selection with the Freehand tool and then chose Edit Selection from the Selections menu. When you select the Edit Selection option, the available colors in the Materials palette change to 256 shades of grey, and the selected element is displayed with a semitransparent color representing the initial selection made with a tool called an **overlay** (like you see in Figure 30).

The overlay is a greyscale bitmap, with fully selected areas represented as white, feathered areas as grey, and unselected areas as black. This method has many advantages, one of which is being able to refine your selection pixel by pixel. Another is being able to store the greyscale mask information to the **alpha channel** for reuse or editing later (either on the original or another image). You take a closer look at masks, the alpha channel, and color channels in Chapter 4.

Zooming in for a Closer Look

When you edit an image, you should have a good view of the area that you are focusing on. Paint Shop Pro has several methods that allow you to reduce or enlarge your current view. The simplest is the

Zoom tool located at the very top of your main toolbar. You can use the Zoom tool by clicking the image to zoom out, enlarging the image view, and right-clicking the image to zoom in, reducing the image view.

It is important to understand that zooming enlarges or reduces your *view* of the image—not the actual image. The current zoom percentage appears in the image's title bar, as shown in Figure 31. The Zoom

tools option bar also contains an Actual Size icon that immediately takes you back to normal (100%) view.

FIGURE 30
Edit Selection mode

Toggle Edit selection

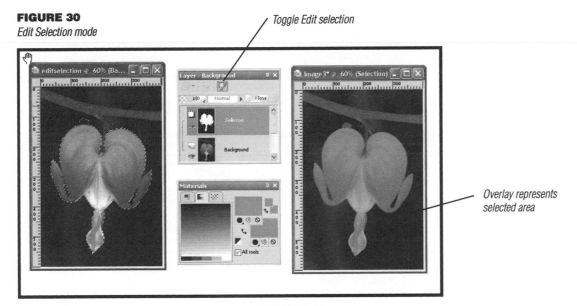

Overlay represents selected area

FIGURE 31
Zoom tool options

Current zoom percentage

Actual size

Use the Edit Selection command

1. Open **PSP3-9.PSPImage**, then save it as **Bird**.

   Your image opens with the selection intact.

2. In the Layers palette, click **Edit Selection**.

   The Materials palette colors change to 256 shades of grey, the Selection channel appears as its own layer in the Layers palette, and the red overlay on your bird represents the selected area. See Figure 32.

   > TIP Instead of using the Edit Selection icon on the Layers palette, you can choose Selections, then Edit Selection.

3. Click the **Paint Brush** ✏ on the main toolbar.

FIGURE 32

Edit Selection command with overlay

New channel

Match these settings

FIGURE 33

Paint Brush options: Set black and white

4. In the tool options palette, choose **20** for Size, **79** for Hardness, **10** for Step, **100** for Density, Thickness and Opacity, **0** for Rotation, and **Normal** for Blend mode.

Your settings should match those in Figure 33.

5. In the Materials palette, click the **Set to Black & White icon** ▣.

The foreground color changes to black and the background color changes to white.

6. Click and paint to remove any area that is not the bird, getting as close as you can without removing any of the bird itself.

The overlay disappears as you paint. Since you are painting with black, you deselect.

> TIP For detailed areas, adjust your brush size by pressing the Alt key while dragging. If that doesn't help, adjust other brush settings such as hardness, which softens the brush edges. If you accidentally remove part of the bird, right-click and paint with white to reselect. You just paint the area back into the selection.

Using the Edit Selection command, you refined an existing selection to isolate an element in your image, keeping more detail in your selection and allowing much softer edges.

Use the Zoom tool

1. Open **Bird.PSPImage** (if necessary).

2. Click the **Zoom tool** 🔍▾, then click the **beak** until the zoom reaches 500%.

   The zoom percentage appears in the title bar of your image. The image enlarges so you can see the finer detailed areas around the beak.

3. Click the **Paint Brush** 🖌▾ on the main tool-bar.

4. Starting at the beak, paint around the bird.

5. In the Layers palette, click the **Edit Selection icon** 🖉.

   The overlay disappears and the marquee reappears around the bird.

6. Click **Edit**, **Copy**, **Edit**, then **Paste as New Image**.

   Your newly isolated image opens on a transparent background, as shown in Figure 34.

Using the Zoom tool, you got as close as possible when painting a detailed area.

FIGURE 34
Newly isolated element

CHAPTER SUMMARY

In this chapter, you learned about some of Paint Shop Pro's most powerful tools, selections, and masks.

What You Have Learned

- How to make shape selections with the Shape Selection tool.
- How to hide the marquee when working at a high zoom ratio.
- How to select with the Freehand tool.
- How to turn rulers on and off.
- How to change the size of the selection marquee.
- How to move a marquee without moving its contents.
- How to use selections to create a vignette.
- How to use Paint Shop Pro's Picture Frame Wizard.

Key Terms

channels Layers of the primary colors that compose an image.

composition Combining one image with another or many others.

marquee The dashed lines that represent the selection.

masking Allows you to protect or modify parts of an image and is created using a selection marquee.

matte A decorative border placed around an image to serve as a frame or to provide contrast between the image and the frame.

selection An area of the image surrounded by a marquee.

chapter

4 USING LAYERS
AND MASKS

1. Learn layer basics.

2. Add and delete layers.

3. Understand layer visibility and layer sets.

4. Work with layer odds and ends.

5. Use layers and masks.

6. Edit mask visibility.

chapter 4 USING LAYERS
AND MASKS

Understanding Layers

You can create complex images by taking advantage of one of Paint Shop Pro's most powerful features: layers. You will probably use layers in the majority of your projects and if your work involves any type of graphic design, nearly all your image editing will involve them. Layers make it possible to manipulate the tiniest detail within your image, which gives you tremendous flexibility. By placing images, effects, and other elements on separate layers, you can modify each individually, without affecting the other image components. The disadvantage to using multiple layers is that your file size can increase dramatically. To remedy this, you flatten—also known as merging or combining—all the layers.

Layering Elements in Images

Think of layers as a clear plastic sheet on which you can paint. A multilayered image is like a stack of those sheets, each with its own element. Unpainted areas of the sheets are transparent, allowing the lower sheets to show through. Areas of the sheet that are opaque block out elements of the lower sheets. Figure 1 shows an image with two layers. The top layer is completely opaque, not letting you see anything else. The iPod stands alone, even though there is a layer underneath it.

You can add, delete, and move layers within your image, or move layers from one image to another. Copying layers from one image to another makes it easy to transfer a complex effect, a simple image, or text. You can also hide and display each layer or change its opacity. The flexibility offered by layers is worth its weight in gold.

Tools You'll Use

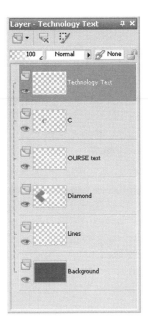

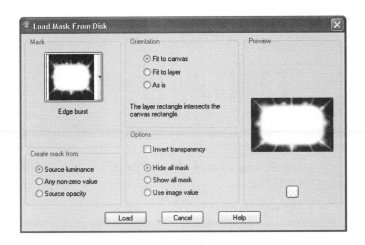

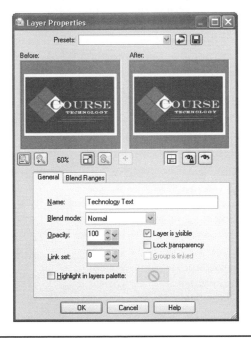

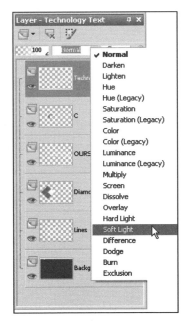

LEARN LAYER
BASICS

What You'll Do

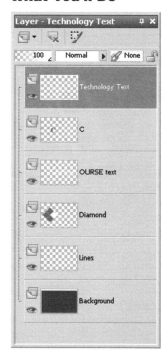

 In this lesson, you'll get familiar with the Layers palette layout, read about different layers, and learn how to organize layers.

Learning about the Layers Palette

The Layers palette lists all the layers within a file and enables you to edit one or more layers at a time. By default, the palette is invisible unless you have an image open. The Layers palette appears when you open a multilayered image. You can also make the Layers palette appear by closing the Learning Center on the default workspace. The Layers palette then appears docked to the right side of your workspace, as shown in Figure 1. Each layer has a **thumbnail**, a miniature picture of the contents, to the left of its name. Two icons appear to the left of the thumbnail. One indicates the layer type (raster, vector, art media, or adjustment) and the other, which looks like an eye, controls the layer's visibility. If the Layer Visibility icon's eye is open, the layer appears; if a Null icon covers the eye, the layer isn't visible. The Layers palette also contains buttons, such as Delete Layer, Create New Layer, and Edit Selection.

Customizing the Layers Palette Layout

If your computer is running slowly when working with layers, you can hide or resize the Layers palette thumbnails to improve performance. To keep them from showing automatically, right-click anywhere on a toolbar, select the General Program Preferences, then click Palettes for the category. Under Layers palette, remove the checkmark from Palette Thumbnails. Alternately, you can reduce thumbnail size by entering a lower number in the numerical value box. The palette's right pane moves the opacity, blend mode, and links sliders to the right of each layer instead of being above all the layers. Figure 2 shows two Layers palettes, one with the right pane checked and one with it not checked. You also see it with automatic thumbnails disabled.

FIGURE 1

Default workspace with the Layers palette docked

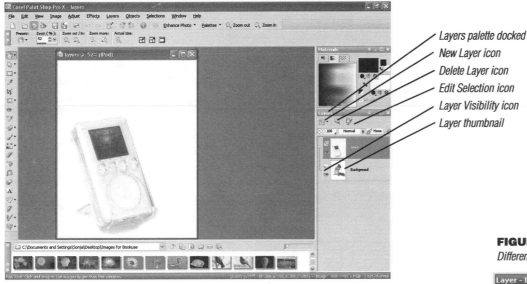

Layers palette docked
New Layer icon
Delete Layer icon
Edit Selection icon
Layer Visibility icon
Layer thumbnail

QUICKTIP   If you choose not to display the thumbnails automatically in the Layers palette, you can still see what's on each layer without leaving the palette. Hold your cursor over a layer. A small thumbnail of the image will appear, as shown in Figure 2.

Converting the Background Layer

The Layers palette allows different types of layers, the first and most basic of which is the background. This special layer is created when you either open a new image with an opaque background or flatten a

FIGURE 2

Different Layers palette setups

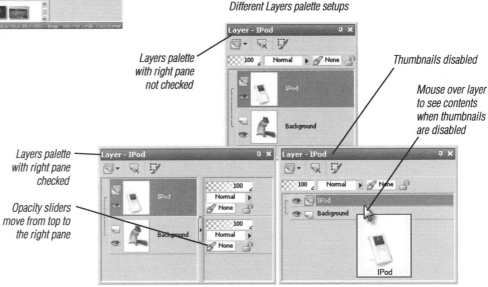

Layers palette with right pane not checked

Thumbnails disabled

Mouse over layer to see contents when thumbnails are disabled

Layers palette with right pane checked

Opacity sliders move from top to the right pane

layered image that does not have a transparency channel. The background layer's opacity cannot be changed unless it is promoted, or changed, to an image layer. Promote it by right-clicking any background layer, then selecting the Promote Background Layer option; if you move the opacity slider down, Paint Shop Pro automatically promotes the background layer to an image layer with a transparency channel. In doing so, the name changes from Background Layer to Raster 1 (or whatever number is sequentially next relative to the other layer names).

Organizing Layers

One of the benefits of using layers is creating different effects by arranging their order in the palette. Each logo in Figure 3 contains the same layers, but each is arranged differently. On the first logo, the C is not visible because I moved it behind the Diamond layer. On the second logo, I moved the C back up above the Diamond layer, so it is visible and reads *Course* instead of *ourse*.

FIGURE 3
Layers in different arrangements

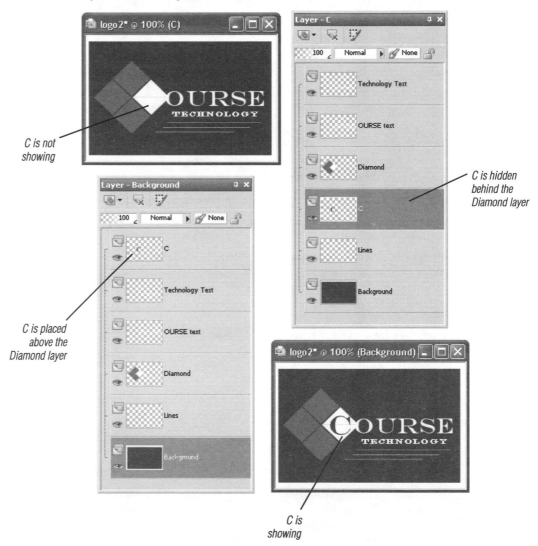

C is not showing

C is hidden behind the Diamond layer

C is placed above the Diamond layer

C is showing

FIGURE 4

Background layer becomes active (left) and is promoted (right)

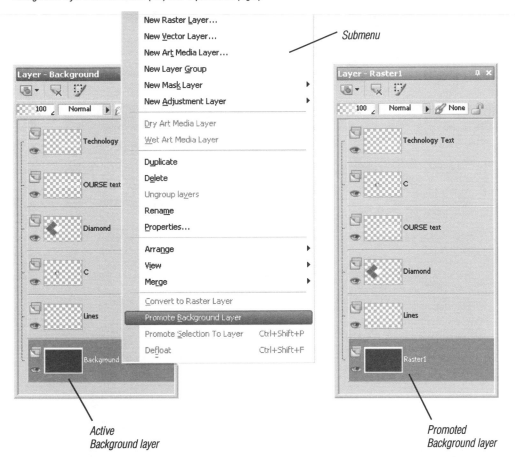

Submenu

*Active
Background layer*

*Promoted
Background layer*

1. Open **PSP4-1.PSPImage**, then save it as **Logo1**.

2. In the Layers palette, click the **Background layer**.

    The Background layer becomes active and is highlighted in the Layers palette.

3. Right-click the **Background layer**.

    A submenu appears, as shown in Figure 4.

4. Click **Promote Background Layer**.

    The background layer promotes to an image layer and is renamed Raster1, as shown in Figure 4.

You promoted a background layer to an image layer, enabling all editing functions.

Organize layers

1. Open **PSP4-1.PSPImage**, then save it as **Rearranged**.

2. Click the **C layer** in the Layers palette.

   The C layer becomes active.

3. Click and drag the **C layer** above the Diamond layer.

   The C is visible, as shown in Figure 5.

4. Save your image.

You rearranged layers so you could see different options without having to create a new image.

FIGURE 5
Rearranged layers

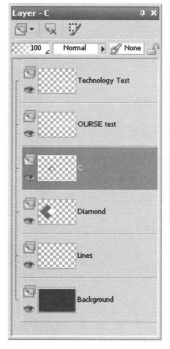

C is visible

ADD AND
DELETE LAYERS

What You'll Do

In this lesson, you'll add, delete, and flatten layers.

Adding Layers to an Image

Because it's so important to make the most of layers, Paint Shop Pro makes it easy to add and delete them. You can create layers three ways:

- Use the New command on the Layer context menu.
- Use the New Layer button on the Layers palette menu.
- Use an assigned combination key.

Elements on a new layer have a default opacity setting of 100%, which means that elements on lower layers will not be visible. Each new layer has the Normal (default) blending mode applied to it. A blending mode is a feature that affects a layer's underlying pixels, and is used to lighten, darken, and blend layers together.

Flattening Layers

You can combine, or flatten, multiple layers into a single layer using the merging process. Merging is useful when you want to make specific edits permanent. To merge, layers must be visible in the Layers palette. You can merge all visible layers within an image, or select specific layers and merge only those. Vector layers cannot be merged until they are rasterized—turned into bitmapped image layers. To merge layers, make invisible any one you do not want merged by clicking the Layer Visibility icon, which looks like an eye, so that a Null icon appears over the eye. Click Layers on the menu bar, select Merge, then select Merge Visible. To merge two layers next to one another, click the top layer, click Layers in the menu, select Merge, then select Merge Down. Merging options are also available if you right-click.

Naming a Layer

Paint Shop Pro assigns a sequential number to each new layer name, but you can rename a layer at any time. Calling it "Raster 4" is fine, but you might want to give it a more unique, descriptive moniker so it is easier to distinguish. If you use the New Layer command, you can name it when you create it. The New Raster Layer dialog box, shown in Figure 6, appears if you choose this option. Rename any other time with one of these methods:

- Right-click the layer you want to rename, choose the Rename option, then type in the new name.
- Double-click the layer in the Layers palette. When the dialog box appears, type in the new name.

Deleting Layers

You may decide you no longer want to use a specific layer; or maybe you changed your mind about adding the layer element to your image. You can use any of four methods to delete a layer:

- Right-click the layer you want to delete in the Layers palette. Choose Delete from the menu.
- Click and drag the layer you want to delete to the Delete Layer icon on the top of the Layers palette. See the icon in Figure 7.
- Click the layer you want to delete in the Layers palette, then click the Layers context menu, then select Delete.
- Assign and use a customized combination key. Chapter 2, "Controlling Menus, Toolbars, and Palettes," tells you how to do that.

Before deleting a layer, be certain that you no longer need it. If you delete by accident and realize it immediately, you can restore it using the Undo command or by deleting the Delete layer state in the History palette. In Figure 7, I had deleted the Raster 1 layer and then decided I wanted to keep it. I restored the previously deleted layer by clicking the Delete layer state in the History palette.

QUICKTIP If your History palette is not visible, activate it with the shortcut key command [F3].

FIGURE 6
Naming your layer upon creation

Type layer name

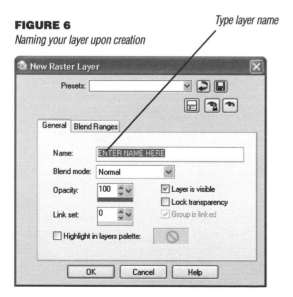

FIGURE 7
Deleting layer options

Delete Layer icon

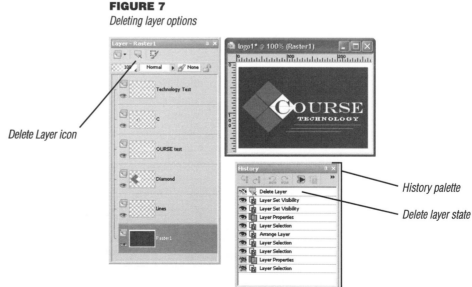

History palette

Delete layer state

FIGURE 8

Create a new raster layer and put it at the top

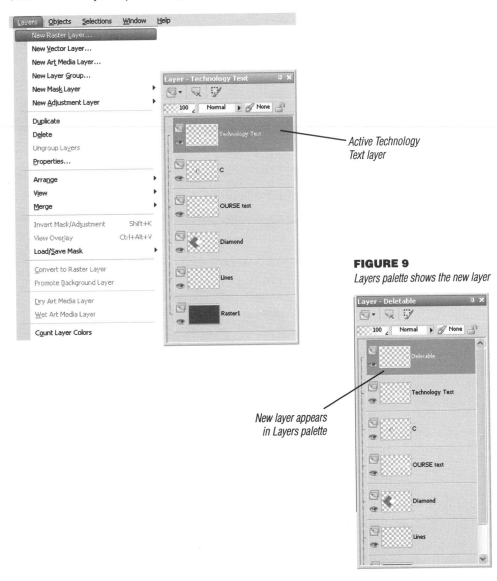

Active Technology
Text layer

FIGURE 9

Layers palette shows the new layer

New layer appears
in Layers palette

1. Open **PSP4-2.PSPImage**, then save it as **Addlayer**.

2. Click the **Technology Text layer** in the Layers palette, as shown in Figure 8.

   The layer becomes active.

   > TIP Clicking the top layer in the Layers palette ensures that any new layer goes directly above that layer.

3. Click the **Layers menu**.

   The submenu opens.

4. Click **New Raster Layer**.

   The Layer Properties dialog box opens.

5. Type **Deletable** for the name.

6. Click **OK**.

   The Layer Properties dialog box closes and the new layer appears in your palette with the appropriate name, as shown in Figure 9.

7. Save your file.

You created a new layer using the New Raster Layer command. You named the layer as you created it, which made identifying it easier.

Delete a layer

1. Open **Addlayer** (if necessary), then save it as **Delete**.

2. Click the **Deletable layer** in the Layers palette.

   The layer named Deletable becomes active.

3. Click the **Delete Layer icon** ☒ at the top of the Layers palette, as shown in Figure 10.

   A Delete Layer dialog box asks if you are sure you want to delete the current layer; see Figure 11.

   > TIP   To avoid the Delete Layer warning dialog box in future sessions, place a checkmark in the Don't ask about this anymore checkbox.

4. Click **Yes**.

   The warning closes and the layer is removed from your Layers palette.

5. Save and close your image.

You deleted an unneeded layer using the Delete Layer icon.

FIGURE 10
Use the Delete Layer icon to cut a layer

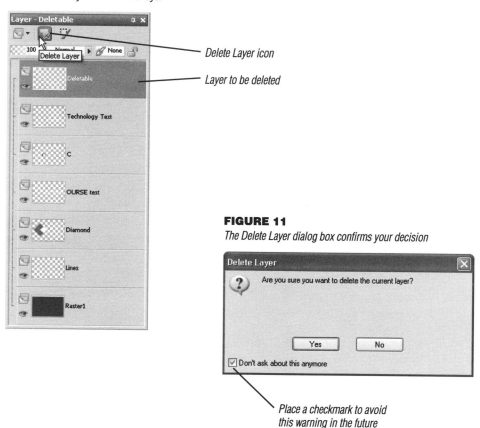

Delete Layer icon

Layer to be deleted

FIGURE 11
The Delete Layer dialog box confirms your decision

Place a checkmark to avoid
this warning in the future

FIGURE 12

Choose from the New Layer icon submenu

New Layer
icon

Submenu lists
different layer
types available

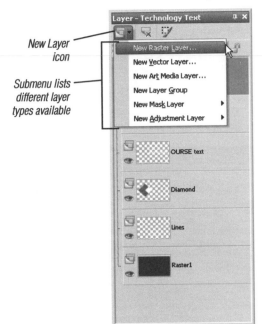

FIGURE 13

New layer in the Layers palette

Newly created
layer appears in
Layers palette

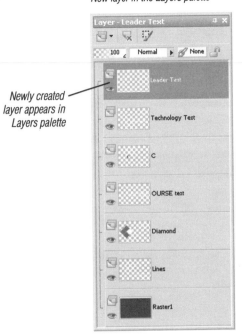

1. Open **PSP4-2.PSPImage**, then save it as **Addlayer2**.

2. Click the **New Layer icon** 🔲▾ in the Layers palette.

   A submenu like that shown in Figure 12 lists the different layer types.

3. Click **New Raster Layer**, type **Leader Text** for the name, then click **OK**.

   The New Raster Layer dialog box closes and the palette shows the layer with the appropriate name. See Figure 13.

4. Click the **Text tool** A, then chose **10** for Miter limit, **0** for Offset, **Engravers MT** for Font, **3** for Size, **Points** for Units, **Bold** for Font style, **Left-aligned** for Alignment, **Off** for Anti-alias, **1** for Stroke width, then **Floating** for Create as.

   These options match settings shown in Figure 14.

5. Set foreground/stroke to **null** and background/fill to white.

6. Place your cursor in the top left of your image, then click.

   The Text Entry dialog box appears.

7. Type **Leading the way in IT Publishing**, then click **OK**.

   The Text Entry dialog box closes and the text appears on your image as a floating selection.

   | TIP If you are having trouble viewing the text, hide the marquee using [Ctrl+Shft+M].

8. Right-click the **Floating Selection layer** in the Layers palette, then click **Defloat**.

   The Floating Selection text merges with the Leader Text layer you created in Steps 4 and 5.

9. Save your image.

You created a raster layer with the New Layer icon, enabling the Text tool. With that tool, you added floating text to the new layer, then defloated the text, merged it with the underlying layer, and repositioned the text.

FIGURE 14

Text tool settings

Match the text option settings

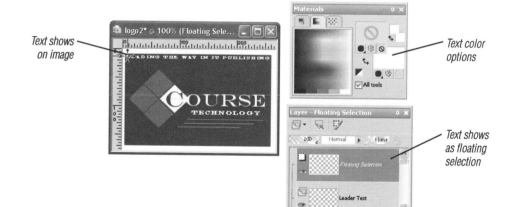

Text shows on image

Text color options

Text shows as floating selection

FIGURE 15

Flattened layers as they are in the Layers palette

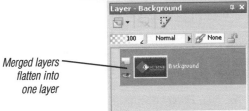

Merged layers
flatten into
one layer

1. Open **Addlayer2.PSPImage** (if necessary), then save it as **Flatten**.

2. Right-click the **Background layer**, click **Merge**, then click **Merge All (flatten)**.

   The seven separate layers merge together to form one—the layer named Background, shown in Figure 15.

   TIP If you have previously promoted the Background layer to an image layer, Paint Shop Pro automatically names the newly merged layer Merged. Double-click the layer. When the Layer properties dialog box appears, type a new name.

3. Save your image as **Logo.gif**.

4. Close your image.

   You flattened all layers, then saved your logo as a GIF file, reducing the size from the original .PSPImage file. You saved 39 kilobytes.

UNDERSTAND LAYER
VISIBILITY AND LAYER SETS

What You'll Do

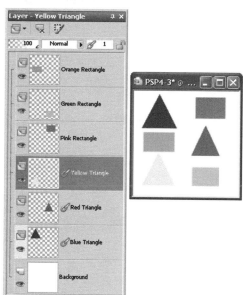

In this lesson, you'll hide, show, and highlight layers. You'll also create, add, and move layer sets.

Toggling Layer Visibility

Each layer in the Layers palette has its own Layer Visibility icon, which looks like an eye. Figure 16 shows the Layer Visibility icon in both the on and off states. One reason to hide a layer is to simply get

FIGURE 16
Visibility turned off and on

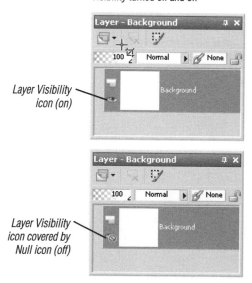

Layer Visibility icon (on)

Layer Visibility icon covered by Null icon (off)

elements out of your way while you are working on another layer. Another reason, as shown in Lesson 2, is so you can merge together only the visible layers of your image.

Highlighting Layers

If your image has few layers, it's easy to locate each one. However, if it contains several, you might need some organizing help. You can organize by highlighting or color coding, which make it easier to distinguish layers from each other in the Layers palette. For example, you could put all triangles in red (the bottom three bars on the left) and all rectangles in blue (the top three bars on the left), as I did in Figure 17.

Creating, Adding, and Moving Layer Sets

A layer set allows you to organize your layers on the Layers palette. In the same way that a folder on your hard drive contains individual files, a layer set contains individual layers. Clear as mud? Try this: If you have several layers of text in your image, you could create a layer set that contains all your text layers. When you click any one of the elements in a set with the Move tool, all the other layers in the set shift also.

Creating a layer set is simple. Determine which you want to group together, then click the first layer you want in the set.

Then, on the Layers palette, you will see the Layer Link button, as shown in Figure 18. Clicking it once gives you the number 1. Each click after that gives you incremental numbers, and the number of clicks until you return to the None setting is determined by the number of layers in your image. My first triangle is 1; simply repeat the process to link it the other triangles— click the next triangle layer, then click the Layer Link button. As you add layers to the

set, you will see the Layer Link icon appear next to the layer name in the palette. Now if I select the Move tool and click any one of the triangles, all three of them go together.

You can have more than one set of linked layers. To create a second (or third, or fourth, or more), click the first layer you want in the set, then click the Layer Link button until it is different from the other set. In Figure 19 it is 2.

FIGURE 17
Color-coded layers help identify sets

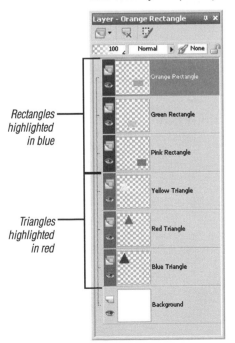

Rectangles highlighted in blue

Triangles highlighted in red

FIGURE 18
Click the Layer Link button to add links

Layer Link button

Linked layers

FIGURE 19
The second linked set

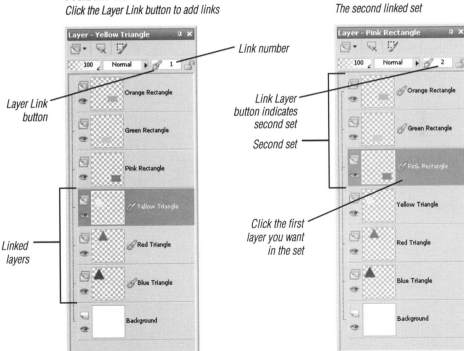

Link number

Link Layer button indicates second set

Second set

Click the first layer you want in the set

Toggle and highlight layers

1. Open **PSP4-3.PSPImage**, then save it as **Toggle**.

2. Click the **Layer Visibility icon** on the Red Triangle layer.

   The Null icon appears over the Layer Visibility icon, and the red triangle element disappears from your image.

3. Double-click the **Blue Triangle layer** in the Layers palette.

   The Layers property dialog box appears, as shown in Figure 20.

4. Click the **Highlight in layers palette checkbox**, then click **OK**.

   > TIP To highlight a background layer, you must first convert it to a regular layer. Paint Shop Pro does this for you if you select the Highlight in Layers Palette option.

   The Layers property dialog box closes and the palette shows the yellow highlight, as shown in Figure 21.

5. Save your image.

You turned off an unneeded layer, then highlighted a different layer, distinguishing it from others.

FIGURE 20
The Layers property dialog box

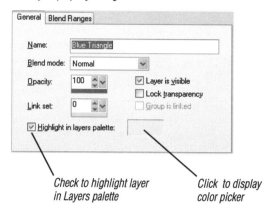

Check to highlight layer
in Layers palette

Click to display
color picker

FIGURE 21
Highlighted layer

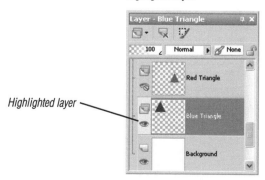

Highlighted layer

FIGURE 22

Move shapes together

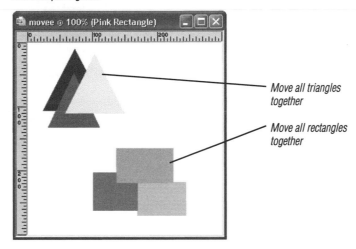

Move all triangles together

Move all rectangles together

1. Open **PSP4-3.PSPImage**, then save it as **Move**.

2. Click the **Move tool** ⊕ on the main toolbar.

3. Click and drag the **yellow triangle** up to the blue triangle.

4. Using the **Move tool** ⊕, move the last **triangle**.

5. Move the **rectangles** together, as shown in Figure 22.

    Each shape is moved independently from the others, then grouped together in the image.

6. Save your image.

You used the Move tool to shift each layer's elements and group shapes together.

Create a layer set

1. Open **Move** (if necessary), then save it as **Move2**.

2. Click the **Blue Triangle layer** in the Layers palette, then click the **Link Layer button** [None].

   The number 1 appears in the link layer box, and the icon appears next to the Blue Triangle layer's name, as shown in Figure 23.

3. Click the **Red Triangle layer** in the Layers palette, then click the **Link Layer button** [1].

   The number 1 appears in the link layer box, and the Link Layer icon appears next to the Red Triangle layer's name.

4. Click the **Yellow Triangle layer** in the Layers palette, then click the **Link Layer button** [1].

   A Link Layer icon appears next to each triangle layer, as shown in Figure 24.

   TIP If you accidentally click past 1 when linking layers, keep clicking to rotate through all numbers back to None, then click once to show the number 1 again.

5. Click the **Move tool** [⊕].

6. Click and drag any of the **triangles** in your image to the opposite side of the canvas.

   All the triangles move.

7. Save your image for the next objective.

You created a layer set by linking common elements, which lets you easily move the combined elements all at once, instead of one at a time.

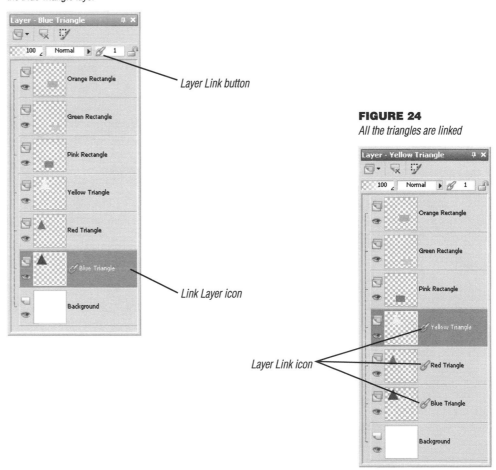

FIGURE 23
The Link Layers icon accompanies the Blue Triangle layer

Layer Link button

Link Layer icon

FIGURE 24
All the triangles are linked

Layer Link icon

FIGURE 25

All the rectangles are linked

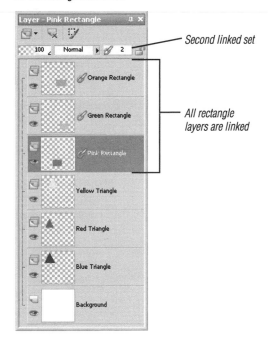

Second linked set

All rectangle
layers are linked

1. Open **Move2** (if necessary), then save it as **Move3**.

2. Click the **Pink Rectangle layer** in the Layers palette, then click the **Link Layer button** `None` until you see the number 2.

   The Link Layer icon appears next to the Pink Rectangle layer's name.

3. Repeat until all rectangle layers are linked, as shown in Figure 25.

4. Save your image.

You created a second layer set by linking common elements, which allows you to easily move the combined elements all at once, instead of one at a time.

WORK WITH LAYER
ODDS AND ENDS

What You'll Do

▶ *In this lesson, you'll adjust images, work with filters, and use blend modes.*

Adjusting Image Content

As you work in Paint Shop Pro, you will find that some images have more complex problems, while others just need a little enhancement. For example, you might want to colorize a dull photo or sharpen a blurred one. You can use a variety of techniques to change the way an image looks. For example, you can use the Adjust commands or Adjustments layer to modify a hue, saturation, brightness, and contrast.

Dabbling in Basic Native Filters

Filters are commands that alter an image's appearance. Experimenting with the filters can become quite addictive, so proceed with caution. You start here with just a couple simple sharpening and blurring filters. In Chapter 6, "Adding Effects with Filters, Plug-ins, and Deformation," you take a more in-depth look at the other native filters, in addition to several must-have plug-in filters. Native filters are those that come with Paint Shop Pro; plug-ins don't.

Sharpen filters work by giving the appearance of definition to a dull, blurry image. In Figure 26, the Sharpen filter increases the contrast of each adjacent pixel and focuses a blurry picture; Sharpen More does so even further. Be careful not to overuse any of the filters. Bad results can occur. For example, since sharpen filters increase contrast, excessive use can create high contrast lines or add grain or brightness to the color.

Choosing Blend Modes

A blend mode controls how pixels are either made darker or lighter, based on the colors underneath. Paint Shop Pro provides a variety of blend modes, which you can see in Figure 27 and read in Table 1.

Each mode blends the pixel colors in the current layer with those in the layers beneath it. You can see a list of blend modes by clicking the arrow in the Blend Mode section on the Layers palette.

Consider a few things when working with blend modes:

- **Base color**, which is the image's original color

- **Blend color**, which is what you apply with a painting or editing tool such as Flood Fill
- **Resulting color**, which is the color created when you blend

FIGURE 26
Sharpen effects get progressively sharper

Original　　　　*Sharpen filter*　　　　*Sharpen More filter*

photo by Ron Lacey

FIGURE 27
Blend mode options

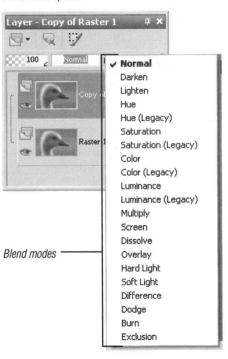

Blend modes

TABLE 1: Blend Modes

Mode	Description
Normal	Displays underlying layer's pixels based on the selected layer's pixel opacity. This is the default setting.
Darken and Lighten	Darken selects a new color based on whatever color is darkest (base or blend). Lighten displays a chosen layer's pixels that are lighter than pixels underneath; any pixels darker than the underlying layers do not show.
Hue and Hue*	Creates a resulting color with the luminance of the base color and the hue of the blend color.
Saturation and Saturation*	Creates a resulting color with the luminance of the base color and the saturation of the blend color.
Color and Color*	Creates a resulting color with the luminance of the base color, and the hue and saturation of the blend color.
Luminance and Luminance*	Creates a resulting color with the hue and saturation of the base color, and the luminance of the blend color.
Multiply	Creates semitransparent shadowed effects. This mode assesses the information in each channel, then multiplies the value of the base color by the blend color resulting in an overall darker image.
Screen	The opposite of Multiply, the result is much lighter.
Dissolve	At random intervals, pixels from the underlying layers are displayed. The degree of the dissolve effect increases as the layers opacity decreases.
Overlay	Dark and Light values (luminosity) are preserved, dark base colors are multiplied (darkened), and the light areas are screened (lightened).
Soft Light and Hard Light	Soft light lightens a light base color and darkens a dark base color. Hard Light works much the same way but provides greater contrast between the base and layer colors.
Difference	Subtracts the value of the layer's pixels from the value's or lower pixels, depending on which pixel is lower. This affects the hues in an image.
Dodge	Brightens the base color to reflect the blend color.
Burn	Darkens the base color to reflect the blend color.
Exclusion	Similar to the Difference mode, but with less contrast between the blend and base colors.

*Legacy modes show behavior that matches Paint Shop Pro 7.

FIGURE 28

Setting brightness and contrast

Brightness slider   Contrast slider

1. Open **PSP4-4.PSPImage**, then save it as **Adjust1**.

2. On the context menu, click **Adjust, Brightness and Contrast**, then click **Brightness and Contrast**.

   The Brightness/Contrast dialog box displays.

3. Drag the **Brightness slider** until +5 appears in the text box.

   > TIP The Brightness and Contrast commands can be a negative value, resulting in the opposite effect. Drag the slider to the left to darken the brightness and contrast.

4. Drag the **Contrast slider** until 3 appears in the Contrast dialog box, as shown in Figure 28.

5. Click **OK** to close the Brightness/Contrast dialog box.

6. Save your image.

You increased the brightness in your image to lighten up the photo, then adjusted the contrast to enhance it.

Dabble with a filter

1. Open **PSP4-4.PSPImage**, then save it as **Sharpened**.

2. Click **Adjust**, **Sharpness**, then click **Sharpen**.

   The image becomes vivid, like what you see in Figure 29.

3. Save your image and move to the next objective.

You adjusted the image with the Sharpen command to bring out more detail.

Vivid details
stand out

FIGURE 29
Sharpened image

photo by Ron Lacey

FIGURE 30
Embossed layer

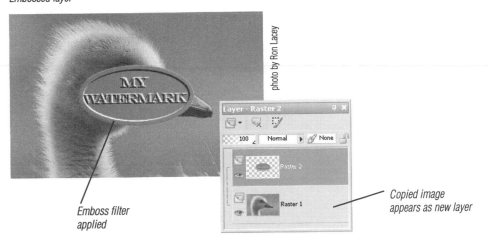

photo by Ron Lacey

Emboss filter
applied

Copied image
appears as new layer

FIGURE 31
Soft Light mode applied to the watermark

photo by Ron Lacey

Soft Light mode

Semitransparent
copied layer

Choose blend modes and opacity settings

1. Open **PSP4-5.PSPImage**, then save it as **Watermarked**.

2. Click **Edit**, then click **Copy**.

   The image copies to the Windows Clipboard.

3. Click the **title bar** of the sharpened image to make it active.

   The sharpened image becomes active.

4. Click **Edit**, then click **Paste as New Layer**.

   The copied image appears on your image and as a new layer in the Layers palette.

5. Click **Effects**, **Texture Effects**, then click **Emboss**.

   The Emboss filter applies to the image, giving the effect shown in Figure 30.

6. Click the **Blend Modes arrow** in the Layers palette to reveal the options, then click **Soft Light**.

   The copied layer changes to reflect the Soft Light mode, becoming semitransparent, as shown in Figure 31.

   TIP   If Soft Light does not give you enough of the effect you are looking for, change to Hard Light and reduce the Hard Light layer's opacity.

7. Click **Layers**, **Merge**, then click **Merge All (flatten)**.

   All your layers merge into one.

8. Save your image.

You applied the Emboss filter to an image, copied and pasted the image onto another image, then changed the blend modes to create a watermark effect to further personalize.

Use blend modes

1. Open **PSP4-4.PSPImage**, then save it as **White**.

2. Click **Layer**, then click **New Raster Layer**.

   The New Layer dialog box prompts you to name the layer.

3. Name the layer **Fill**, then click **OK**.

   The dialog box closes.

4. Click the **Flood Fill tool** 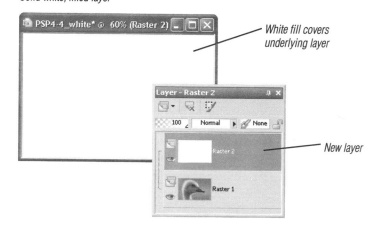, then set the foreground/stroke color in the Materials palette to white.

5. Click the **image** to fill the layer with white.

   The new layer fills with solid white, covering the underlying layer. See Figure 32.

6. Click the **Blend Modes arrow** in the Layers palette to reveal the options, then click **Color (L)**.

   The solid white fill layer disappears and your underlying layer shows through as black and white, as shown in Figure 33.

7. Merge your layers, then save your image.

You added a layer to your image, filled it with white, and then changed the blend mode to Color (L). What used to be a color image was made black and white.

FIGURE 32
Solid white, filled layer

White fill covers
underlying layer

New layer

FIGURE 33
Color mode applied to create a black and white image

photo by Ron Lacey

USE LAYERS
AND MASKS

What You'll Do

In this lesson, you'll use standard masks and make your own mask.

Working with Masks

We've all used masks in one way or another. At Halloween you wear a mask that hides your face but lets your eyes and mouth to show through. When you use a stencil to spray paint some letters on a sign, you are using a mask. When you paint your house and want to keep the trim clean, you use—what else?—masking tape. In the graphics world, artists use masks to protect portions (or all parts) of an image.

Using Standard Masks

Figure 34 shows just a few of the great time-saving masks included with Paint Shop Pro. Additionally, you can add to the predefined mask collection by creating your own and saving it to a disk. When you save an image that includes a mask in the .PSPImage format, the mask is saved as well; however, if you save your image in a format that doesn't support layers, Paint Shop Pro flattens the image, merging all layers, including the mask. JPEG and TIFF do not support layers. Additionally, you can save a mask to an alpha channel or as a separate image file on a disk, which is really beneficial if you want to use the mask again.

If you apply a mask to a background layer, the area being masked out becomes transparent, and when you save it to a file format that doesn't support the transparency, Paint Shop Pro turns the transparency to a solid color. For that reason, you should get in the habit of making a solid-colored background image for your masked image. Make it the same size as the photograph or image you are going to use. Then copy and paste your image as a new layer on the solid-colored background. Luckily, Paint Shop Pro doesn't limit you to its selection of predefined masks. You can create your own and save it for future use.

Knowing the Makings of a Mask Layer

Paint Shop Pro supports masking, which are greyscale layers hiding portions of other layers without deleting or modifying them. Masks can hide and show parts of a layer, fade between layers, and create other special effects. You can create a mask from a selection (as you did in Chapter 3), the alpha channel, or an existing image, and it can completely cover a layer or cover it with varying layers of opacity. A mask applies to all layers below it that are at the same level:

- If a mask layer is in a layer set, the mask applies only to the layers within the set that are lower in the stacking order.
- If the mask layer is at the main level (rather than in a layer set), the mask applies to all layers below it.

Painting a Layer Mask

After you add a mask to a layer, you can reshape the mask with the Brush tool, much like you did with the Edit Selection command in Chapter 3. Paint Shop Pro offers loads of brush tips. For example, you can create a smooth transition between the hidden and visible areas using a soft-edged brush. Keep these things in mind when using masks:

- When you paint the image with a black foreground/stroke, the mask size increases and each brush stroke hides pixels on the image layer. Paint with black to hide pixels.
- When you paint an object using a white foreground/stroke, the mask size decreases. Paint with white to reveal pixels.
- When you use a grey value (between black and white), the mask is semi-transparent.

FIGURE 34
Masks included with Paint Shop Pro

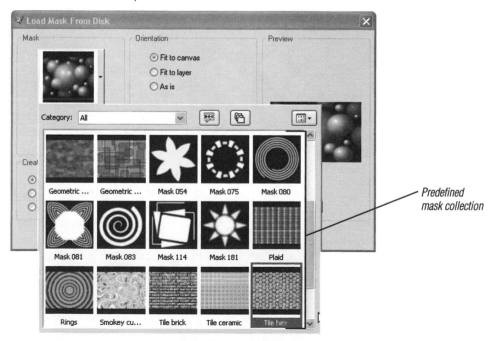

Predefined mask collection

FIGURE 35

Edge burst mask applied

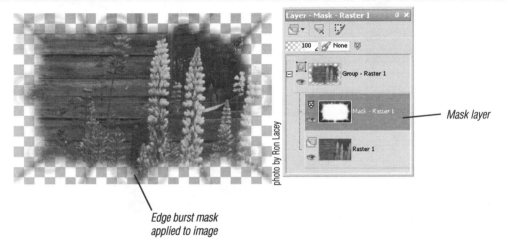

photo by Ron Lacey

Mask layer

Edge burst mask applied to image

1. Open **PSP4-6.PSPImage**, then save it as **Loadmask**.

2. Click the **Layers menu**, click **Load/Save Mask**, then click **Load Mask from Disk**.

   The Mask dialog box opens.

3. Click the **arrow** next to the mask you want to use.

   The list expands to show all masks.

4. Click the **Edge burst mask** to select it.

5. Click the **Fit to Layer radio button**, then click **Load**.

   The Mask dialog box closes and the Edge burst mask is applied to your image, as shown in Figure 35.

6. Save your image.

You loaded a standard mask onto your image, giving it a rugged look.

Create and paint a layer mask

1. Open **PSP4-6.PSPImage**, then save it as **Layermask**.

2. Click **Layers**, **New Mask Layer**, then click **Hide All**.

   Your image becomes invisible and the new mask layer is added to the Layers palette, as shown in Figure 36.

3. Click the **Paint Brush** 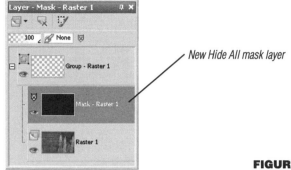.

4. Click the **Set to Black and White icon** ▣ in the Materials palette.

5. Click the **Swap Materials icon** ⬑ to make your foreground/stroke color white.

   The foreground/stroke and background/fill colors in the Materials palette swap places.

6. Click and drag the **Paint Brush** across the canvas to reveal the underlying image.

   The underlying layer is revealed, as shown in Figure 37.

7. Save your image.

You created a new mask, hiding all the contents of your image so you could use the Paint Brush to reveal only the areas you want in the image.

FIGURE 36
New mask with Hide All

New Hide All mask layer

FIGURE 37
Painted with white

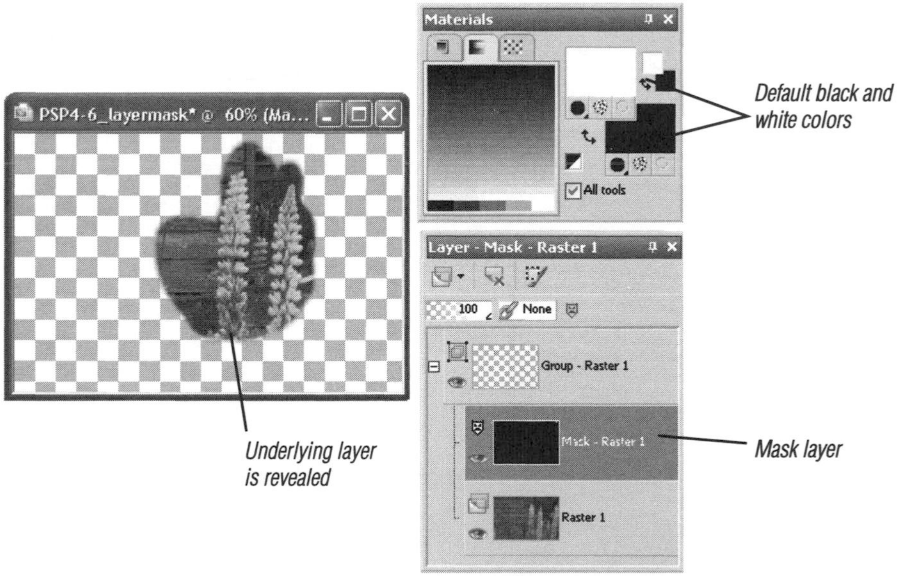

Default black and white colors

Underlying layer is revealed

Mask layer

FIGURE 38

New mask layer Show All

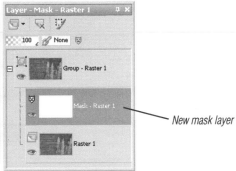

New mask layer

photo by Ron Lacey

FIGURE 39

Paint out areas

Contents of the
underlying layer
are removed

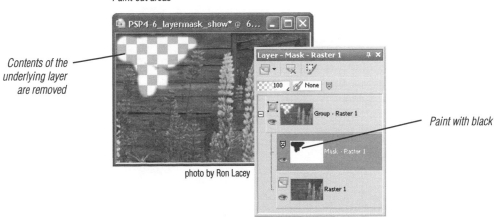

Paint with black

photo by Ron Lacey

1. Open **PSP4-6.PSPImage**, then save it as **Layermask_show**.

2. Click **Layers**, click **New Mask Layer**, then click **Show All**.

   The new mask layer appears in the Layers palette, with your image still completely visible. See Figure 38.

3. Click the **Paint Brush** ⬚.

4. Click the **Set to Black and White icon** ⬚ in the Materials palette.

5. Click the **Swap Materials icon** ⬚.

   The foreground/stroke and background/fill colors in the Materials palette swap places and your foreground/stroke color becomes black.

6. Click and drag the **Paint Brush** across the canvas to reveal the underlying image.

   The contents of the underlying layer are removed, as shown in Figure 39.

7. Save your image.

You created a new mask, showing all of the image so you could remove areas you didn't want with the Paint Brush.

Create your own mask with the Rectangle Marquee Selection tool

1. Create a new, 500 × 600 pixel image with a black background, then save it as **Mymask**.

2. Click the **Shape Selection tool** ⬚⦁, then select the **Ellipse shape**.

3. Draw a selection in the black image.

   The marquee appears, in the shape of an ellipse, on the black image.

4. Click the **Flood Fill tool** ⬚, then set your foreground/stroke color to white (if necessary).

5. Click once inside the selection.

   The selection is filled with white, and all elements in this area show through.

6. Click **Layers**, **New Mask Layer**, then click **From Image**.

   The Add Mask From Image dialog box appears, as shown in Figure 40.

7. Click the **Source window arrow**, then click your **image name**, then click **OK**.

   The Add Mask from Image dialog box closes. The black areas of your image become transparent, indicated by the grey and white checkerboard pattern.

8. Click **Layers**, click **Load/Save Mask**, then click **Save Mask to Disk**.

   The Save Mask To Disk dialog box prompts you to name your mask, as shown in Figure 41.

9. Enter a unique name for your mask, then click **Save**.

   Your new mask appears in the Load/Save Mask from Disk option.

You created your own mask, then saved it to disk so you can use it later.

FIGURE 40
Mask from image source

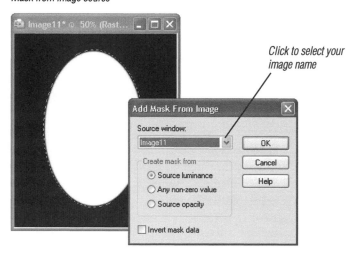

Click to select your image name

FIGURE 41
Save Mask To Disk dialog box

Enter name for mask

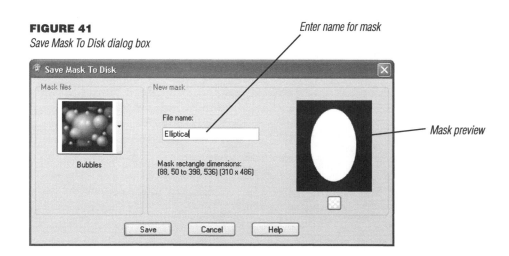

Mask preview

EDIT MASK
VISIBILITY

What You'll Do

In this lesson, you'll disable, enable, and delete a mask, and toggle a mask overlay.

Disabling and Enabling a Mask

You can temporarily disable a mask to view the layer without the mask. When you disable a mask, Paint Shop Pro uses the same icon that indicates that image layers are still in place: the Layers Visibility icon, which looks like an eye. Temporarily disabling a mask has many advantages. For example, if you have several mask layers, you can enable and disable each, applying different effects until you get the look you want. Assume you're working on a poster that promotes healthy eating. You aren't sure if you want peppers on the poster. You could create different mask layers for peppers, view the background layer, and enable and disable the pepper mask layer. That way you see all your available options. Figure 42 shows both an enabled and disabled layer mask.

Removing a Layer Mask

If you are certain you no longer need your mask, you can permanently remove it by dragging it up to the Delete icon in the top of the Layers palette. However, Paint Shop Pro gives you the following options for deleting a mask:

- Apply the mask to the active layer, permanently making it a part of the layer.
- Discard the mask and its effect completely.

If you do one of those things and then apply the mask, the layer will keep the appearance of the mask effect, but it will no longer contain the actual mask layer. If you discard the mask completely, you delete the effect you created with the layer mask and return the layer to its original state.

QUICKTIP   Each layer mask increases the file size, so it's a good idea to perform some routine clean-up before saving your image. Get rid of any unused, empty layers or any other mask that you do not want to use by dragging it to the Delete icon in the Layers palette.

Finessing a Mask Overlay

When you created a new layer mask using the Hide All option, you might have noticed that something was missing: the overlay. An overlay represents masked and non-

masked areas. You can toggle this overlay off and on through the Layers menu by choosing the View Overlay option. You can also change the color to anything you want through the Layer properties dialog box.

FIGURE 42
Enable and disable

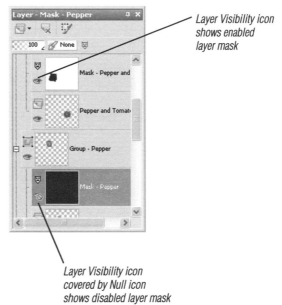

Layer Visibility icon shows enabled layer mask

Layer Visibility icon covered by Null icon shows disabled layer mask

FIGURE 43

Disable mask layer

Layer Visibility icon covered
by Null icon shows Disabled
Pepper layer mask

1. Open **PSP4-7.PSPImage**, then save it as **Disable**.

2. Click the **Mask-Pepper layer** in the Layers palette.

   The Mask-Pepper layer becomes active.

3. Click the **Layer Visibility icon** .

   The Mask-Pepper layer disables, as shown in Figure 43.

4. Save your image and move to the next objective.

You disabled a mask using the Layer Visibility icon, removing the effect and bringing back an image that was previously masked out. You got to see both options without committing to either.

Enable a layer mask

1. Open **Disable.PSPImage** (if necessary).
2. Click the **Mask-Pepper layer** in the Layers palette.

   The Mask-Pepper layer becomes active.
3. Click the **Layer Visibility icon** 👁.

   The Mask-Pepper layer is enabled, as shown in Figure 44.

You enabled a mask using the Layer Visibility icon to restore the effect. You hid an image that you no longer needed.

FIGURE 44
Enable mask layer

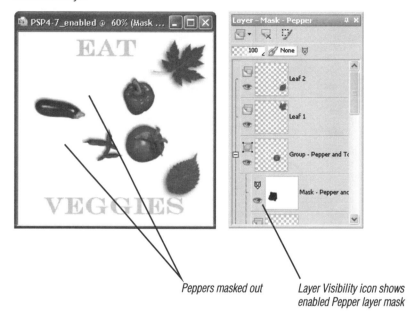

Peppers masked out

Layer Visibility icon shows enabled Pepper layer mask

FIGURE 45

Drag to the Delete Layer icon

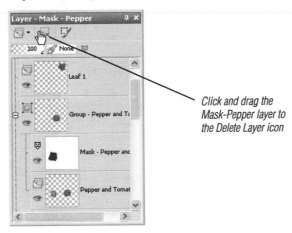

Click and drag the
Mask-Pepper layer to
the Delete Layer icon

1. Open **PSP4-7.PSPImage**, then save it as **Removedmask**.

2. Click the **Mask-Pepper layer** in the Layers palette.

    The Mask-Pepper layer becomes active.

3. Click and drag the **Mask-Pepper layer** to the **Delete Layer icon** in your Layers palette, as shown in Figure 45.

    The Mask-Pepper layer disappears completely from your image.

4. Save your image.

You removed an unwanted mask from your image using the Delete icon, returning an image to the way it was before you applied the mask.

View and change overlay color

1. Open **PSP4-7.PSPImage**, then save it as **Overlay**.

2. Click the **Mask-Pepper layer** in your Layers palette.

   The Mask-Pepper layer becomes active.

3. Click **Layers**, then click **View Overlay**.

   The overlay appears on your image, as shown in Figure 46, representing the mask.

4. Double-click the **Mask-Pepper layer** in the Layers palette.

   The Layer Properties dialog box appears with the Overlay tab displayed, as shown in Figure 47.

5. Click the color swatch from the Overlay color area.

   The color picker displays.

6. Select a color, then click **OK** to exit the Overlay dialog box.

   The dialog box closes and your chosen color replaces the red.

   > TIP To remove the preview images from the Layers dialog box (or any of Paint Shop Pro's dialog boxes), click the Show/Hide Previews icon.

7. Save your image.

You enabled the overlay through the Layers menu, then changed the overlay's color to something more pleasing to you.

FIGURE 46
Overlay appears

The overlay appears on your image

FIGURE 47
Overlay color

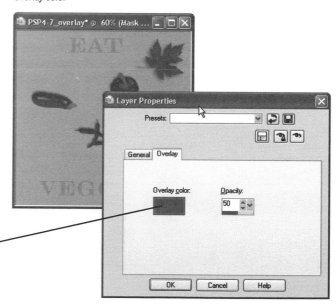

Click the color swatch to display the color picker

CHAPTER SUMMARY

In this chapter you learned how to customize the Layers palette to best suit your workflow needs. You also learned how to organize your layers, as well as how to add and delete layers you no longer need. You have learned about different kinds of layers and used the mask layer to isolate image elements. Finally, you know how to use the layer blend modes to create your own watermarks.

What You Have Learned:

- How to organize and customize your Layers palette
- How to convert a background layer to a regular raster layer
- How to add a new layer
- How to delete a layer
- How to apply blending modes to layers
- How to create layer sets to simplify your workflow
- How to apply a mask from the disk
- How to create your own mask using the Selection tool

Key Terms

blend modes Controls how pixels are either made darker or lighter, based on the underlying colors.

flatten Completely flattens an image to one layer

layers Separate layers of different elements

merge Merge together layers without flattening

thumbnail Small image representation of a layer's contents

5

CONSTRUCTING VECTOR
GRAPHICS AND TEXT

1. Venture into vectors.

2. Select and move objects.

3. Bring order to objects.

4. Perform vector text tricks.

chapter 5

CONSTRUCTING VECTOR
GRAPHICS AND TEXT

Comparing Vector to Raster

Computer graphics and their file formats are probably the most complicated aspects of graphic design. Most computer graphics fall into one of two distinct categories: vector or raster. It's important to understand the basic differences between them and to know what you can do with each. At this point in the book, you have worked mostly with raster objects, which use pixels to store image information. Each pixel has a color, and the pattern they create results in the image you see. **Raster** images are always rectangular or square, with every pixel assigned a color. If no other color is assigned to the pixel, it is colored white.

On the other hand, a **vector** image contains no pixels. Instead, a vector file contains mathematical instructions that tell the computer how to draw the image. The instructions describe a line's path: where it starts, where it ends, and the route it takes

between. It also contains information about **stroke** width and color. Is the fill a solid color, a pattern, or a texture? Is the path **closed**, meaning it starts and ends at the same place? Figure 1 shows a vector rectangle with a solid blue stroke and a **duotone** (two-toned color) dark-blue gradient as the fill.

Touting Vector Features

Resizing is a great vector feature. Since vectors don't rely on pixel information, the computer simply sends a different set of instructions to Paint Shop Pro, telling it how to draw the object. Rotating is another important difference between vector and raster images. Vector images are easily rotated at any angle, and because there are no pixels to deal with, the image retains its high-resolution sharpness. Figure 2 shows a resized image in vector and raster.

FIGURE 1

A solid stroke and duotone gradient fill

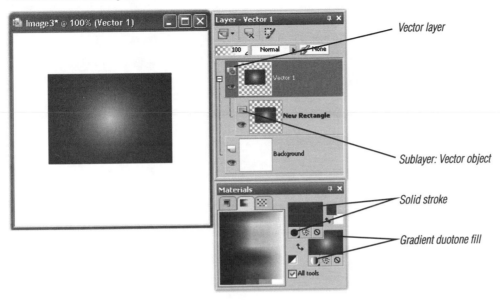

Vector layer

Sublayer: Vector object

Solid stroke

Gradient duotone fill

FIGURE 2

Compare a resized vector and raster image

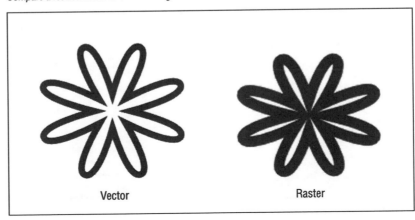

Vector   Raster

Tools You'll Use

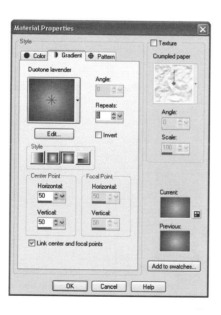

VENTURE INTO VECTORS

What You'll Do

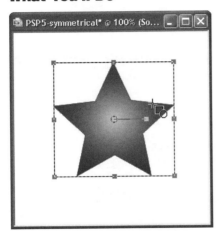

In this lesson, you'll use different tools to draw shapes on vector layers, and then add fills and gradients.

Defining Vector Paths

A vector path, or object, is made up of one or more **contours**, which are line segments with start and end points. If the points are in the same place, then the path is considered **closed**, or **contiguous**. If the start and end points are at different places, then the path is considered open.

You don't actually see a path or contour— you see its properties. These properties define the appearance of the stroke and fill, and the stroke and fill properties are defined by the foreground (stroke) and background (fill) colors in your Materials palette at the time the path is laid down. The foreground/stroke and background/fill can have any of the following attributes: solid color, gradient, patterns, and textures. Although a single path can contain any number of contours, it can only have one set of stroke and fill properties. All the contours in a single path share the same stroke and fill attributes.

Adding Vector Shapes to Layers

A single image can contain both raster and vector objects. However, vector and raster objects cannot be mixed on any layer. Vector objects must be on a vector layer. If you try to create a vector object on a raster layer, Paint Shop Pro automatically creates and places the object on a new vector layer. If the current layer is vector, Paint Shop Pro adds the object to the current layer. Paint Shop Pro files can have many vector layers, and each layer can have many objects.

QUICKTIP   Every object displays as a sublayer in the Layers palette.

Drawing Common Shapes

A few common shapes are included: rectangles, squares, ellipses, circles, polygons, and stars. The fourth tool from the bottom on the Tools toolbar gives you quick access to these commonly used shapes. The first three tools work similarly to each other. The Rectangle tool draws rectangles or squares, the Ellipse tool draws ellipses or circles, and the Symmetric tool draws polygons and stars. The last tool, Preset Shape, provides additional shapes and options.

The tool options palette is where you select the preferred shape, decide whether you want it to draw as a vector—you do!—and depending on which tool you select, whether the corner radius is square or round. Rectangular- and square-corner radius values vary from 0, which is completely square, to 1000, which is rounded, and the symmetrical star shape radius values are from 0 to 100. For symmetrical shapes, you can also select the number of sides you want the star or polygon to have.

QUICKTIP For more editing flexibility on basic shapes, use the Preset Shape tool instead of Rectangle or Ellipse. Shapes made with Rectangle or Ellipse cannot be node edited. A node is a control point on a vector object. Node editing is a powerful but somewhat advanced technique for editing vector objects. When using the Pen tool in Edit mode, you can move the nodes and change their properties (which determines how the lines before and after the node behave). With the vector control arms on the nodes, you can change the angle, curve, and length of the line segments on either side of the node. In addition, you can copy and paste nodes and change contours' and paths' directions. All those options are at Edit > Node Type and Transform > Objects menu.

Drawing Preset Shapes

Another way to draw the rectangular, elliptical, and symmetrical shapes is to use the Preset Shape tool. With it you get options that you do not get with the regular Rectangle or Ellipse tools: inkblots, callouts (talk balloons), flowers, gears, and starfish. Keep in mind the following facts when you're drawing a preset shape:

- If you click the top of the canvas and drag toward the bottom, the shape will be drawn from corner to corner.

- If you click the bottom of the canvas and drag toward the top, the shape will be drawn upside down.

- If you click and drag using the right mouse button instead of the left mouse button, the shape will be drawn from its midpoint to the outer edges.

Figure 3 shows just a few of the many shape options in Paint Shop Pro, as well as the tool options palette for the Symmetric tool.

FIGURE 3

Shape options and the Symmetric tool's options palette

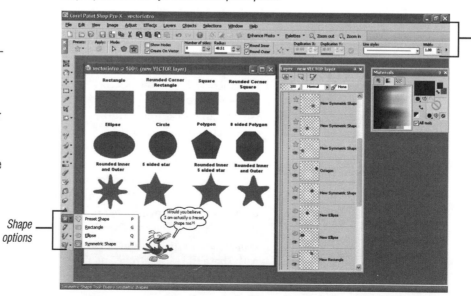

FIGURE 4
Choose a rectangle option

Rectangle mode

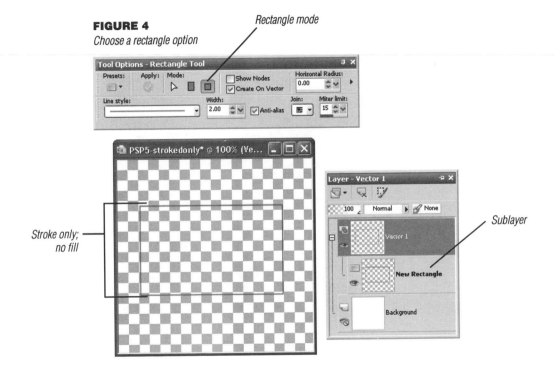

Stroke only; no fill

Sublayer

1. Create a 300 × 300 raster image with a white background, then save it as **Strokeonly**.

2. Click the **Rectangle tool** ▭▾.

   The tool options palette appears.

3. In the Materials palette, click the top color swatch.

   The color picker appears.

   > TIP To bypass the color picker, right-click the color swatches in the Materials palette. You get a selection of your most recently used materials, as well as some of the most commonly used colors.

4. Select a color, then click **OK** to close the color picker dialog box.

5. Choose a **rectangle**, then set Mode, Line Style, and Join to match the settings in Figure 4.

6. Check **Create on Vector**, enter **0** for Horizontal radius, **2** for Width, check **Anti-alias**, then enter **15** for Miter limit.

   These settings match those shown in Figure 4.

7. Draw out the shape on your canvas.

   The stroked rectangle shape appears on your canvas with no fill.

   > TIP If your shape has a white fill instead of no fill, disable the background layer. The white disappears and is replaced with the grey and white transparency checkerboard.

8. Save the image.

Using the Rectangle tool in vector mode, you created a stroked rectangle. By creating the vector object on a raster layer, you prompted Paint Shop Pro to automatically create the new vector layer, saving you clicks.

Add a vector layer

1. Create a 300 × 300 raster image with a white background, then save it as **Vectorlayer**.

2. Click the **New Raster Layer icon** ⬜️ in the Layers palette, then click **New Vector Layer**.

   The vector layer properties dialog box opens.

3. Type a name for the new layer, then click **OK**.

   The dialog box closes and the new vector layer appears in your Layers palette, as shown in Figure 5.

4. Save your image and move to the next objective.

You added a new vector layer to a raster image, which enabled you to draw vector objects.

FIGURE 5
The new vector layer appears in your Layers palette

New vector layer ──────

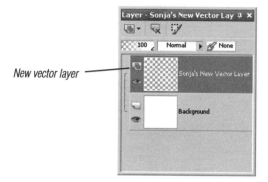

FIGURE 6
The settings shown here produce a gradient-filled star

Tool icon

Match these settings

Click here

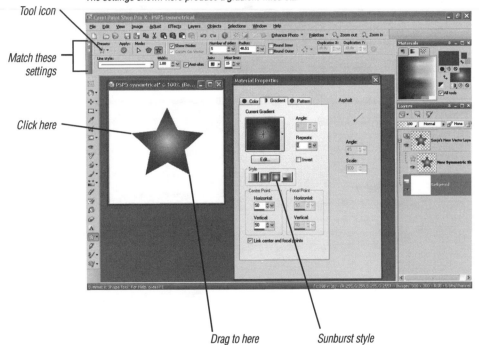

Drag to here

Sunburst style

1. Open **Vectorlayer.PSPImage** from objective 2 (if necessary), save it as **Symmetrical**, then click the **Symmetric tool** ⬚.

   The Symmetric tool option appears.

2. Set Presets to **star shape**, Apply to **checkmark**, Mode to **star shape**, Number of sides to **5**, Radius to **48.51**, Width to **1.00**, and Miter limit to **15**.

3. Check **Show Nodes** and **Anti-alias**, then set Line style and Join to match Figure 6.

4. In the Materials palette, click the foreground/stroke color swatch, then set it to dark blue.

5. Click the **fill arrow** on the background/fill color swatch, then select the **gradient** option.

   The Material Properties dialog box appears, with the Gradient tab selected, as shown in Figure 6.

6. Click the preview box **arrow**, then click the **duotone dark blue gradient**.

7. Click the **Sunburst icon** ⬚, then click **OK**.

   The Material Properties dialog box closes and the Materials palette reflects the changes.

8. Click in the shape's upper-left corner and drag until it resembles Figure 6.

9. Save your image.

Using the Symmetric tool, you created a star shape with a dark blue stroke and a duotone blue gradient fill.

Draw a preset shape

1. Open **PSP5-1.PSPImage**, save it as **Preset-shape**, then click the **Preset Shape tool** 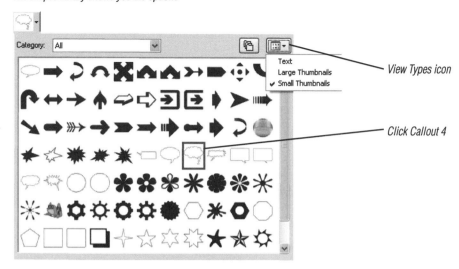.

   The Preset Shape tool is active and the tool options palette appears.

2. Click the **arrow** next to the shape preview window.

   The library of shapes appears, as shown in Figure 7.

3. Click **Callout 4**.

   The previews close and the chosen callout shape appears in the preview window.

4. In your tool options, uncheck **Retain Style**.

   Now you can choose colors.

5. Click the **Line Width arrow**, then increase your line width to **2**.

6. In the Materials palette, set foreground/stroke color to black, then set background/fill color to white.

7. Click the **Fish layer**, click the **New Vector Layer icon** , then select **New Vector Layer**.

   The New Vector Layer dialog box appears.

8. Type **Callout** for the layer name, then click **OK**.

   The dialog box closes and the layer appears in the Layers palette.

9. Draw your shape, then save your image.

   The callout shape appears on your image, as shown in Figure 8.

You used the Preset Shape tool, selected your own colors, and added a callout to an image.

FIGURE 7
The shapes library shows you the options

View Types icon

Click Callout 4

FIGURE 8
The callout, or talk balloon, lets your fish chat

Callout shape

New vector layer

SELECT AND
MOVE OBJECTS

What You'll Do

In this lesson, you'll use the Object Selection tools to choose objects and then move those objects.

Selecting Vector Objects

Before you can modify a vector object, you must select the object. Paint Shop Pro offers a couple methods for doing this: the Pick and the Object Selection tools. The Pick tool, new to Paint Shop Pro, is a hybrid of the Object Selection and Raster Deform tools, which were in previous versions. The Pick tool allows you to select raster layers and vector objects. Unlike Object Selection, Pick is available at all times. Object Selection is available only if you are on an active vector layer.

QUICKTIP If you are new to Paint Shop Pro, bring back the old Object Selection tool. The Pick tool can cause conflicts when working with multiple layers that contain both vector and raster data.

When you activate the Object Selection tool, the mouse pointer turns into a white cross with a boxed arrowhead beside it. When you click an object, a bounding box and selection handles appear around it,

indicating that it is selected. The bounding box lets you rotate and deform the object. If the object you want to select contains a fill, you can click anywhere on the object to select it. If the object has no fill, click the image outline. Figure 9 shows a selected vector object.

QUICKTIP You can get to the Object Selection tool by pressing O. You can add it to your toolbar, which makes for easier vector selections. See Chapter 2, "Controlling Menus, Toolbars, and Palettes," which tells you how to customize your toolbars.

Using the Object Selection Tool

In addition to the simple click-select option, Paint Shop Pro offers two more methods for selecting objects. Both methods require activating the Object Selection tool, which you do by clicking the icon shown in Figure 10. One method is to draw a bounding box around the objects you want to select. Paint Shop Pro selects all the objects that are *completely* surrounded by the bounding box. This can be tricky if you want to select a lot of objects that are scattered around the canvas. The other method uses the Layers palette. Click the object name in the Layers palette and the name becomes bold, indicating that it has been selected.

QUICKTIP   Easier picking from the stack is another good reason to name each layer relative to its contents.

Moving Vector Objects

Keep in mind that moving vector objects is a bit different than moving raster objects. With raster objects, you can use the Mover tool. With vector objects, you don't use the Mover tool. Instead, choose the object with the Object Selection tool and place your mouse over it. Drag the mouse when its pointer becomes a four-headed arrow. You see an outline of your shape as it moves. Release the mouse when you have the object in the new position.

FIGURE 9

The vector object is selected and the Layers palette reflects that

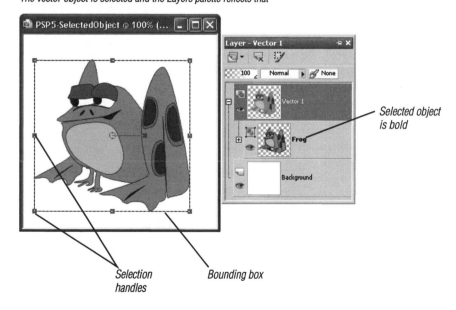

Selection handles

Bounding box

Selected object is bold

FIGURE 10

Customize your toolbar by dragging the Object Selection icon there

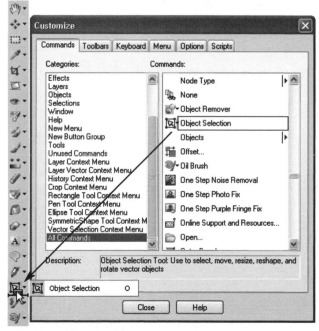

Drag Object Selection tool to toolbar

FIGURE 11
Select the circle

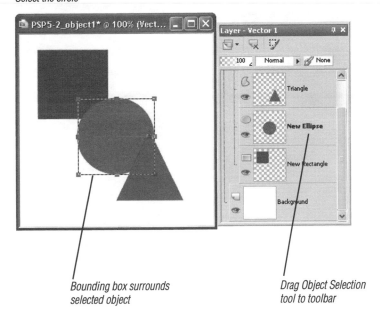

Bounding box surrounds
selected object

Drag Object Selection
tool to toolbar

1. Open **PSP5-2.PSPImage**, then save it as **Object1**.

2. Click the **Object Selection tool** 🔲.

3. Click the **square**.

   The square is surrounded by the bounding box.

4. Click **Selections**, then click **Select None**.

   The object is deselected and the bounding box disappears.

5. Click the **circle**.

   The circle is surrounded by the bounding box, as shown in Figure 11.

   TIP To select more than one object at a time, make your first selection, press Shift, then click the shape you want to add.

6. Click **Selections**, then click **Select None**.

   The object is deselected and the bounding box disappears.

7. Save your image and move to the next objective.

You used the Object Selection tool to choose individual vector objects, then deselected them.

Select an object using the Layers palette

1. Click **Selections**, then click **Select None** (if necessary).

2. In the Layers palette, click the **Triangle layer**.

   The triangle is selected. The name becomes bold in the Layers palette, as shown in Figure 12.

3. Save your image and move to the next objective.

You used the Layers palette to select a single vector object.

FIGURE 12
Select the triangle

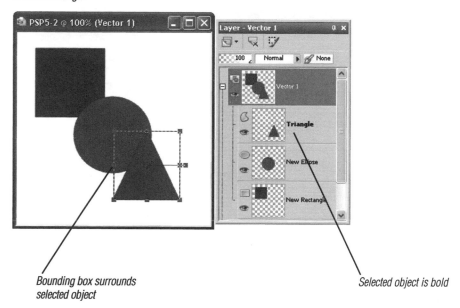

Bounding box surrounds
selected object

Selected object is bold

FIGURE 13

Select the square and the circle

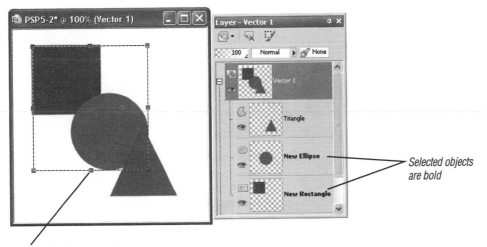

Bounding box surrounds
selected objects

Selected objects
are bold

FIGURE 14

Moving objects with the four-headed arrow

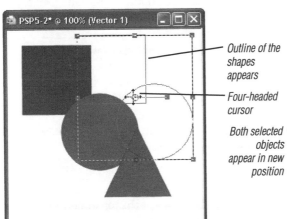

Outline of the
shapes
appears

Four-headed
cursor

Both selected
objects
appear in new
position

FIGURE 15

The square and the circle appear in their new position

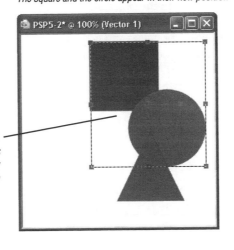

1. Click **Selections**, then click **Select None** (if necessary).

2. Click the **Object Selection tool** 🔲.

3. Click and drag to draw out a selection around the **square** and **circle**, then release the mouse button.

   The bounding box surrounds the square and the circle, as shown in Figure 13.

4. Place your cursor in the middle of the bounding box that surrounds the square and circle.

   The cursor becomes a four-headed arrow.

5. Click and drag to move the shapes to a new position.

   As you drag objects across the canvas, an outline of the shapes appears, as shown in Figure 14.

6. Release the mouse button.

   The square and circle appear in their new position, as shown in Figure 15.

7. Save your image.

Using the Object Selection tool, you chose two objects together, keeping them correctly aligned as you moved them. You saved time by moving both objects together.

BRING ORDER
TO OBJECTS

What You'll Do

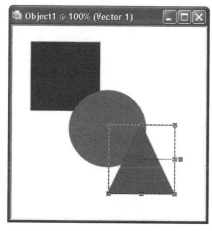

In this lesson, you'll align, resize, and distribute objects.

Aligning Objects

At some point you will want to position an object in the exact center of your canvas, or align one object with another, or evenly space a group of objects on the canvas. Making a navigation bar for a Web site is an example of when you might need to do these things. These functions work only when two or more objects are selected; otherwise, the object alignment options are greyed out in the tool options palette. The icons in the Objects tool options palette will give you a good idea of what each function does and how the objects can be aligned in different ways: top, bottom, left, right, centered vertically, or centered horizontally. The thumbnail in the lower right of Figure 16 shows the shapes' original position, then shows them being top aligned.

Distributing Objects

Distributing objects means to place equal distance between them. This option is available only after you've selected two or more objects. You can vertically distribute objects by their top, center, or bottom. When you distribute, the edge or center of the upper- and lowermost objects remain in place, while any objects between them are arranged for equal distance from another.

Resizing Objects

Changing a vector object's size is easy. From a corner, you can change the size an equal, uniform amount, or you can change only its width or its height. Use your mouse and the bounding box handles to change size. A bounding box with handles surrounds the image once it's selected. If you point to a corner handle, the cursor changes into a four-headed arrow with a small attached square, but if you point to a side or top handle, the cursor becomes a double-headed arrow.

- Use the handle on either side to resize the width.
- Use the handle at the top or bottom to resize the height.

- Use a corner handle to resize both width and height at the same time.

QUICKTIP Right-click to choose a corner handle, which helps maintain height-to-width proportions.

In addition to the bounding box, you can use the Make Same Size options. These options are available on the tool options palette after you select an object, but you can find them in the context menu under Objects > Make Same Size. Three options

are available: Horizontal, Vertical, and Both. Like the distributing option, these are available only after you select two or more objects.

Selection order is the secret to working with most multiple-object features. The object you select first is considered the base object—the one all others will mimic. Figure 17 shows the Make Same Size option. The square was the base; all the other shapes conformed to equal it.

Arranging Objects

Objects are arranged from front to back on the canvas, so where they overlap, the object at the front will block any objects behind it. Objects at the top of the Layers palette are in front. You can rearrange a couple of ways. Either drag the layers into a new order or select an object and use the Objects > Arrange menu commands. For example, Objects > Arrange > Bring to Top puts the selected object at the top of the layer stack.

FIGURE 16

The inset shows the shapes before they were top aligned.

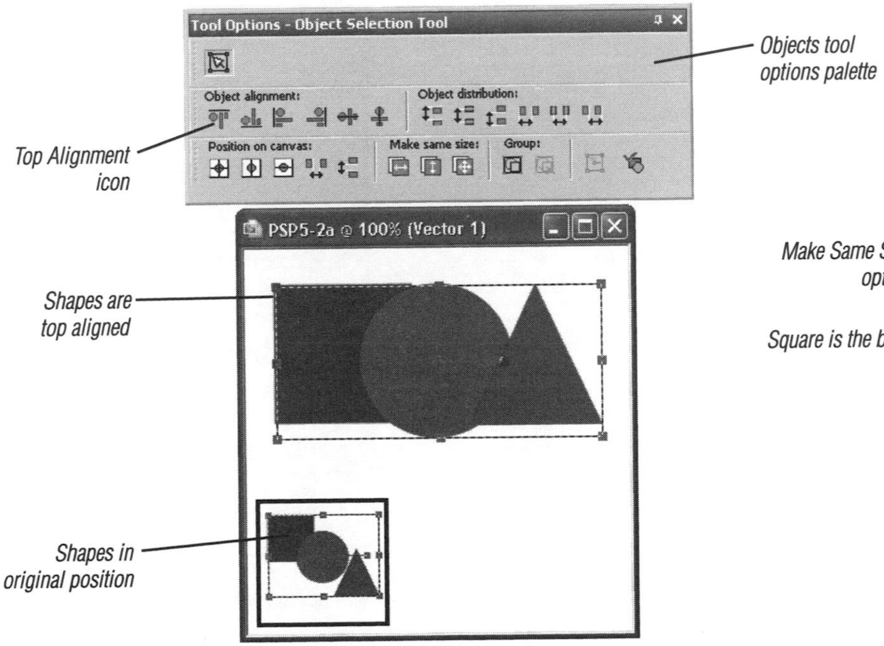

Objects tool options palette

Top Alignment icon

Shapes are top aligned

Shapes in original position

FIGURE 17

The circle and triangle are resized

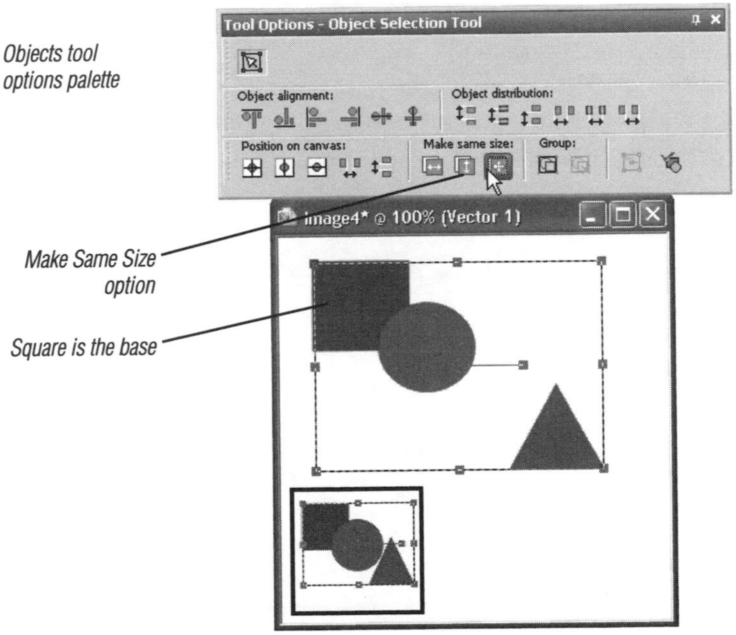

Make Same Size option

Square is the base

Align objects

1. Create a 300 × 300 raster image with a white background, then save it as **Aligned**.

2. Click the **Preset Shape tool** 🖌️.

3. Draw three different shapes.

   Paint Shop Pro automatically adds a vector layer as you draw shapes.

4. Click the **Object Selection tool** 🔲.

5. Click the **topmost shape** on your canvas, press the **Shift key**, then click the other **two shapes**.

   The shapes are selected. The alignment options are available on the Object Selection toolbar, as shown in Figure 18.

6. Click the **Align Top icon** 🔲.

   The objects align to the topmost shape, as shown in Figure 18.

7. Save your image.

You used the Object Selection tool to select multiple objects, then aligned all the objects to the top, clearing space for more shapes.

FIGURE 18
Objects align to the topmost shape and distribute vertically from the center

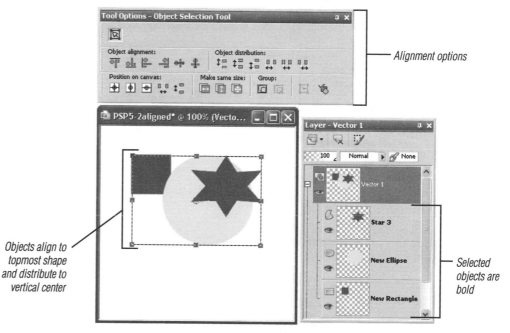

Alignment options

Objects align to topmost shape and distribute to vertical center

Selected objects are bold

FIGURE 19

The shapes distribute to horizontal center

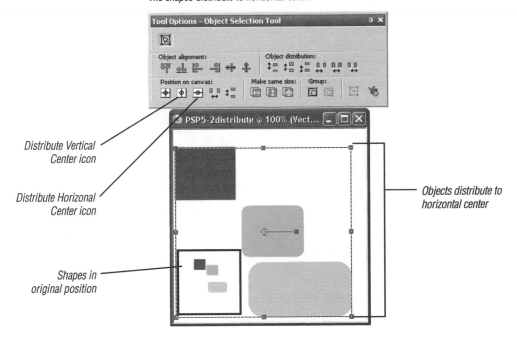

Distribute Vertical
Center icon

Distribute Horizonal
Center icon

Objects distribute to
horizontal center

Shapes in
original position

1. Create a 300 × 300 raster image with a white background, then save it as **Distribute**.

2. Click the **Rectangle Shape tool** ▢.

3. Draw three different rectangular shapes.

    Paint Shop Pro automatically adds a vector layer as you draw.

4. Click the **Object Selection tool** ▣.

5. Drag a selection around your **shapes**.

    The bounding box appears, and each shape's name is bold in the Layers palette.

    | TIP If you have trouble grabbing any of your objects, press Shift and click more shapes.

6. Click the **Distribute Vertical Center icon** ▣

    The shapes distribute to vertical center, as shown in Figure 18.

7. Click the **Distribute Horizontal Center icon** ▣.

    The shapes distribute to horizontal center, as shown in Figure 19.

8. Click **Selections**, then click **Select None**.

    The shape objects are deselected and the bounding box disappears.

9. Save your image.

You used the Distribute command to precisely center your objects horizontally and vertically on the canvas.

Resize an object using the bounding box

1. Open **Distribute.PSPImage** (if necessary), then save it as **Resize1**.
2. Click the **Object Selection tool** 🔲.
3. Click a **shape**.

   The shape is selected.
4. Right-click any **corner handle** of the bounding box, then drag inward.

   The shape becomes smaller, as shown in Figure 20.
5. Click a **different shape**.

   The shape is selected, as shown in Figure 21.
6. Right-click any **corner handle** of the bounding box, then drag outward.

   The shape becomes larger, as shown in Figure 22.
7. Save your image.

You used the Object Selection tool to select objects, then used the bounding box handles to increase and decrease their size.

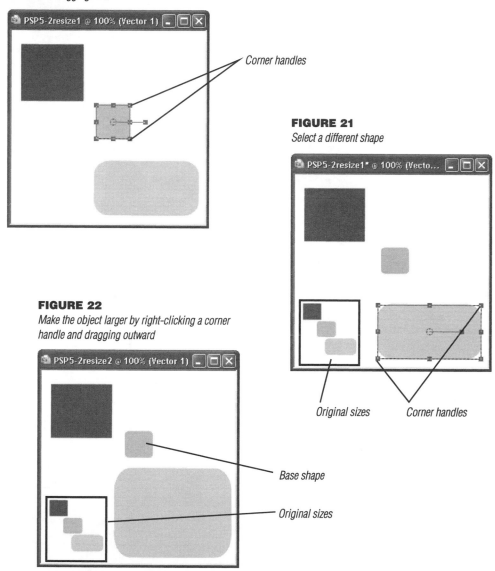

FIGURE 20
Make the object smaller by right-clicking a corner handle and dragging inward

Corner handles

FIGURE 21
Select a different shape

Original sizes   Corner handles

FIGURE 22
Make the object larger by right-clicking a corner handle and dragging outward

Base shape

Original sizes

FIGURE 23

Sizes are changed according to the base selection

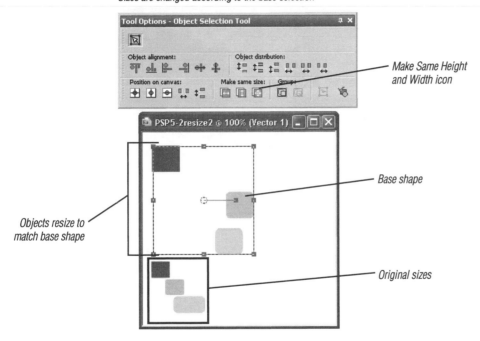

Make Same Height
and Width icon

Base shape

Objects resize to
match base shape

Original sizes

1. Open **Resize.PSPImage** (if necessary), then save it as **Resize2**.

2. Click the **Object Selection tool** 🔲.

3. Click the **smallest shape**.

   The shape is selected.

4. Press the **Shift key**, click the **second shape**, then click the **final shape**.

   The shapes are added to the already selected shape.

5. In Make same size, click the **Make Same Height and Width icon** 🔲.

   All the objects resize to match the base shape, which is smallest. See Figure 23.

6. Save your image.

You used the Make Same Size command to precisely resize all of your objects to a uniform size.

Arrange objects through the Objects menu

1. Open **PSP5-3.PSPImage**, then save it as **Arrange**.

   The image opens.

   | TIP Don't panic: The image looks odd, but you are going to fix that.

2. In the Layers palette, click the **Chest layer**.

   The layer name bolds.

   | TIP If you do not see a layer named Chest, click the plus sign (+) on the Vector 1 layer, then select Chest.

3. Click **Objects**, **Arrange**, then click **Move Up**.

   The Chest layer is visible on the body, as seen in Figure 24.

4. Save your file and move to the next objective.

Using the Arrange context menu, you hid a layer.

FIGURE 24
You can see the Chest layer

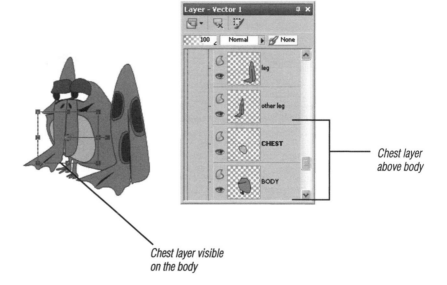

Chest layer visible on the body

Chest layer above body

FIGURE 25

Select the other leg and put it where it belongs

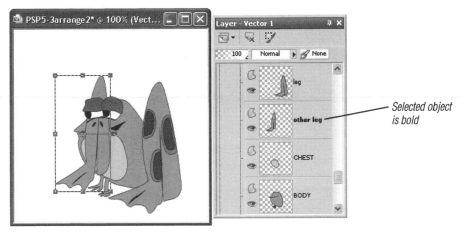

Selected object
is bold

FIGURE 26

The other leg is now behind the body

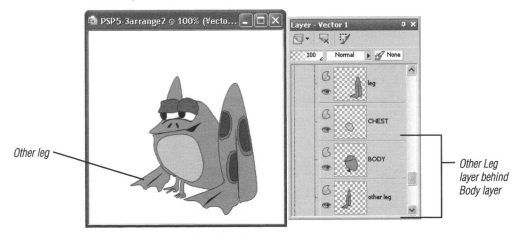

Other leg

Other Leg
layer behind
Body layer

1. Open **Arrange.PSPImage** (if necessary),
   then save it as **Arrange2**.

2. In the Layers palette, click the **Other Leg
   layer**.

   The layer name bolds, as shown in
   Figure 25.

3. Click and drag the **Other Leg layer** below the
   Body layer, then release the mouse.

   The Other Leg layer is behind the Body layer,
   as shown in Figure 26.

4. Save your image.

*You used the traditional drag-and-drop method to
move layers.*

PERFORM VECTOR
TEXT TRICKS

 In this lesson, you'll create and convert vector text and modify it to follow a path.

Working with Vector Text

You use the Text tool to create text in Paint Shop Pro. Similar to the other tools you have used so far, when you select Text, you have additional options. You get to determine things such as font, style, stroke, kerning, leading, and alignment. Table 1 explains each of these options.

Adding text to just about any image is simple. Paint Shop Pro offers three Create As methods with the Text tool.

- **Floating** creates raster text that hovers above the active layer and is filled with whatever material is currently set as the background/fill in the Materials palette. If you drag floating characters with the Text tool, the colored text moves and the layer underneath remains intact.
- **Selection** creates a raster text selection in letter shapes. If you drag with the Text tool, the pixels within the

selection move and the areas left behind are filled either with the current background material or with transparency.
- **Vector** creates vector text on a vector layer and is most editable.

This section is devoted to the vector method, which offers you the most flexibility and the ability to edit the text, even after you have deselected the Text tool.

Creating Vector Text

Vector text doesn't work the same as selected or floating text. Vector text works more like a word-processing program that enables you to edit characters after they are laid down. It offers all the normal options that you have with floating or selected text, with a few extras thrown in. Figure 27 shows various setting examples. Table 1 offers a description of some of the most commonly used attributes.

TABLE 1: Text Attributes

Attribute	What It Does
Font	Sets the font, such as Times New Roman.
Size	Sets point or pixel size.
Units	Sets point or pixel size.
Font style	Sets **bold**, *italics*, underline, and strikethrough.
Stroke width	Sets the stroke width around each character.
Leading	Sets the amount of space between lines of text.
Kerning	Sets the spacing between adjacent characters.
Align left	Aligns text left; left edge of the first line is the spot you clicked when activating the tool.
Center	Centers all text; first line is centered horizontally around the spot you clicked when activating the tool.
Align right	Aligns text right; right edge of the first line is the spot you clicked when activating the tool.
Horizontal and down	Places text horizontally, with subsequent lines below.
Vertical and left	Places each character vertically, with subsequent lines to the left.
Vertical and right	Places each character vertically, with subsequent lines to the right.

FIGURE 27

Text options include kerning, leading, alignment, and more

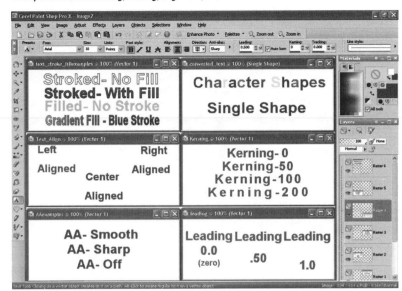

Converting Vector Text

Unlike vector objects, vector text is not editable with the Pen tool, but a simple and effective workaround for this is to convert text to an object. When converting, Paint Shop Pro gives you two options: single or character shapes. If you choose character shapes, each letter becomes a separate object. A single shape converts all the text entered into a single vector object. This means that the text takes on the properties of the first character in the string of text. With character shapes, however, you can make each letter a separate color.

Wrapping Text Around a Shape

You can easily wrap text around any vector object. Wrapping it around shapes or lines is referred to as text on path, and it can create some fun and interesting effects. You can create text on a path two ways: Create the shape or line, then the new text, or create the path and text as separate objects, then fit the text to the shape.

Create vector text

1. Create a 400 × 200 raster image with a white background, then save it as **Simpletext**.

2. Click the **Text tool** [A].

   The Text tool becomes active and the tool options appear.

3. In the Materials palette, click the foreground/stroke color swatch, choose a **dark blue**, then click **OK**.

   Clicking the swatch brings up the color picker; choosing OK closes it.

4. In the Materials palette, click the background/fill color swatch, then choose a **light blue**.

   The Materials palette swatches reflect your choices.

5. Choose **Engravers MT** for Font, **12** for Size, **Points** for Units, **B** for Font style, **Centered** for Alignment, **Sharp** for Anti-alias, **2** for Stroke width, **Vector** for Create As, **10** for Miter limit, and **0** for Offset, Leading, Kerning, and Tracking.

6. Check **Warp text** and **Auto kern**, then set Direction, Line Style, Join, and Presets to match those shown in Figure 28.

7. Click the **canvas**, type **Course Technology**, then click the **Apply button**.

   Your cursor becomes a cross with an attached A; the Text Entry dialog box opens. When you click Apply, the dialog box closes and your text appears, as shown in Figure 29.

8. Save your image.

Using the Text tool, you created text with a dark stroke and a lighter fill to give the text a 3D look.

FIGURE 28

Text tool options help you customize characters

Match these settings

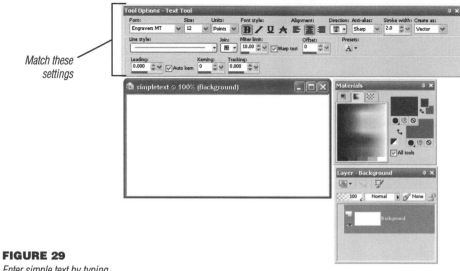

FIGURE 29

Enter simple text by typing

Type text appears here

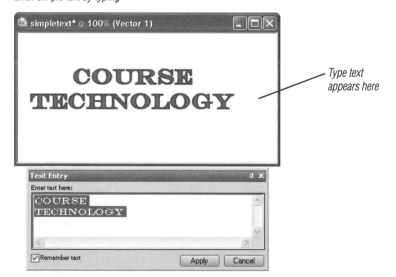

FIGURE 30

Choose underline and highlight text to apply the style

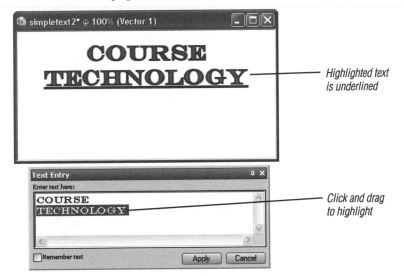

Highlighted text
is underlined

Click and drag
to highlight

1. Open **Simpletext** (if necessary), then save it as **Simpletext2**.

2. Click the **Text tool** A.

3. Click the words **Course Technology**, which you created in Objective 1.

   The Text Entry dialog box shows you the previously made text.

4. Click once inside the **Enter text here box**.

   The Course Technology text is no longer highlighted.

5. Click and drag to highlight only the word **Technology**, as shown in Figure 30.

6. In the Text tool options palette, click the **Underline icon** U.

7. Click the **Apply button**.

   The Text Entry dialog box closes and the highlighted word is underlined, as shown in Figure 30.

8. Save your image.

You highlighted, then underlined the word Technology to bring attention to it.

Convert text to a single shape

1. Open **Simpletext2** (if necessary), then save it as **Convert2shape**.

2. Click the **Text tool** .

3. Choose **Engravers MT** for Font, **5** for Size, **Points** for Units, **B** for Font style, **Centered** for Alignment, **Sharp** for Anti-alias, **2** for Stroke width, **Vector** for Create As, **10** for Miter limit, and **0** for Offset, Leading, Kerning, and Tracking.

4. Check **Warp text** and **Auto kern**, then set Direction, Line Style, Join, and Presets to match those shown in Figure 31.

5. Click the **Vector1 layer**, click the **New Vector Layer icon** , then click **New Vector Layer**.

   The Vector1 layer is active and the New Layer dialog box appears.

FIGURE 31

Text tool options for creating a single shape

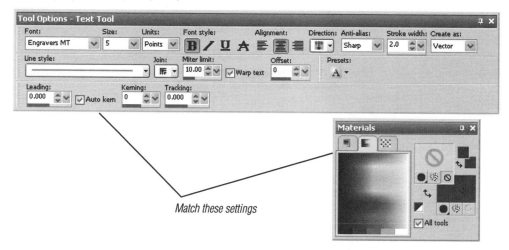

Match these settings

FIGURE 32
Text is converted

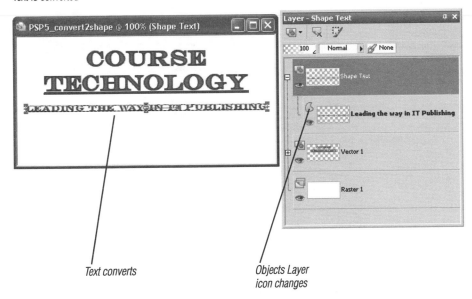

Text converts

Objects Layer
icon changes

6. Type **Shape Text**, then click **OK**.

The dialog box closes and the new layer appears above Vector1.

7. Click the **canvas**, type **Leading the Way in IT Publishing** in the Text Entry dialog box, then click the **Apply button**.

TIP If you want Paint Shop Pro to remember the text you last typed, mark the Remember Text checkbox.

The dialog box closes. The bounding box surrounds the text, and the new layer is in the Layers palette.

8. Click **Objects**, click **Convert Text to Curves**, then click **As Single Shape**.

The text converts and the Objects Layer icon changes in the Layers palette, as shown in Figure 32.

9. Save your image.

You created new vector text, then converted it to a single shape so that you can later node edit.

Create text and convert it to shapes

1. Create a 400 × 200 raster image with a white background, then save it as **Textcharacter**.

2. Click the **Text tool** 🅰.

   The Text tool is active and the tool options appear.

3. In the Materials palette, click the foreground/stroke color swatch, then choose a **dark blue**.

4. In the Materials palette, right-click the background/fill color swatch; from Recent Materials, select the same color you chose for foreground/stroke.

   The foreground/stroke and background/fill colors are the same.

5. Choose **Arial** for Font, **14** for Size, **Points** for Units, **Centered** for Alignment, **Sharp** for Anti-alias, **2** for Stroke width, **Vector** for Create As, **10** for Miter limit, **0** for Leading and Tracking, then **25** for Kerning.

6. Check **Auto kern**, then set Direction, Line Style, Join, and Presets to match those shown in Figure 33.

FIGURE 33

Text tool options for converting text to shapes

Match these settings

FIGURE 34

Text converts and the Objects Layer icon changes

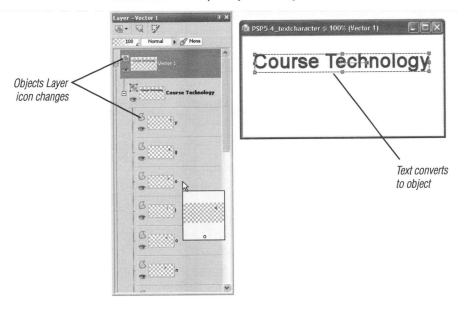

Objects Layer
icon changes

Text converts
to object

7. Click your **canvas**, type **Course Technology** in the dialog box, then click the **Apply button**.

The text appears on the canvas and the text dialog box closes.

8. Click **Objects**, click **Convert Text to Curves**, then click **As Character Shapes**.

The text converts and the Objects Layer icon changes in the Layers palette, as shown in Figure 34.

TIP To change the color of each letter, right-click the letters layer in the Layers palette, choose Properties, then select the new colors from the Properties dialog box.

You created, stroked, and filled vector text, then converted the text to character shapes so you could edit each letter individually.

Create a shape for text on a path

1. Create a 400 × 400 raster image with a white background, then save it as **Textonpath1**.

2. Click the **Preset Shape tool** 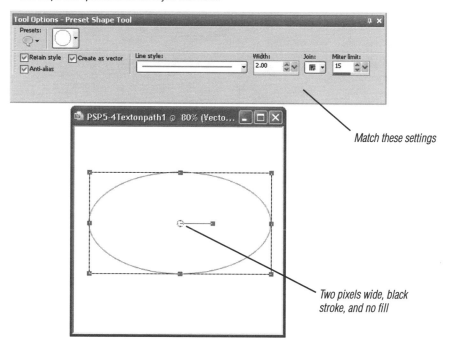.

   The Preset Shape tool is active and the tool options display.

3. Check **Retain Style**, **Anti-alias**, and **Create as New Vector**.

4. Continuing with settings, enter **2** for Width, then **15** for Miter limit.

5. Continuing with settings, set Presets, Shape, Line Style, and Join to match those shown in Figure 35.

6. Draw your shape.

   The shape is 2 pixels wide with black stroke and no fill. A new vector layer appears in the Layers palette showing the new shape.

7. Save your image and move to the next objective.

Using the Preset Shape tool, you created a shape—a path—for your text to follow in the next objective.

FIGURE 35

Preset shape tool options create an object with no fill

Match these settings

Two pixels wide, black stroke, and no fill

FIGURE 36

Place your cursor as shown here to change it to the text on path cursor

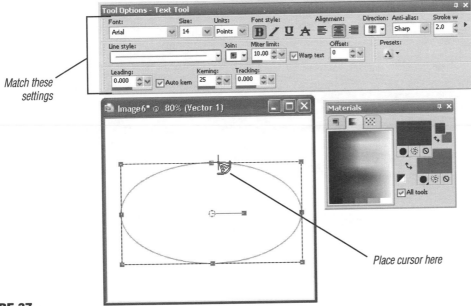

Match these settings

Place cursor here

FIGURE 37

Text follows the path

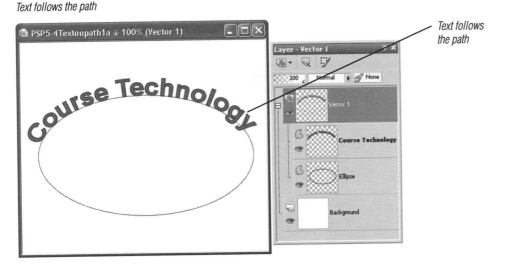

Text follows the path

Wrap text to a shape

1. Open **Textonpath1.PSPImage** (if necessary), then save it as **Textonpath1a**.

2. Click the **Text tool** [A].

   The Text tool is active and the tool options palette appears.

3. Choose **Arial** for Font, **14** for Size, **Points** for Units, **B** for Font Style, **Centered** for Alignment, **Sharp** for Anti-alias, **2** for Stroke width, **Vector** for Create As, **10** for Miter limit, **0** for Offset, Leading, and Tracking, and **25** for Kerning.

4. Check **Warp text** and **Auto kern**, then set Direction, Line Style, Join, and Presets to match settings shown in Figure 36.

5. Place your cursor as shown in Figure 36.

6. When the Text tool cursor [A] changes to the text on path cursor [b], click.

   The Text Entry dialog box appears.

7. Type **Course Technology**, then click the **Apply button**.

   The dialog box closes and the text follows the path, as shown in Figure 37.

8. Right-click the **Course Tech layer**, then click **Convert to Path**.

9. Save your image and move to the next objective.

You created text to follow the path you made in Objective 5. You converted text to a path so you can use the shape to create text on a path without affecting existing text.

PAINT SHOP PRO X REVEALED   179

Wrap more text to a shape

1. Open **Textonpath1a.PSPImage** (if necessary), then save it as **Textonpath2**.

2. Click the **New Vector Layer icon** ⬛▾, then name the layer **Leading**.

   The layer appears above the Course Tech layer.

3. Click and drag the **Ellipse layer** under the Leading layer, as shown in Figure 38.

4. Click **Image**, then **Flip**, then click the **Text tool** [A].

   The ellipse shape flips, the Text tool is active, and the tool options palette appears.

5. Choose **Arial** for Font, **8** for Size, **Points** for Units, **B** for Font style, **Centered** for Alignment, **Sharp** for Anti-alias, **1** for Stroke width, **Vector** for Create as, **10** for Miter limit, **0** for Offset, Leading, and Tracking, then **25** for Kerning.

6. Check **Warp text** and **Auto kern**, then set Direction, Line Style, Join, and Presets to match settings shown in Figure 38.

7. Place your Text tool cursor ⊞ᴀ at the bottom until it changes to the text on path cursor 🖹, then click.

   The Text Entry dialog box appears.

8. Type **Leading the way in IT Publishing**, then click the **Apply button**.

   The dialog box closes and the text follows the path, as shown in Figure 39.

9. Save your image.

You moved and flipped the path (shape) to a new layer, then created new vector text to follow the new path, creating a professional look.

FIGURE 38
Text tool options for wrapping text to a shape

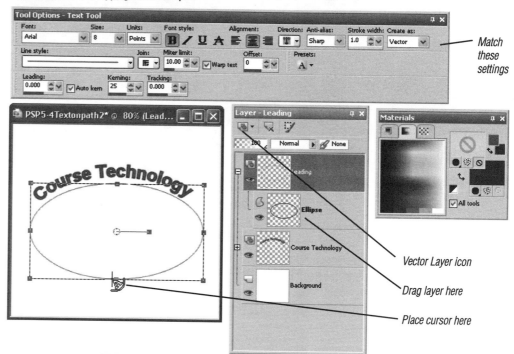

Match these settings

Vector Layer icon

Drag layer here

Place cursor here

FIGURE 39
Adding to the text on path

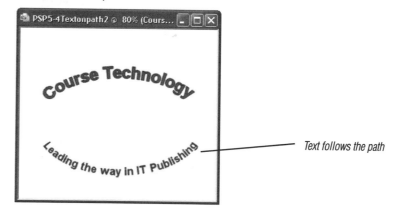

Text follows the path

CHAPTER SUMMARY

In this chapter, you have learned that resized vector images maintain quality better than do resized raster images. You have learned how to add vector layers, as well as how to evenly rearrange and distribute objects in the sublayers. You have learned how to create vector text and how to wrap text to a path. You have also learned to convert text to a shape so that it can later be edited.

What You Have Learned

- How to use the Preset Shape tool
- How to add vector layers
- How to create a symmetrical shape
- How to select vector objects with the Object Selection tool
- How to select vector objects with the Layers palette
- How to align vector objects
- How to distribute vector objects
- How to resize vector objects using the bounding box
- How to move vector objects
- How to create vector text
- How to change existing text properties
- How to convert text to a single shape
- How to wrap text to a shape

Key Terms

bounding box A box with handles for rotating and deforming objects

closed A path with the same starting and ending points

contiguous Continuous; linked together

contours A line segment with starting and ending points

distribute To space objects evenly

duotone Two-toned color

chapter

6

ADDING EFFECTS WITH
FILTERS,PLUG-INS, AND DEFORMATION

1. Use and view effects.

2. Explore special effects.

3. Plug it in.

4. Use third-party filters, cropping, and colorizing.

5. Blur with filters.

ULTRASONIC

Explaining Filters

Filters are just small subprograms that you can run either on an entire image layer or a selected part of an image. Some of these important correction and creativity tools can also be run on individual color channels and layer masks, as you saw in Chapter 4. Filters modify the color or position of pixels in an image, with sometimes practical and sometimes impractical results. Though not always practical, it can be a lot of fun experimenting with them!

Many cameras, especially those used by professional photographers, have lots of filters. The function of the filter is to change the way the camera sees the subject. Some filters are tinted and can block certain colors; others can blur the image or even add distortion and other special effects. But there's no need to have one of the expensive cameras to get your shots when you can easily add the effects later in Paint Shop Pro.

Distinguishing between effects and filters

In Paint Shop Pro, the terms *effects* and *filters* basically mean the same thing; you will hear the words used interchangeably. Although not a hard and fast rule, the Effects menu holds effects, and the Adjust menu holds filters. Complicate this with the fact that the Adjust menu items appear within the Effect Browser (which you learn about later in this chapter). Clear as mud? That's understandable. Try thinking of all of them as filters and the names given under the Effects menu as an end result of the filter.

Finding the Right Filter for You

Paint Shop Pro offers many creative and sometimes mystical filters designed to radically change images. Some are subtle, while others jump right off the screen! If you are mostly using Paint Shop Pro for photography, then you probably won't use those filters much, if at all. In some special circumstances, though, you might find them helpful or downright entertaining.

Filters work on selections or on individual layers, so you can apply an effect for each layer or apply multiple effects to one layer. With the majority of filters, your image needs to be a **raster** (bitmap) and at least 16 million colors or certain grayscale settings; not all filters work with 16 bit. Paint Shop Pro includes over 80 different effects in 11 categories:

- 3D
- Art Media
- Artistic
- Distortion
- Edge
- Geometric
- Illumination
- Image
- Photo
- Reflection
- Texture

Tools You'll Use

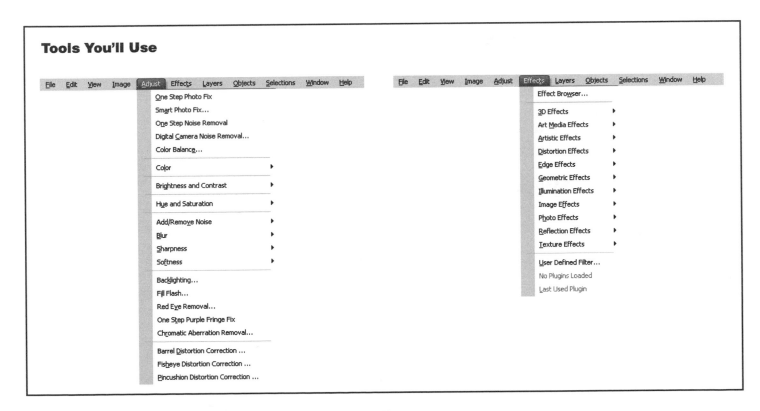

185

Tools You'll Use

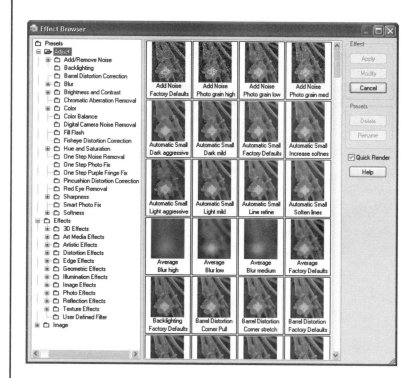

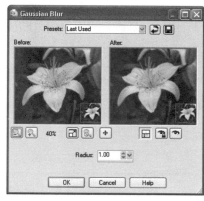

USE AND VIEW
EFFECTS

What You'll Do

In this lesson, you'll take a look at dialog boxes that display when using filters and explore the Effect Browser.

Setting Options in Dialog Boxes

Since this chapter can't show every effect, I'll review the categories and the type of effect within each. Some, like the Edge effects, apply with no dialog box. Others require input from you. The dialog box shown in Figure 1 is one of the simpler kinds; only a single option appears. Other

FIGURE 1

Aged Newspaper offers one option; it's a simple dialog box

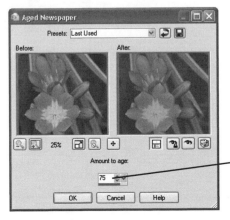

A single option

dialog boxes provide a wealth of options to create the effect you want. For example, the dialog box in Figure 2 is for Rough Leather. In it you can adjust seven different settings. This may seem a bit overwhelming at first, but more options provides more flexibility.

Previewing with the Effect Browser

With such a massive number of effects to choose from, it would be impossible to go through each and every filter, apply it to an image, then undo and go to the next to see how each would affect your image. The easiest way to see what an effect will do to your image is look at it with the Effect Browser. The **Effect Browser** displays a **thumbnail** (a small version) of your open image with a sample of each effect and its default settings and other presets.

The Effect Browser, the first option under the Effects menu, takes a few moments to load, but you'll find it's worth the wait. Check out Figure 3. On the left side you have a hierarchy, or tree, view of all the adjustments and effects categories. Click the plus sign to expand that category and click the minus sign to collapse it. When

you locate and click the effect you like, click Apply; Paint Shop Pro automatically applies the default settings to the image and closes the Effect Browser. If the default setting is almost what you want but not quite, click the Modify button (instead of Apply) to get the respective dialog box.

QUICKTIP A filter comes with a default setting (also known as an **initial setting** or **preset parameter**). When you save the parameters as a custom setting, you're creating a **preset**.

FIGURE 2
Rough Leather offers several options; it's a more complex dialog box

FIGURE 3
The Effect Browser shows thumbnails of various effects

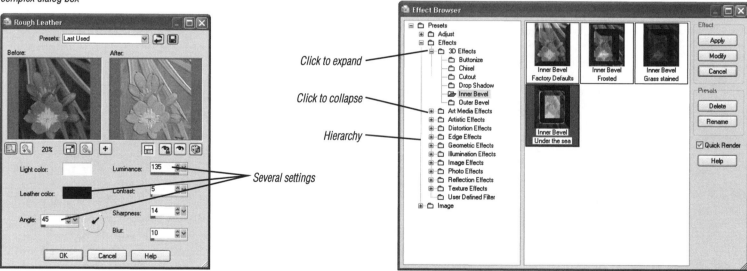

Counting on user-defined filters

All image editing is a result of math. Paint Shop Pro makes mathematical calculations for almost every command you use, and filters are no exception. If you are a whiz at math and really want a challenge, create your own filters. Paint Shop Pro includes a User Defined Filter dialog box, where you can enter your own values. Click the Effects menu, then select User Defined Filters. A dialog box appears, looking like the one shown in Figure 4. You can find out more about the basics by visiting Lori Davis's web site, which runs through the basics and even shows how to create a couple decent filters. You can view the tutorials at http://loriweb.pair.com/8udf-basics.html.

FIGURE 4

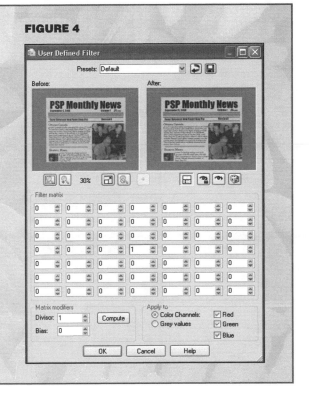

Set options in the Blinds Effect dialog box

1. Open **PSP6-1.PSPImage**, then save it as **Blinds**.

2. Click the **Blinds Effect layer** in the Layers palette.

   The Blinds Effect layer becomes active.

3. Click **Effects**, **Texture Effects**, then click **Blinds**.

   The Blinds dialog box displays, as shown in Figure 5.

4. Enter **2** for Width, then enter **100** for Opacity.

5. Click **OK**.

   The Blinds effect applies to the Blinds Effect layer.

6. Save your image.

You used the Blinds effect, applying it to a solid-colored object to give it depth and direction.

FIGURE 5

The Blinds dialog box lets you enter width and opacity settings

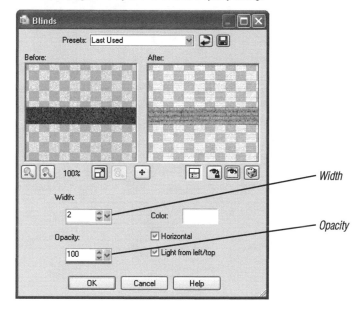

Width

Opacity

FIGURE 6

The Effect Browser offers a preview

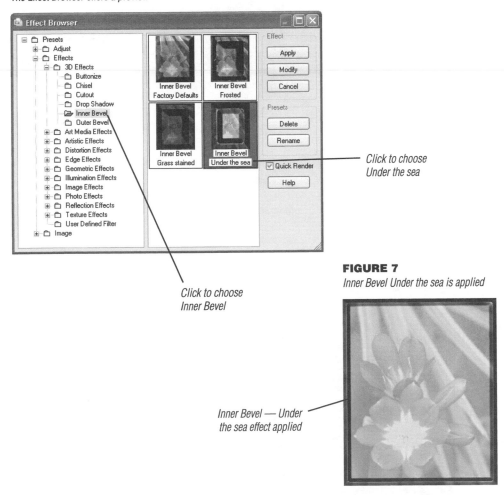

Click to choose Under the sea

Click to choose Inner Bevel

FIGURE 7

Inner Bevel Under the sea is applied

Inner Bevel — Under the sea effect applied

1. Open **PSP6-6.PSPImage**, then save it as **Underseabevel**.

2. Click **Effects**, then click **Effect Browser**.

   The Effect Browser opens, as shown in Figure 6. It might open slowly, so give it a few minutes.

3. Click **Effects**, then **3D Effects**, then click **Inner Bevel**.

   The open image appears, with all the Inner Bevel presets applied.

4. Click the **Inner Bevel Under the sea preset**, then click **Apply**.

   The dialog box closes and the setting applies to your image, as shown in Figure 7.

5. Save your image.

You used the Effect Browser to view variations and presets. You then selected the one you preferred and applied it directly from the Effect Browser, saving a lot of trial and error.

Preview and modify from the Effect Browser

1. Open **PSP6-6.PSPImage**, then save it as **Modifybrowser**.

2. Click **Effects**, then click **Effect Browser** (if necessary).

   The Effect Browser appears.

3. Click the **Effects arrow**, then **Contours**, then click **Artistic Effects**.

4. Click the **Contours Busy black preset**.

   The thumbnail is highlighted and the Modify and Apply buttons are available, as shown in Figure 8.

5. Click the **Modify button**.

   The Effect Browser closes and the Contours dialog box appears.

6. Adjust the settings for something that appeals to you.

7. Click **OK**.

   The Contours dialog box closes and modifications are visible, as shown in Figure 9.

8. Save your image.

You used the Effect Browser to view variations and presets, found one close to what you wanted, and used the Modify button to tweak the image.

FIGURE 8

The Effect Browser's Modify and Apply buttons are active

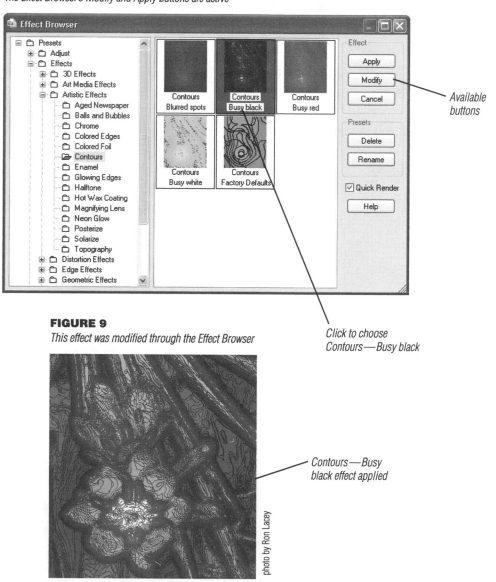

Available buttons

Click to choose Contours—Busy black

FIGURE 9

This effect was modified through the Effect Browser

Contours—Busy black effect applied

photo by Ron Lacey

EXPLORE
SPECIAL EFFECTS

What You'll Do

photo by Ron Lacey

▶ *In this lesson, you'll explore various available Paint Shop Pro effects and use them to turn an ordinary image into a work of art.*

Applying Texturing Effects

Most of the 15 different texture effects make your image appear as if it were on a textured canvas. You also can take a plain rectangle and give it depth using one of the 3D effects—instant web site button! These are your choices:

- Blinds
- Emboss
- Fine Leather
- Fur
- Mosaics
- Polished Stone
- Rough Leather
- Sandstone
- Sculpture
- Soft Plastic
- Straw Wall
- Texture
- Tiles
- Weave

Getting Artsy with Artistic Effects

This is one of the most fun categories to play around in, as well as one of the largest, with 16 possible effects. Table 1 lists them.

Creating 3D Effects

The 3D category includes special effects designed to give your selection or image a sense of depth and dimension. Outer Bevel requires a selection. You can use the remaining effects—Buttonize, Cutout, Chisel, Drop Shadow, and Inner Bevel—on both layers and selections. (See Chapter 3 for selection information and Chapter 4 for layer information.) Figure 10 shows the

FIGURE 10
Buttonize applied to selected rectangle

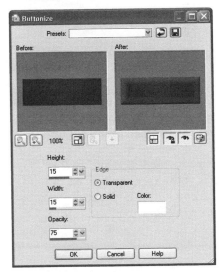

TABLE 1 Artistic Effects Categories

Effect	What it does
Aged Newspaper and Sepia Toning	Apply a yellow-colored coating, giving an aged look.
Balls and Bubbles	Let you create reflective, transparent bubbles over your image.
Chrome	Gives your image a metallic look.
Color Edges	Locates and enhances the edges of your photo.
Colored Foil and Enamel	Gives the image a shiny, merged look.
Contours	Gives your image an outline.
Glowing Edges	Applies to the image's edges and gives the appearance of a blacklight.
Neon Glow	Similar to Glowing Edges, applies a glow to the image's edges. Also applies a speckled pattern.
Halftone	Provides gradations of light, as if the photo were taken through a fine screen or mesh-type filter.
Hot Wax Coating	Makes your image appear as if a layer of hot wax were poured on it.
Magnifying Lens	Simulates placing a magnifying lens over a portion of the image.
Solarize	Gives the appearance of double exposure.
Topography	Provides a graphic representation of the image surface features.

Buttonize effect applied to a selected rectangle. The Buttonize effect is great for making buttons and banners on the fly—quickly and easily! Have you made a button you really like? You can save any effects you create as a preset so that next time there is no fiddling with all the controls: All you have to do is apply the preset to your image, and you are in business.

Using Art Media Effects

The six Art Media effects are an artist's dream. Use them to make your image look as if it were hand painted or drawn. Choices include Black Pencil, Brush Strokes, Charcoal, Colored Chalk, Colored Pencil, and Pencil. Wow all your friends and let them think you worked for hours on your images, when in reality Paint Shop Pro has done all the work for you. Figure 11 shows

the Colored Pencil effect used on a floral image. The inset shows you how the image looked before the effect was applied.

Enhancing with Edge and Illumination Effects

None of the edge effects offer options or controls that you can adjust. Paint Shop Pro simply applies the effect. Select from Dilate, Enhance, Enhance More, Erode,

FIGURE 11

The Colored Pencil effect makes this image look drawn by hand

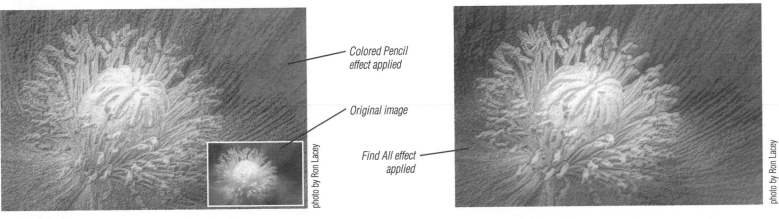

— Colored Pencil effect applied

— Original image

photo by Ron Lacey

FIGURE 12

Find All Edges effect highlights this image

Find All effect applied

photo by Ron Lacey

Find All, Find Horizontal, Find Vertical, High Pass, and Trace Contour. Figure 12 shows the Find All effect applied to the same floral image in the Figure 11 inset.

The illumination effects category has only two options: Lights and Sunburst. Both add lighting to your entire image or to selected areas. Figure 13 shows the Lights effect applied to the floral image. You can see where the cursor's placed in the top-left corner in the Before window. The pinpoints of light appear in those spots in the After window. The horizontal and vertical controls adjust the direction, or angle, that the light comes from. The intensity setting controls the amount of light. A lower setting gives less light, while a higher setting gives more.

FIGURE 13

The Lights effect has illuminations coming from different spots

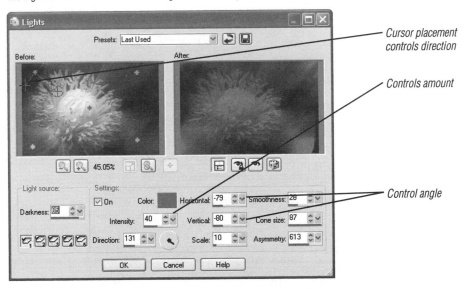

— Cursor placement controls direction

— Controls amount

— Control angle

Warping with Distortion Effects

Just as the name implies, distortion effects contort your image. This is another large category of effects to play with, many of which can turn your image into an unrecognizable but artistic form. For example, you can take an image of a flat leaf and use a distortion effect to make it appear to be falling from a tree. Or take pictures of family and friends and apply distortion effects to make some interesting-looking characters. Figure 14 shows four of the possible effects (each is named after its effect), which includes 13 choices:

- Curlicues
- Displacement Map
- Ripple
- Spiky Halo
- Lens Distortion
- Pinch
- Pixelate
- Polar Coordinates
- Punch
- Twirl
- Warp
- Wave
- Wind

Giving Perspective with Geometric Effects

Don't worry . . . you don't have to be a mathematics whiz to use the geometric effects included with Paint Shop Pro. This category includes eight options you can use to transform your images into various shapes, including circles, cylinders, pentagons, and spheres. You can also use the Perspective filters in Geometric effects to show perspective.

Thinking about Reflection Effects

Remember when you were a young kid and had the kaleidoscope that twisted and turned? It's back! From twisting your images with Kaleidoscope to mirroring them with Feedback (the old mirror-reflecting-mirror effect), the four reflection effects make it seem as if you have multiple images. Choices also include Pattern and Rotating Mirror.

Applying Effects That Are Tough to Categorize

Think of Image Effects as the "Everything Else" category. It offers three options: Offset, Page Curl, and Seamless Tiling. I think Page Curl is the most interesting and fun one to use. It gives the appearance of one of the image's corners curling. This is great for creating digital scrapbook components. Figure 15 shows Page Curl applied to a map image; this will make any treasure hunt feel like the real thing.

FIGURE 14
Distorting effects offer many options

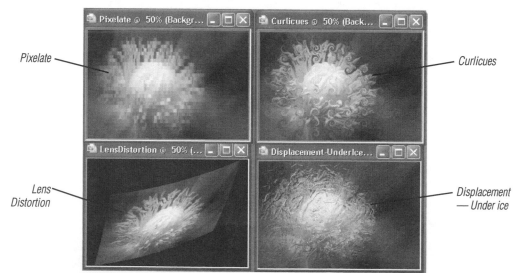

Pixelate

Curlicues

Lens Distortion

Displacement — Under ice

FIGURE 15
A Page Curl effect can add fun and realism

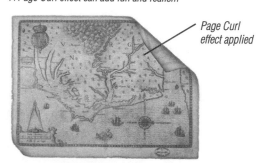

Page Curl effect applied

FIGURE 16

Use the Buttonize dialog box for your web page components

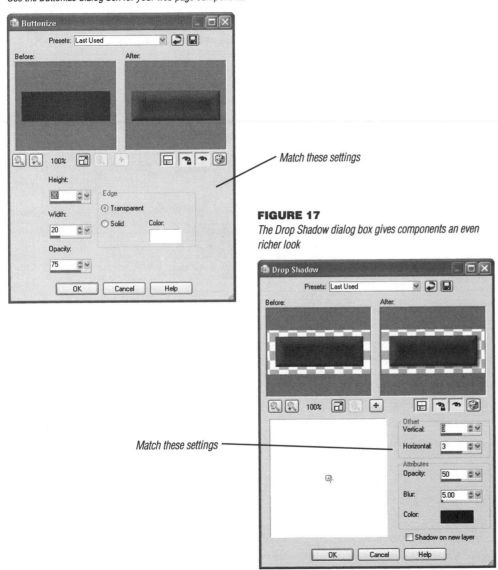

Match these settings

FIGURE 17

The Drop Shadow dialog box gives components an even richer look

Match these settings

Create a button

1. Open **PSP6-2.PSPImage**, then save it as **Buttonize**.

2. Click **Effects**, **3D**, then click **Buttonize**.

   The Buttonize dialog box displays.

3. Enter **20** for Height and Width, enter **75** for Opacity, then select the **Transparent radio button** to match the settings shown in Figure 16.

   > TIP   To see other random effects on this image, click the Randomize icon 🎲 (which looks like a di). Paint Shop Pro chooses from the possible effects and applies it.

4. Click **OK**.

   The Buttonize dialog box closes and the effect is applied to your image.

5. Click **Effects**, **3D**, then click **Drop Shadow**.

   The Drop Shadow dialog box appears.

6. Enter **3** for Horizontal and Vertical, **50** for Opacity, then **5** for Blur, matching settings in Figure 17.

7. Click **OK**.

   The Drop Shadow dialog box adjusts the shadow to new settings, then closes.

8. Save your image.

You used the Buttonize effect to give a plain-looking image a 3D look, then applied a drop shadow to enhance the button even more, making it perfect for use on a web site.

Get artsy with the aged newspaper look

1. Open your **Blinds** image, then save it as **Newspaper**.

2. Click the **Layer Visibility icon** 👁 to turn on hidden layers.

   The hidden layers display, looking like the newspaper shown in Figure 18.

3. Click **Layers**, **Merge**, then click **Merge All (Flatten)**.

   The layers merge to one layer.

4. Click **Effects**, **Artistic**, then click **Aged Newspaper**.

   The Aged Newspaper dialog box appears, as shown in Figure 19.

   TIP To preview an effect, click the Proof icon in the Aged Newspaper dialog box. The effect appears on the image open in Paint Shop Pro, in addition to that in the dialog box preview.

5. Type in an **age**, then click **OK**.

   The dialog box closes and the aged look is applied to your image.

   TIP For even more fun, review Chapter 4, "Using Layers and Masks," then try applying a mask to the edges of your newspaper to give it that used look.

6. Save your image.

You used the Aged Newspaper effect to decide exactly how old you wanted your paper to look.

FIGURE 18
Turn on hidden layers

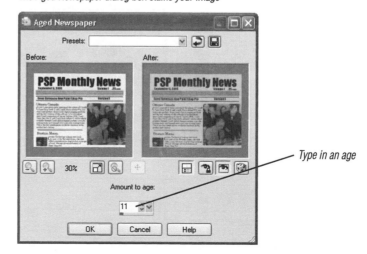

Layer Visibility icon

FIGURE 19
The Aged Newspaper dialog box stains your image

Type in an age

FIGURE 20

The Charcoal effect makes your image look drawn by hand

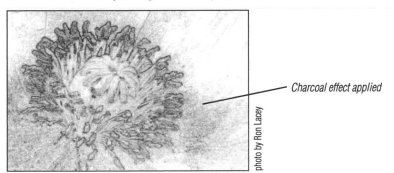

Charcoal effect applied

photo by Ron Lacey

1. Open **PSP6-3.PSPImage**, then save it as **Artmedia**.

2. Click **Effects**, **Art Media Effects**, then click **Charcoal**.

   The Charcoal dialog box displays.

3. Enter **100** for Detail, then **20** for Opacity.

4. Click **OK**.

   The Charcoal dialog box closes and the effect is applied to your image, as shown in Figure 20.

5. Save your image.

You used the Charcoal effect to make your image look as if it had been drawn by hand.

Enhance image edges

1. Open **PSP6-4.PSPImage**, then save it as **Enhanceedges**.

2. Click **Effects, Edge Effects**.

3. Click **Enhance**.

   The Enhance Edges effect is applied, as shown in Figure 21.

   > TIP When you see an effect name followed by three periods in the Effects menu, Paint Shop Pro is telling you that a dialog box requires your input. If you don't see the periods, PSP automatically applies the effect with no input from you.

4. Save your image and contact the Smithsonian Institute. Tell them you have a new masterpiece to display.

   You created a more artistic look with the Enhance Edges effect.

FIGURE 21

Use the Enhance Edges effect to pinpoint an outline

— *Enhance Edges effect applied*

photo by Ron Lacey

FIGURE 22

The Sunburst dialog box belongs to the illumination effects category

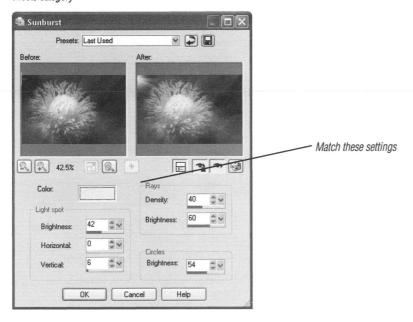

Match these settings

1. Open **PSP6-4.PSPImage**, then save it as **Sunburst**.

2. Click **Effects**, **Illumination Effects**, then click **Sunburst**.

   The Sunburst dialog box displays, as shown in Figure 22.

   TIP To easily move the direction from which the light is coming, click and drag the crosshair in the preview pane to the new location.

3. Enter **42** for Brightness, **0** for Horizontal, then **6** for Vertical.

4. Continuing in the dialog box, enter **40** for Density, **60** for Brightness, then **54** for Circles: Brightness.

5. Click **OK**.

   The applied settings give the appearance of light shining down on the image, as shown in Figure 23.

You used the Sunburst effect to give the illusion of light.

FIGURE 23

The Sunburst effect is applied to image

Sunburst effect applied

Create an artistic twirl

1. Open **PSP6-4.PSPImage**, then save it as **Distort**.

2. Click **Effects, Distortion Effects**.

3. Click **Twirl**.

   The Twirl dialog box appears, as shown in Figure 24.

4. Enter **180** for Degrees.

5. Click **OK**.

   The Twirl dialog box closes and the effect is applied to your image.

6. Save your file.

You used the Twirl effect to create a psychedelic image.

FIGURE 24
The Twirl effect makes things psychedelic

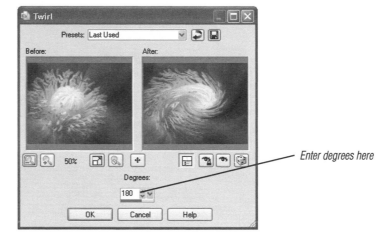

Enter degrees here

FIGURE 25

The Circle effect is psychedelic, too

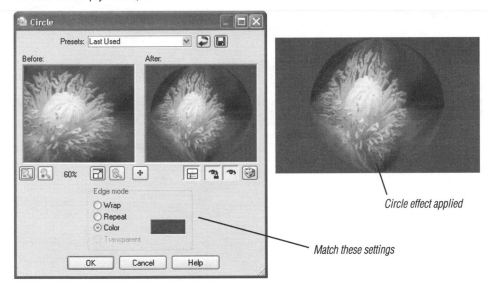

Match these settings

Circle effect applied

1. Open **PSP6-4.PSPImage**, then save it as **Geometric**.

2. Click **Effects**, then click **Geometric Effects**.

3. Click **Circle**.

   The Circle dialog box displays.

4. Select the **Color radio button**, then choose black.

5. Click **OK**.

   Your image becomes circular, as shown in Figure 25. The Circle dialog box closes.

You used the Circle effect to give your image the appearance of being stirred.

Think about the Kaleidoscope effect

1. Open **PSP6-4.PSPImage**, then save it as **Reflection**.

2. Click **Effects, Reflection Effects**, then click **Kaleidoscope**.

   The Kaleidoscope dialog box opens.

3. Click the **Randomize icon** 🖼.

   Paint Shop Pro randomly adjusts settings, as shown in Figure 26.

   > TIP   Paint Shop Pro randomly adjusts settings each time you click the Randomize icon. Continue clicking the icon for more options.

4. Click **OK**.

   The Kaleidoscope dialog box closes and the effect is applied to your image.

5. Save your image.

You used the Kaleidoscope effect with random settings to get a fun image with chance.

FIGURE 26

The Kaleidoscope effect mimics a childhood toy

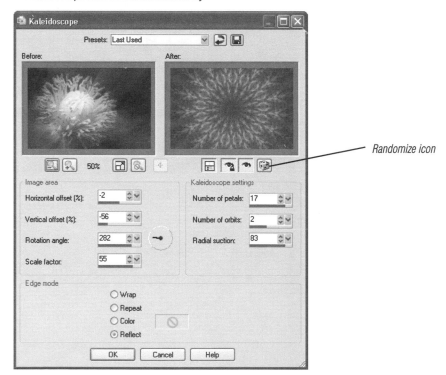

Randomize icon

FIGURE 27

The Page Curl dialog box lets you choose how many curls to add

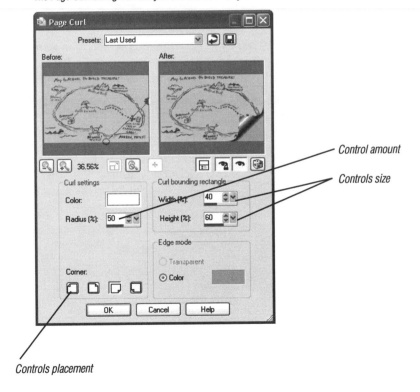

Control amount

Controls size

Controls placement

1. Open **PSP6-5.PSPImage**, then save it as **Curled**.

2. Click **Effects**, **Image Effects**, then click **Page Curl**.

   The Page Curl dialog box displays, as shown in Figure 27.

3. Enter **40** for Width, **60** for Height, then **50** for Radius.

4. Continuing in the dialog box, choose white for Curl settings Color.

5. Choose tan for the Edge mode color.

   > TIP   Radius controls the amount of curl applied. Height and width determine the curled portion's size. The preview window controls represent where you want to place the curl. Click to move or adjust the controls.

6. Click **OK**.

   The Page Curl dialog box closes and the effect is applied to your image.

7. Save your image.

You added a Page Curl effect, giving your image a richer, three-dimensional look.

PLUG
IT IN

What You'll Do

 In this lesson, you'll learn how to install third-party plug-ins with a wizard. In addition, you'll install a plug-in that does not have an automatic installer.

Plugging into Creativity with Third-Party Plug-ins

If the over 100 filters supplied with Paint Shop Pro aren't enough for you, you can add plug-in filters. Third-party plug-ins come from outside developers; they're not originally part of Paint Shop Pro. Generally, plug-ins require an image-editing program, but a few work alone, as well as being accessible through the Effects > Plug-In menu.

Some plug-in filters are quite pricey, whereas others are free or very inexpensive (usually less than $5). Typically, you won't find plug-ins available at your local software or discount store, but the Internet offers an abundance of them, and in many cases you can get a trial copy before laying out your hard-earned money. Most third-party filters are compatible with Paint Shop Pro and typically have the file extension .8bf, such as SuperBlade-Pro.8bf. Table 2 lists some popular plug-ins and some that the graphics industry deems "must haves." Figure 28 shows a SuperBladePro effect applied to text.

FIGURE 28
SuperBladePro applied to text

SuperBladePro effect applied

TABLE 2 Affordable, Popular, Must-have Plug-ins

Site name	Site address	Site description
Alien Skin	www.alienskin.com	Provides a wider variety of photorealistic textures, such as snakes; has glass, bevels, and 3D effects; Xenofex 2 collections simulate nature.
Amphisoft Plug-In Filters	http://photoshop.msk.ru/	Offers a nice variety of photo-fixing filters.
Auto FX	www.autofx.com	Carries some really unique effects, like wrinkle, tape, and gels.
Av Bros	www.avbros.com	Hands down the best Page Curl and Puzzle plug-in on the Internet today. Examples shown in the Gallery.
Flaming Pear	www.flamingpear.com	Includes unusual filters, such as kinds that create planets or give the illusion of flooding.
Namesuppressed	www.namesuppressed.com	Useful for photo enhancement and pattern creation.
The Plug-In Site	www.thepluginsite.com	Offers many free and commercial plug-ins, including its own very popular ColorWasher and Focal Blade.

Downloading plug-ins

When getting a plug-in from the Internet, you'll encounter steps that seem to require a fairly deep commitment. With viruses galore, you want to know what's normal. Here's what you can expect: Most filter vendors offer the opportunity to take their filter for a test drive. Most demos and trial versions are full working versions that either apply a watermark to the image until you purchase it or expire within a certain timeframe. Once your timeframe is up, you can no longer use the filter until you buy a purchase code from the vendor. The timeframe is usually between 15–30 days.

Installing Plug-in Filters

Each filter manufacturer provides its own method and directions for installing its filters. When you install, make a note of the file location; you will need to tell Paint Shop Pro where to find the files on your computer. Paint Shop Pro stores its instructions to the file locations in Preferences, as you saw in Chapter 1, "Getting Started with Paint Shop Pro X." Once a file location is set and your plug-ins are installed, they will appear under Effects > Plug-ins. Figure 29 shows one plug-in filter installed: Flaming Pears' SuperBladePro.

An installer automatically puts the files on the computer for you with a step-by-step walkthrough. Not all filters come with an installer. For instance, Flaming Pears' Flood does not install by itself. You must download it to the drive, then copy and paste it to the folder where your plug-in filters are stored.

QUICKTIP I recommend creating your own filter folder on your hard drive, outside Corel folder paths. Doing so ensures faster loading when you launch Paint Shop Pro.

FIGURE 29
Once installed, plug-ins display in the Effects menu

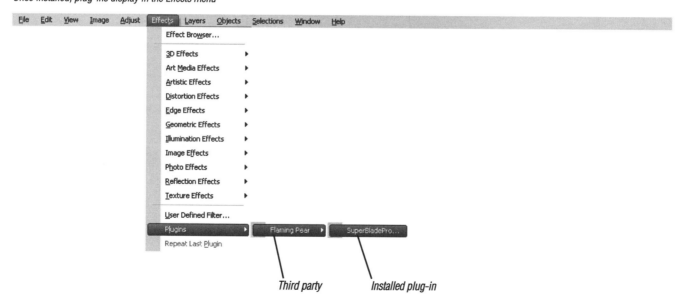

Third party   Installed plug-in

FIGURE 30

The destination folder is where you want to store the plug-in

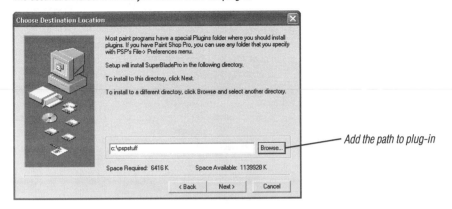

Add the path to plug-in

FIGURE 31

The newly installed plug-in displays in Effects menu

Listed plug-in

1. Download **Filters4Readers.zip** from the Course web site, save it to your desktop, then double-click the **file**.

   Three folders are revealed.

   > TIP To ensure a smooth installation, close all programs (including Paint Shop Pro) and any open windows.

2. Double-click the **SuperBladePro folder**.

   The folder displays a file.

3. Click and drag the **SuperBladePro file** onto your desktop, then close the folder window.

4. Double-click the **SuperBladePro file**.

   A dialog box says that the installer is starting, then the install screen appears.

5. Click **Next** until you see the Choose Destination Location dialog box shown in Figure 30.

6. Add the path for your plug-in folder.

   > TIP If the location is not where you need it, click the Browse button, then go to the place on your hard drive where you want to store the plug-in.

7. Click **Next**, then click **Next** again, then click **Close**.

   SuperBladePro installs, the Finished screen appears, the installer closes, and your desktop appears.

8. Open Paint Shop Pro (if necessary), then click **Effects**, **Plug-ins**.

   The SuperBladePro plug-in is listed, as shown in Figure 31.

You downloaded and installed a demo copy of Flaming Pears' SuperBladePro plug-in so you can try it before deciding whether to buy it.

Install a plug-in without installer

1. Double-click the **Filters4Readers.zip file** on your desktop.

   The zip file displays three folders.

2. Double-click the **FloodFilter folder**.

3. Right-click the **Flood folder**, then click **Copy**, as shown in Figure 32.

   The folder copies to your clipboard.

4. Using Windows Explorer, navigate to the drive and folder where your plug-in filters are stored.

5. Right-click, then click **Paste**.

   A progress window appears, as shown in Figure 33. Copying can take a few minutes. The window closes when the function is complete. The copied file is pasted on the drive and folder where your plug-in filters are stored.

6. Close all windows, then open Paint Shop Pro.

   You see the Flood filter in the Effects menu, as shown in Figure 34.

You manually installed a demo copy of Flaming Pears' Flood Fill plug-in filter, because there was no installer to guide you through setup.

FIGURE 32

Copying the Flood plug-in folder

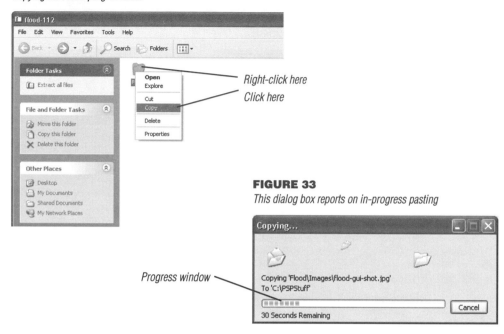

Right-click here

Click here

FIGURE 33

This dialog box reports on in-progress pasting

Progress window

FIGURE 34

The Flood plug-in is added

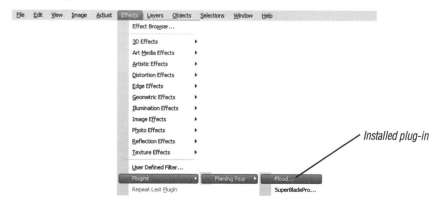

Installed plug-in

USE THIRD-PARTY FILTERS,
CROPPING, AND COLORIZING

What You'll Do

 In this lesson, you'll learn to use newly installed filters to create 3D effects with text and frames.

Accessing and Using Third-Party Filters

Just like native Paint Shop Pro filters, each third-party filter performs differently. Some require you to make a selection before working; others require no selection. One commonality all filters share is that your image is required to be high color depth (more than 256 colors). Some filters work on 16-bit images with Paint Shop Pro, but not all.

Each filter's interface varies depending on who created it. Figure 35 shows the SuperBladePro interface. Does it look a bit overwhelming? It's not. I won't cover each SuperBladePro slider and option, but I think you will find it comes equipped with a nice stock of premade settings (commonly referred to as presets) for using again and again until you muster up the courage to start moving all those sliders and bars around. They're just begging for your attention.

Colorizing

Remember the old days, when everything was in black and white? Despite all the technological advances, nowadays we are seeing some of those old black and white programs come back—but in full color! Paint Shop Pro offers a Colorize feature that works well on selected, color-neutral (grey) areas. One of the many advantages is that you can create text, buttons, and other web components in greyscale, then use Colorize. Do you want your web site to be red this week and blue the next? Pull out your greyscale components and colorize them. This way you don't have to create new components from scratch each time you want to change the colors.

Cropping from Selections

You can lop off any unwanted areas of an image with the Crop tool. When you crop unwanted areas, you take away parts of the image, thus reducing the actual file size. That data is no longer stored in the image.

Increasing Your Canvas Size

Oftentimes you will have created something really nice by applying a filter to it but think something is lacking. Say you create some text and apply some effects from SuperBladePro. Thinking this could be another prospective masterpiece for the Smithsonian Institute, you need to add that finishing touch. Thinking for a moment,

you have an epiphany. A frame! That would be the perfect accent; after all, you wouldn't catch the Mona Lisa with her frame down, would you? You could make the frame to match your text. That's it! But—there's always a *but*, isn't there?—when looking at your image, you notice you have already cropped the extra space. The image is quite small and you don't know how to add a

frame that matches the image. You need just a bit more symmetrical space around the image. What to do? Paint Shop Pro offers an option for resizing your canvas (the bottommost background layer).

QUICKTIP If there is no background layer, a dialog box says that you need to flatten your layers before you can resize your canvas.

FIGURE 35

The SuperBladePro interface offers many sliders and bars

Sliders

Having plug-in nightmares

Be careful not to acquire so many plug-ins that it becomes an organizational nightmare. Try demos. If you like them, then by all means purchase them. Just don't spend a lot of money on anything right away. Get familiar with Paint Shop Pro first. It offers many of the same effects that most third-party plug-ins do. There are, however, exceptions to that rule. It's been my experience that there are a couple "must-have" filters out there that perform a function that PSP can't, or perform a function a bit better, or provides more flexibility and control. I have listed my "must-have" plug-ins in Table 2, earlier in this chapter.

FIGURE 36
Access a plug-in with the SuperBladePro dialog box

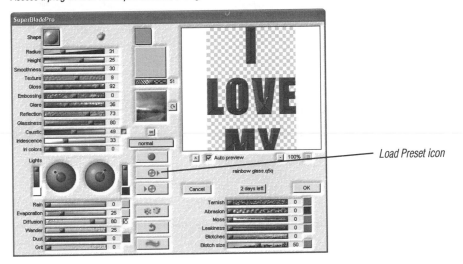

Load Preset icon

FIGURE 37
Loading a preset

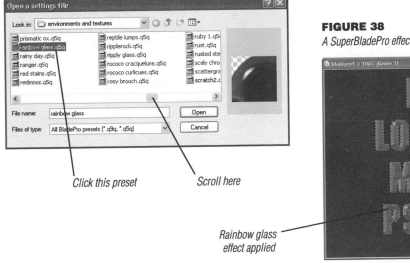

Click this preset

Scroll here

FIGURE 38
A SuperBladePro effect applied to text

Rainbow glass
effect applied

Access and use a newly installed plug-in

1. Open **PSP6-7.PSPImage**, then save it as **Bladepro1**.

   The image opens with selected text on a black background.

2. Click **Effects**, **Plug-ins**, **Flaming Pear**, then click **SuperBladePro**.

   The SuperBladePro dialog box appears, as shown in Figure 36.

3. Click the **Load Preset icon**.

   A small dialog box appears, as shown in Figure 37.

4. Scroll through the presets, click the **rainbow glass** setting, then click **Open**.

   When you click the setting, a thumbnail previews the effect. When you click Open, the dialog box closes and that effect is applied to the text.

   > TIP The preset preview is not 100-percent reliable. When SuperBladePro does its thing, it considers several factors: size and base color just to name two. You can apply a preset; then, if needed, tweak your settings to get the desired results.

5. Click **OK**.

   The effect is applied to your text, as shown in Figure 38. You remedy its darkness in the next objective.

   > TIP If you forget which preset you are using, look directly below the preview window in the SuperBladePro interface to see its name.

6. Save your image.

You used one of your newly installed plug-ins to add definition to text.

Colorize your text

1. Open **Bladepro1.PSPImage** (if necessary), then save it as **Colorize**.

2. Click **Adjust**, **Hue and Saturation**, then click **Colorize**.

   The Colorize dialog box displays.

3. Click, then hold down the mouse button on the **Hue arrow**.

   A small gradient color bar displays under the Hue box, as shown in Figure 39.

4. Slide to the desired color.

5. Click the **Saturation arrow** to desired level of saturation, then click **OK**.

   The Colorize dialog box closes and the color is applied to your text, as shown in Figure 40.

6. Save your image.

You added color to your dry, dark image, bringing it to life.

FIGURE 39
Colorizing with the Hue slider

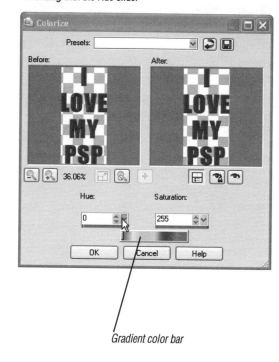

Gradient color bar

FIGURE 40
Colorized text

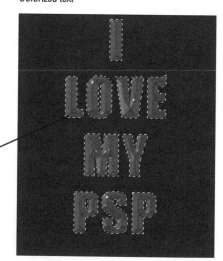

Colorized Rainbow
glass effect applied

FIGURE 41

When placed on the bounding box, your cursor becomes a two-sided arrow

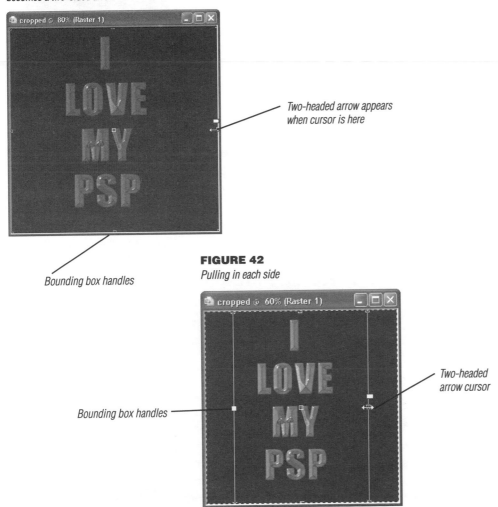

Two-headed arrow appears when cursor is here

Bounding box handles

FIGURE 42

Pulling in each side

Bounding box handles

Two-headed arrow cursor

Lesson 4 Use Third-Party Filters, Cropping, and Colorizing

Crop off extra space

1. Open **Colorize.PSPImage** (if necessary), then save it as **Cropped**.

2. Click **Selections**, then click **Select None** (if necessary).

   The marquee disappears, indicating the text is no longer selected.

3. Click **Selections**, then click **Select All**.

   The marquee appears, indicating that the entire image is selected.

4. Click the **Crop tool** [⊡], then click the **Snap to Selection icon** [⊠].

   The bounding box appears in the same position as your selection marquee.

5. Place your cursor on one of the **bounding box** sides until it turns into the two-headed arrow shown in Figure 41.

   > TIP If you have trouble finding the cropping arrow at the side of the image, resize the window, hold your tongue in your cheek just right, then place the cursor over the midsection again.

6. Click and drag the **bounding box handle** inward; repeat for the other side.

   Your image should appear as shown in Figure 42.

7. Double-click anywhere inside the crop box.

   The crop is applied and the extra space around your image is no longer visible.

8. Save your image.

You used the Crop tool to remove unwanted and unnecessary portions of your image, making the file smaller and saving some hard-drive space.

Increase the canvas to make a frame

1. Open **Cropped.PSPImage**, then save it as **Canvasframe**.

2. Click **Image**, then click **Canvas Size**.

   The Canvas Size dialog box appears, as shown in Figure 43.

3. Enter **400** for Width, **550** for Height, choose **Pixels** from the drop-down arrow, then enter **25** for Top, Bottom, Left, and Right.

4. Click **OK**, click the **Magic Wand tool** , then click any of the added **transparent canvas**.

   The dialog box closes and area is added, as shown in Figure 44.

5. Click the **Flood Fill tool** , set the foreground/stroke color to white, then click once inside the selection.

   The selected area fills with white paint.

6. Click **Effects, SuperBladePro**.

   The SuperBladePro interface displays.

7. Click the **Load Preset icon** , select **Rainbow glass** (if necessary), then click **Open**.

   The dialog box closes and the effect is applied, as shown on the left in Figure 45.

8. Click **Adjust, Hue and Saturation**, then click **Colorize**.

9. Set your color, then click **Close**.

   The preview changes as you adjust settings, then closes when you click Close.

You increased the canvas size, colored it, and inserted a frame to enlarge an image that you wanted to make larger.

FIGURE 43
Choose your area with the Canvas Size dialog box

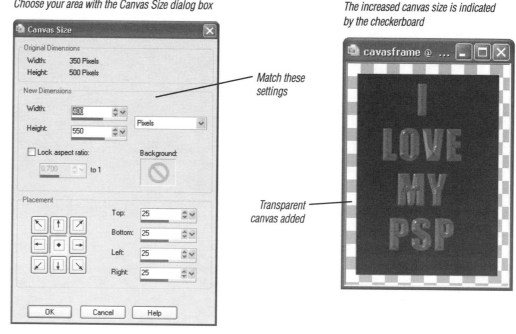

Match these settings

FIGURE 44
The increased canvas size is indicated by the checkerboard

Transparent canvas added

FIGURE 45
Left frame—SuperBladePro applied; right frame—colorized frame

Rainbow glass frame

Colorized frame

BLUR WITH FILTERS

What You'll Do

In this lesson, you'll learn about different blurring methods and how to use them effectively.

Working with Blur

Most images demand clarity. You have a wealth of filters that help clarify the details in your image: Salt and Pepper and DCNR (Digital Camera Noise Remover), just to name two. Sometimes, though, you want to blur, or soften, all or part of a photo. Blur filters work by comparing the average values of adjacent pixels. The value adds noise (graininess) to your image. In turn, contrast between them is reduced. Most of the blur filters focus on high-contrast areas, and all the blur filters work on greyscale and 16 million-plus color images.

Softening Effects Using Blur and Blur More

You can use the blur filters many ways. You might use Blur and Blur More to reduce noise or to focus on one particular element. Blur removes noise by applying a smooth transition and decreasing contrast. As you might expect, Blur More applies the same effect that Blur does, but with greater intensity. Figure 46 shows

examples of the filters. You can especially see the difference when you compare the backgrounds in these shots.

Applying Average Blur

Average Blur really comes in handy for removing dithering and other noise that often occurs when you scan images or increase color depth. By reducing the contrast between pixels, you get fewer unwanted artifacts and a smoother, more consistent appearance. When you use Average Blur, Paint Shop Pro prompts you for an amount measured in aperture. Aperture options run from 3–29. Just like when you take a photo with a camera, the lower the aperture, the more blur you see.

Making Movement with Motion Blur

Today's cameras have built-in features that reduce the chance of getting blur during a motion shot; however, you may want it to add visual impact. Paint Shop Pro includes a Motion Blur filter, which gives the illu-

FIGURE 46
Blur and Blur More effects

No blur filter

Various levels of applied blur

Going far out with Gaussian Blur

Gaussian Blur originated from a German mathematician and astronomer, Karl Friedrich Gauss. Mr. Gauss had many mathematical theories, some of which Paint Shop Pro applies when you use his namesake blur. Gaussian Blur is very similar to Average Blur, but more intense and more realistic. It works by controlling the amount of blurring applied to any given pixel or edge by an adjustable amount, making the blur appear dense in the center, with soft, feathery edges. Like other blurring effects, you can apply it to all or just a portion of your image. Most of the time you wouldn't want to apply the blur to the entire image but only to a selected part, which changes the depth of field (distance between the nearest and farthest objects in focus as seen by the camera lens). Depth of field determines what parts are in focus (the foreground) or not (the background).

sion that the photo has been taken, while the object is moving, using a fixed exposure time. This filter works best when used inside a selection—not on an entire image. The motion effects are applied in a directional manner, and you can adjust not only that direction but the intensity. Figure 47 shows a Motion Blur application. I selected each wing separately, then applied the filter. I set the direction for each wing to be opposite the other. This way the blur gives the illusion of the bird beginning to take off.

Spinning with Radial Blurs

Radial Blur simulates spinning your camera around in circles, or zooming in quickly with a slow shutter speed. Like many other filters, you probably won't use Radial Blur

FIGURE 47
Motion Blur applied to each wing makes this image appear to move

Motion blur applied

much, but with the right photograph you can yield some interesting results. Radial Blur filters provide three options:

- Twirl: A spiral
- Zoom: Away from the center of the image
- Spin: Circularly around the center of the image

FIGURE 48

Inverting the selection can be easier

blur @ 80% (Background)

— Selection to invert

photo by Ron Lacey

FIGURE 49

Blur applied to inverted selection

— Blur and Blur More effects applied

— Original image

photo by Ron Lacey

Soften with Blur and Blur More

1. Open **PSP6-8.PSPImage**, then save it as **Blur**.

   The image opens with a selection already made.

2. Click **Selection**, then click **Invert**.

   The selection around the flower inverts, selecting the opposite from what is chosen in Figure 48.

   TIP   It is often easier to select the part of an image that doesn't need an effect applied. It's more efficient to select that part and then invert the selection.

3. Click **Adjust**, **Blur**, then click **Blur More**.

   The selected area blurs, as shown in Figure 49. The inset shows the original image.

   TIP   For even further drama, apply Blur or Blur More numerous times.

4. Save your image.

You made areas of the image fuzzy with the Blur More filter, bringing focus to the main subject.

Apply Average Blur

1. Open **PSP6-9.PSPImage**, then save it as **Average**.

   The image opens with the selection still active.

2. Click **Selections**, then click **Invert**.

   The selection reverses.

   > TIP   If the marquee is distracting you, hide it without losing the selection via Selections > Hide Marquee.

3. Click **Adjust**, **Blur**, then click **Average**.

   The Average dialog box displays, as shown in Figure 50.

4. Enter **5** for Filter aperture.

5. Click **OK**.

   The Average Blur is applied to your selected area.

6. Save your image.

You applied Average Blur to a selected area, directing focus to a specific object in the image.

FIGURE 50
Average Blur dialog box

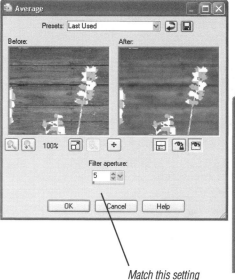

Match this setting

Average blur effect applied

photo by Ron Lacey

FIGURE 51

Motion blur applied

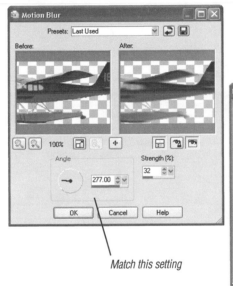

Match this setting

Motion blur effect applied

photo by Ron Lacey

1. Open **PSP6-10.PSPImage**, then save it as **Motion**.

2. Click **Adjust**, **Blur**, then click **Motion Blur**.

   The Motion Blur dialog box displays, as shown in Figure 51.

3. Enter **277** for Angle.

4. Enter **32** for Strength.

5. Click **OK**.

   The dialog box closes and the effect is applied to your image.

6. Save your image.

You created the illusion of movement with Motion Blur.

Spin a Radial Blur

1. Open **PSP6-11.PSPImage**, then save it as **Radial**.

2. Click **Adjust**, **Blur**, then click **Radial**.

   The Radial Blur dialog box appears.

3. Click the **Zoom radio button**.

4. Enter **10** for Strength.

5. Mark the **Elliptical checkbox**.

6. Enter **0** for Horizontal offset, Vertical offset, and Protect center.

   As you change your settings to match those shown in Figure 52, the After window shows the results.

7. Click **OK**.

   The Radial Blur dialog box closes.

You applied Radial Blur to give a more artistic look.

FIGURE 52

Radial blur settings give an artistic look

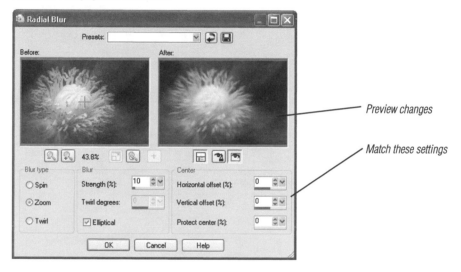

Preview changes

Match these settings

CHAPTER SUMMARY

In this chapter, you learned about programs that can make for some interesting effects when used in conjunction with Paint Shop Pro. You also learned how to use the Effect Browser to see different effects applied to your image at one time, avoiding having to open each filter independently and saving you valuable time. You also learned how to organize your plug-ins and maximize them so they flow smoothly with Paint Shop Pro.

WHAT YOU LEARNED

- How to download and install plug-in filters.
- How to use the Effect Browser to view multiple effects on your image.
- How to create 3D effects with plug-ins.
- How to apply a page curl.
- How to create an older-looking image using colorize filters.
- How to increase your canvas size.
- How to manage plug-ins.
- How to add a blur filter.

KEYWORDS

aperture The lower this setting on a blur filter, the more blur you see.

blur To soften.

canvas Bottommost background layer.

dithering Fuzziness, artifacts, or noise, in a photo.

Effect Browser Displays a small version of an open image with a sample of each effect, and its default settings and other presets.

filter Small subprogram.

presets Premade settings.

third-party plug-in Filter that is not originally part of Paint Shop Pro.

thumbnail A small version of an image.

7

EDITING AND
ENHANCING PHOTOS

1. Learn digital darkroom basics.

2. Get rid of red eye.

3. Remove unwanted objects.

4. Correct specific problems.

5. Improve and enhance photos.

ULTRASONIC

7 EDITING AND
ENHANCING PHOTOS

Taking Pictures On the Fly

Digital cameras are not only fun devices for capturing special moments and beautiful images, they are fast and efficient. Imagine you are driving along the countryside and spot some wild deer. In a matter of moments, you can pull over, capture the image, and resume driving. Gone are the days of loading your traditional camera with film, returning to the same spot, and waiting, all the while hoping that those deer will return to have their picture taken.

Knowing a Good Editing Candidate

Some of the best pictures are totally spontaneous: "Quick, grab the camera!" And these are just the types of images—taken quickly—that may be good candidates for Paint Shop Pro's editing and enhancing tools. How many times have you said to yourself, "If only her eyes weren't so red" or "I wish we had moved the vacuum cleaner out of the way before we took the picture." With Paint Shop Pro, you can perfect your images to your liking by removing red eye, dust, scratches, and unwanted objects. You can also sharpen dull images and correct specific colors. The Smart Photo Fix feature analyzes your image and makes suggestions for fixing it, showing a "before" and "after" image in the Smart Photo Fix dialog box. You can accept the suggestions or even fine-tune the settings. This is a great place to start if you're unsure how to correct an image.

Tools You'll Use

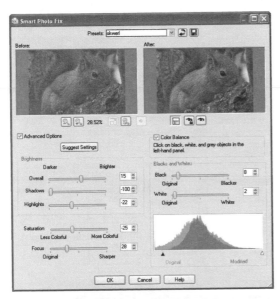

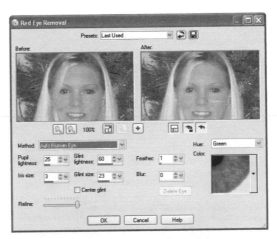

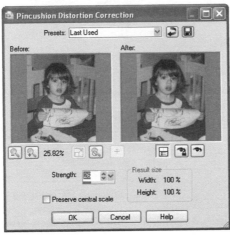

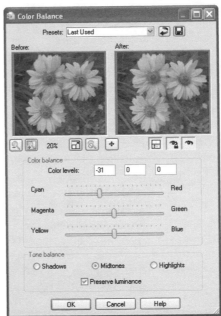

LEARN DIGITAL
DARKROOM BASICS

What You'll Do

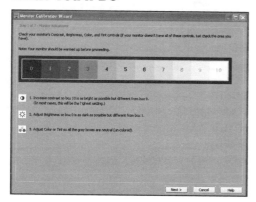

 In this lesson, you'll review the definition of color depth as well as how to calibrate and profile your monitor for better image display.

Understanding Color Depth

As you already know, digital images are composed of pixels, which are capable of displaying a certain number of colors. This number is known as a pixel's **color depth** or **bit depth**. Color depth is defined by the total number of bits per pixel that can be displayed on the computer screen. Data is stored in bits. Each bit represents two colors because it has a value of 0 or 1. The more bits per pixel, the more color can be displayed.

For example, each pixel in a 4-bit image can display one of 16 possible colors, while pixels in a 24-bit image can display one of over 16-million colors. Images with a higher color depth obviously display much better than those with a lower color depth. However, high color depth files are much larger and require more of your computer's resources to display properly. In Paint Shop Pro, you can view your image's color depth in the Overview palette through the Info tab, and you can find out

how many colors are used in an image at Image > Count Image Colors.

So what does this all mean for you? It means you'll probably need an image with a minimum of 16-million colors. Most of Paint Shop Pro's correction and effect features are available only for such images. Another thing it means is that sharing photos via email might be tough. Most Internet service providers set a limit on file size. Also, the amount of time required to download a 20MB image on a dial-up connection would be well over a couple hours and would make for some very unhappy friends and family.

QUICKTIP To decrease an image's color depth, simply click Image on the menu bar, then click Decrease Color Depth. The Decrease Color Depth dialog box opens. In this dialog box, you can see the before and after previews, as well as choose reduction options. However, I recommend exporting the file through the JPEG Optimizer (shown in Figure 1 and discussed in Chapter 1), which uses compression to reduce the size of the file.

FIGURE 1

Reduce file size with the JPEG Optimizer

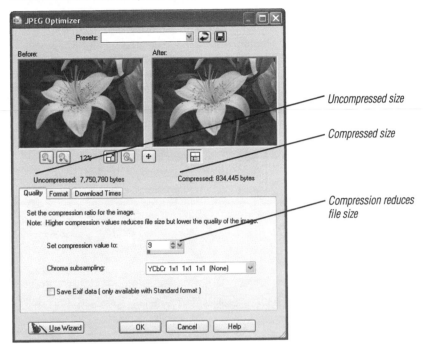

Uncompressed size

Compressed size

Compression reduces
file size

Understanding RAW images

What exactly is RAW? It may surprise you that RAW is not
an acronym for anything, but if you think of the traditional meaning of *raw*, which is something that is
unprocessed and in a natural condition, then you'll have
no trouble remembering what a RAW image is: an image
containing unprocessed data. Think of RAW as the digital
equivalent to a negative.

To understand exactly what makes up a RAW file, you
first need to understand how most current digital cameras
work. Sensors create an image from millions of tiny light-
sensing areas on a chip. Most sensors actually only record
in greyscale values and then use filters and color schemes,
such as the Bayer Pattern (invented by a Kodak scientist
Dr. Bayer in the 1980's) to determine the colors. There are
usually three different colors: red, green, and blue.

RAW files are usually proprietary to the camera manufacturer and sometimes to a specific camera model. That
means that only the camera that captures the picture can
understand the information collected on the sensors. The
settings associated with them, such as shutter speed, aperture, white balance, contrast, sharpening, and saturation
values, are not applied; they are stored for later use. RAW
images are typically used by professional photographers
who prefer more control over their image. Once your digital camera is connected to your computer, you can access
the images through Paint Shop Pro. In the Learning Center, click Get Photos > Download. Paint Shop Pro is now
compatible with more makes and models of digital cameras for the purpose of importing RAW images. See the
appendix for a list of compatible cameras.

Calibrating and Profiling Your Monitor

Now that you've got a handle on image color depth, here's a curve ball. Computer monitors also have a specific color depth that is built into the monitor at the time of production. A monitor's color depth is also determined by display settings in the Control Panel.

Keep in mind that if your image's color depth is higher than that of your monitor, it will not display correctly. Another thing to keep in mind is that no two monitors display color identically. In order for a monitor

to display colors accurately, you have to fine tune its settings. This is known as **calibrating** your monitor. A full monitor calibration is a two-step process: The first step is the calibration (changing the monitor's display settings) and the second step is to profile the monitor so color-managed applications know how to display the colors.

The second step is profiling your monitor. A color profile tells a color managed application like Paint Shop Pro how to display colors (even if the monitor's settings are off). Here's an example: If your monitor displays too much red, the color profile tells

the program that the monitor's red settings are X number of points too high. Paint Shop Pro adjusts the settings and displays your image with X points less red, so the colors onscreen are accurate. Paint Shop Pro has a calibration wizard that helps you calibrate your monitor, as shown in Figure 2. To use this wizard, click File on the menu bar, select Color Management, then click Monitor Calibration.

QUICKTIP Applying the profile is not necessary if things are viewing acceptably. At the time of release, some monitor profiling issues remained.

FIGURE 2
Profile your monitor with the Calibration Wizard

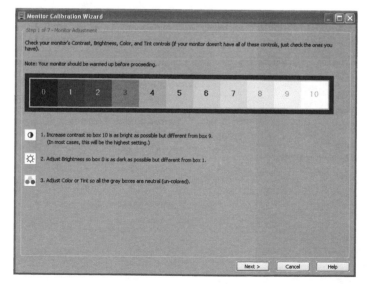

Importing images through TWAIN

TWAIN is an applications programming interface (API) created for image capture. Created in 1992 for both Windows and Macintosh platforms, TWAIN has become the industry standard for getting an image from your scanner onto your computer and into your imaging software. If you want to scan images from your scanner directly into Paint Shop Pro, click File on the menu bar, point to Import, then click TWAIN Source, choose your scanning device in the Select Source dialog box, then click Select. Now you're ready to scan. Go back to the File menu, point to Import, and choose TWAIN Acquire. It's that easy! By the way, TWAIN is not an acronym. It comes from Rudyard Kipling's expression ". . . and never the twain shall meet. . . ."

FIGURE 3

This photo has a color depth of 8 bits

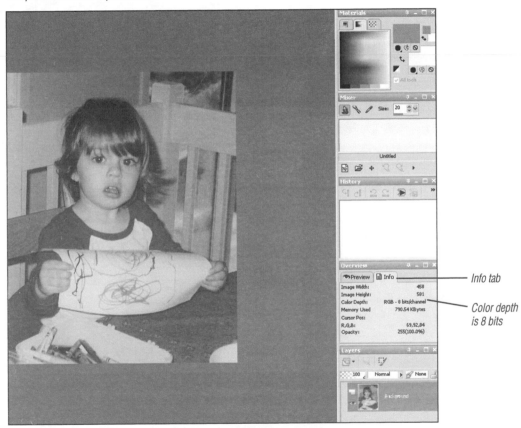

Info tab

Color depth
is 8 bits

Understand color depth

1. Open **PSP7-1.PSPImage**, then save it as **Color Depth**.

2. Click the **Palettes arrow** on the standard toolbar, then click **Overview** (if necessary).

3. Click the **Info tab** in the Overview palette, then locate the color depth information in the Info palette.

   As shown in Figure 3, color depth is an 8-bit image.

4. Click **Image**, then click **Decrease Color Depth**.

5. View the possible color depths you could apply to this image, then release the mouse button.

6. Click **Image**, point to **Increase Color Depth**, then click **RGB – 16 bits/channel**.

7. Notice the change in color depth in the Info palette, then save your work.

8. Close your file.

You viewed an image's current color depth, then learned how to decrease and increase the color depth information for future use.

Calibrate and profile your monitor

1. Click **File**, select **Color Management**, then click **Monitor Calibration**.

   The Monitor Calibration Wizard opens.

2. Click the **Maximize button** in the upper-right corner of the wizard.

3. Click **Next** at each prompt, stopping at Step 7 of 7 - Save Monitor Profile, as shown in Figure 4.

4. Type **My Calibration** in the File name text box, then click **Finish**.

   The wizard closes and your newly created profile is set as the default profile for your monitor.

5. Click the **minimize button** on the top right; if necessary, resize to see your desktop.

   | TIP As an alternate, you can click the Show Desktop button on your taskbar.

6. Right-click an empty space on your desktop, then click **Properties**.

7. Click the **Settings tab**, then click **Advanced**.

8. Click the **Color Management tab**, then locate My Calibration next to the Default monitor profile.

9. Click **Cancel**, then click **OK** in the Display Properties dialog box.

You profiled your monitor so colors display accurately. You opened the Display Settings dialog box to verify that the profile is the default.

FIGURE 4
Stop at this step to name your profile

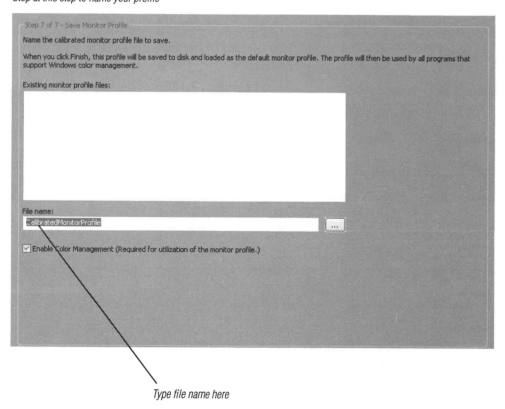

Type file name here

GET RID OF
RED EYE

What You'll Do

In this lesson, you'll learn how to remove red eye from a photograph using the Red Eye tool and the Remove Red Eye command. You'll also learn how to navigate the Red Eye Removal dialog box.

Using the Red Eye Tool

Red eye, which occurs when you take a picture, is a common but frustrating problem. The light resulting from the flash of the camera reflects off of the blood in the back of the eye and is captured in the picture. Many of today's cameras have a red-eye button that sets off a preflash, which closes the retina and helps prevent red eye.

Paint Shop Pro has two features to help you remove that unsightly, unwanted red eye. The first is the Red Eye tool. You simply select the tool, adjust its size, and click away on top of the red pixels, until you are happy with the results. Zoom way in on your subject to clearly see the red pixels.

Using the Red Eye Removal Command

The second method for removing red eye is the Red Eye Removal command on the Adjust menu. Think of this one as the Cadillac of red eye removal, allowing you

much more control over all the properties of the eye, including the color. Want to be blue eyed instead of green eyed? Easy to do with just a few clicks of the mouse. This function also offers a red-eye fix for animals, which is most handy for the beloved four-legged family member who is just as prone to red eye as you and I. Like many other features, it shows a before and after image so you can see the finished result before committing to it. You can choose the color you want from the Hue menu and see a preview right below, in the Color window, as shown in Figure 5.

To get started, you choose your method. The first two: Auto Human Eye and Auto Animal Eye are self-explanatory and the easier two of the four available methods. They change the color of the entire iris to the chosen color. The second two methods are Freehand Pupil Outline and Point-to-Point Pupil Outline. These methods allow you to fine tune the exact area of the iris you want to correct, using a freehand or point-to-point selection around the desired area. Once you choose the method, there are other settings that you can adjust:

- Pupil lightness
- Iris size
- Glint lightness
- Glint size
- Feather
- Blur

The glint is the tiny white part of your eye inside the pupil—the small dark circle in the center of the eye. Have you fixed your eyes to the tune of them looking a little unnatural, like the person's wearing colored contact lenses? The Feather and Blur options are helpful for making a corrected eye look more natural.

QUICKTIP Click the Center glint checkbox to center the glint within the iris.

Navigating the Red Eye Removal Dialog Box

As always when working in smaller, detailed areas, it's recommended you zoom in on problematic areas as much as possible. The Zoom Out and Zoom In buttons allow you to increase or decrease your view each time you click: Zoom in to do the work, then step back with Zoom Out and see how it looks. You can also zoom down to see the entire image by clicking the Fit Image to Window button, then zoom to 100 percent by clicking Zoom Image to 100 percent. When you click the Navigate button, the entire image displays, so you can define the specific area you want in the Before and After windows. Drag the supplied rectangle inside the window to the area you want to zoom in on, as shown in Figure 6.

FIGURE 5
The Red Eye Removal dialog box

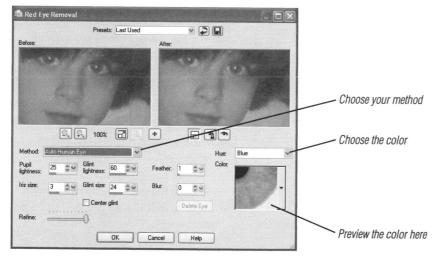

Choose your method

Choose the color

Preview the color here

FIGURE 6
Navigate using the full image

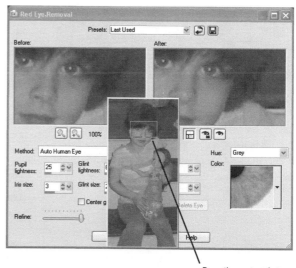

Drag the rectangle to area you want zoomed

FIGURE 7

Zooming in close lets you correct accurately

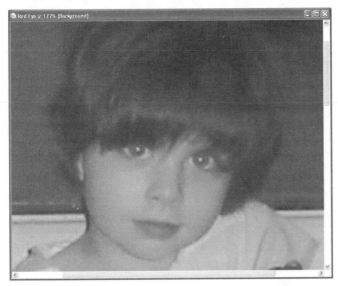

FIGURE 8

Your pointer should match this position

Center of Red Eye
tool pointer

1. Open **PSP7-2.PSPImage**, then save it as **Red Eye**.

2. Click the **Zoom tool** 🔍▾, then zoom in so your screen resembles Figure 7.

3. Click the **Red Eye tool** 👁, then enter **25** in the tool options palette.

4. Position the Red Eye tool pointer in the red areas of the **left eye**, as shown in Figure 8, then click to remove redness.

   The center of the Red Eye tool pointer should be on the pixels you want to remove.

   | TIP Click as many times as you feel necessary to correct the eye.

5. Position the Red Eye tool pointer in the red areas of the **right eye**, then click to remove redness.

6. Click the **Zoom tool** 🔍▾ and zoom out so you see the entire image.

   | TIP Repeat Steps 2–4 again if you are unhappy with your results. You can also use the History palette to undo as many steps as your personal preferences settings allow.

7. Save, then close your document.

You zoomed to be as accurate as possible, then corrected redness in both eyes using the Red Eye tool.

Use the Red Eye Removal command

1. Open **PSP7-3.PSPImage**, then save it as **Redeye2**.

2. Click **Adjust**, then click **Red Eye Removal**.

   The image appears at 100% in the Red Eye Removal dialog box.

3. Click and drag in the After window, so the view resembles Figure 9.

   The cursor becomes a hand.

4. Click the **Hue list arrow**, select **Green**, then make sure **Auto Human Eye** appears in the Method text box.

5. Click the **left eye** in the Before window, enter **60** for Glint lightness, **1** for Feather, then **0** for Blur, matching settings shown in Figure 10.

   TIP   To select a different shade, click the drop-down arrow in the color box. You can also manually adjust the size by using the bounding box in the Before window once you have clicked the eye.

FIGURE 9
Cursor changed to hand

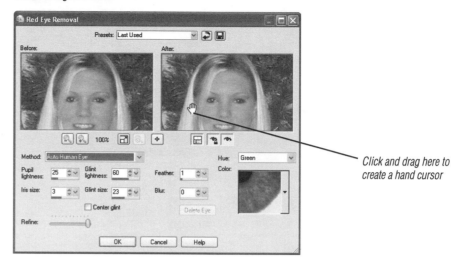

Click and drag here to create a hand cursor

FIGURE 10
The Red Eye Removal dialog box offers many settings

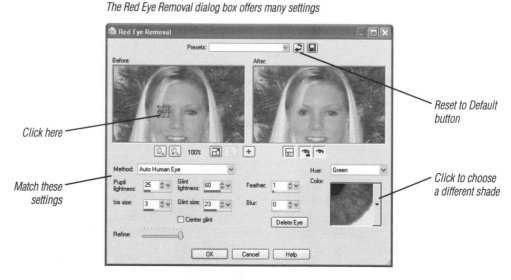

Click here

Match these settings

Reset to Default button

Click to choose a different shade

FIGURE 11

Before (inset) and after red eye removal

Original image

6. Click **OK**.

   The adjustments apply and the Remove Red Eye dialog box closes.

7. Repeat Steps 1–5, adjusting settings (if necessary) until red eye is gone, as shown in Figure 11.

8. Click **OK**.

   The Red Eye Removal dialog box closes.

9. Save your image.

You corrected two red eyes using the Red Eye Removal dialog box, and salvaged a great picture.

REMOVE UNWANTED
OBJECTS

What You'll Do

 In this lesson, you'll learn how to remove scratches and unwanted objects from photos. You'll also learn how to use the retouch tool brushes.

Smoothing Scratches

Lots of things can cause scratches on an image: something getting in the way of the camera lens, such as dust or a piece of lint, or normal wear and tear on a very old photograph. Sometimes scratches like that are desirable for an antique effect (known as Sepia). However, most of the time, scratches (like red eyes) are not particularly attractive in an otherwise great photo. When you examine an image on your monitor, you may see scratches that were caused by the camera lens or you may see scratches that were already part of the image. For example, imagine taking a picture of your bookcase to sell. You notice a scratch in the paint job. You can easily touch that up with paint before selling the bookcase, and you can just as easily remove the scratch from the picture using Paint Shop Pro. You can choose from two Scratch Remover tool presets: Large scratches and Small scratches. You can

choose a width and a type of selection box to use for removing scratches. You simply drag the Scratch Remover tool over the flaw and voila! It's gone.

Retouching Damage

When a photo has been damaged, it needs repair. Repairing part of an image, also known as **retouching**, is easy using the Retouch tools:

- Dodge lightens shadowed areas to bring out more details.
- Burn darkens light areas it passes over and is commonly used to add depth to an image.
- Smudge mixes colors, as if you ran your fingers through wet paint and picked up new color and image info as you moved.
- Push moves existing color and image details over the canvas from the starting point, but does not pick up any new paint.

- Soften smoothes and reduces contrast on the edges, blending them into the background.
- Sharpen brings an area into better focus.
- Emboss makes the foreground appear raised by suppressing color and tracing edges in black.

- Lighten/Darken increases or decreases brightness. The left mouse button lightens; the right mouse button darkens.
- Saturation Up/Down increases or decreases the saturation level by affecting the HSL value of the pixels. The left mouse button increases; the right mouse button decreases.

- Hue Up/Down adjusts the color shade.
- Change to Target changes pixels so they look like the selected target.

Retouching tools are brushes. When you choose a retouching tool, its function is described in the Learning Center and its options are made available in the tool options palette. Figure 12 shows information about the Push tool.

FIGURE 12

The Retouching tools are revealed in the Learning Center

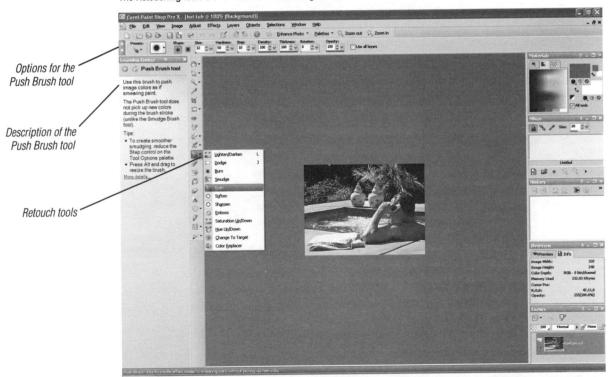

Options for the Push Brush tool

Description of the Push Brush tool

Retouch tools

Removing Unwanted Objects

Like scratches, unwanted objects are just that—unwanted! You can easily remove unwanted objects using the Object Remover tool. The tool works by replacing the area you want to remove with that of a selected area. The selected area can be any other part of your image. In Figure 13, the diamonds on the mime's face are the selected object; you can tell that because of the marquee. Once you select the source, the Object Remover randomizes the patterns with the set source and applies it to the selected area.

FIGURE 13

Diamonds are the selected area to be replaced

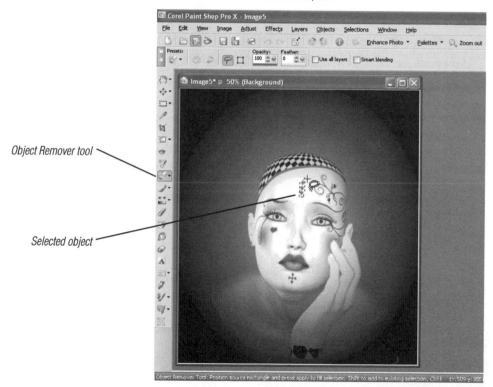

Object Remover tool

Selected object

Using the Makeover tool

What goes through your mind when you hear the word *makeover*? A new hair style or makeup? Maybe a nose job? Makeovers are fun in real life and they're fun in Paint Shop Pro, too. The Makeover tool includes a blemish fixer, a tooth-brush, and a suntan tool. That's right. In a few steps you can remove unsightly blemishes, whiten your teeth, and catch up on your rays! If only you could apply these changes so quickly in real life! To create the new you, click the Makeover tool, then choose the Blemish Fixer, Toothbrush, or Suntan tools in the tool options palette. Each tool lets you change the brush's size and strength. For best results, zoom in on your image and start out with small brush sizes.

FIGURE 14

Zoom in to see the scratch

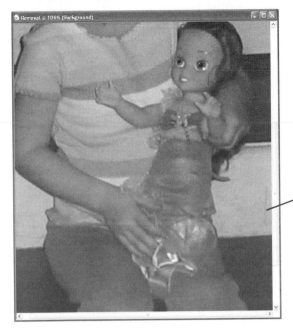

Scratch in step

1. Open **PSP7-4.PSPImage**, then save it as **Scratch**.

2. Click the **Zoom tool** 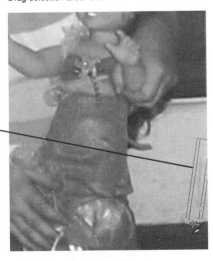, then zoom in to see the scratch in the stair, as shown in Figure 14.

3. Click the **Scratch Remover tool** , then click the **polygon-shaped selection box tool** in the tool options palette.

4. Enter **20** for Width (if necessary).

5. Drag the **Scratch Remover tool** until it completely overlaps the scratch, as shown in Figure 15, then release the mouse.

   The scratch is removed from the image.

6. Save your image.

You used the Scratch Remover tool to remove a scratch and salvage an image.

FIGURE 15

Drag selection around scratch

Drag tool completely over scratch

Retouch damage

1. Open **PSP7-5.PSPImage**, then save it as **Red Flower**.

2. Click the **Soften Brush tool** ⬭, click the **Tool arrow**, then click **Fuzz soft**, as shown in Figure 16.

3. Change the size to **40**, then drag the **Soften Brush tool** over the edges of each petal, as shown in Figure 17.

   As you drag the Soften Brush tool, the sharp yellow borders of each petal disappear.

4. Save your image.

You used the Soften Brush tool to create softer edges.

FIGURE 16

You can choose from several options for the Soften Brush tool

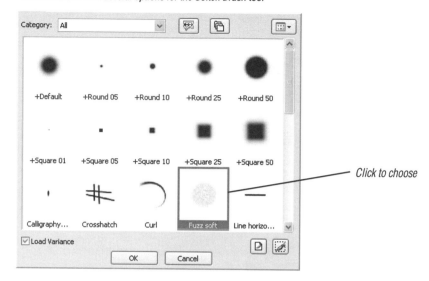

Click to choose

FIGURE 17

Soften the edges

Soft Edges

Edges to be softened

FIGURE 18

Marquee area is removed and replaced with bounding box area

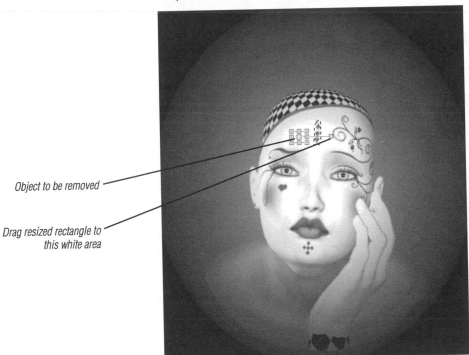

Object to be removed ——————

Drag resized rectangle to
this white area ——————

1. Open **PSP7-6.PSPImage**, then save it as **Object Removal**.

2. Click the **Object Remover tool** ⌖⊿.

3. Your pointer automatically becomes the Selection mode pointer, which looks like a lasso.

4. Drag a selection around the object you want to remove, then click the **Source mode tool** ▢.

5. Resize the **rectangle** and drag it to a small white area near the object, as shown in Figure 18.

6. Click the **Apply button** ⊘ in the tool options palette.

7. Save your work, then close the document.

You used the Object Remover tool to remove an unwanted object in the image.

CORRECT SPECIFIC PROBLEMS

What You'll Do

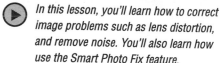 *In this lesson, you'll learn how to correct image problems such as lens distortion, and remove noise. You'll also learn how use the Smart Photo Fix feature.*

Correcting Lens Distortion

Lens distortion is created at the time a picture is taken. It can be the result of an inferior lens, such as one used in a disposable camera, or it can occur when a picture is zoomed. Typically you will find that wide-angle lenses causes barrel distortion and a telephoto or zoom lens causes pincushion distortion. In general, the distortion is most noticeable when you have a very straight edge (such as a building) near the edge of the frame. Figure 19 gives an idea of what each looks like. Another type of distortion is fisheye. Fisheyed images look like they have been pasted onto a sphere. Lines that should be straight are curved, and the edges look compressed. Fisheye distortion is the least common.

Although it sounds like something you need to fix, some photo enthusiast actually use distortion as a dramatic effect. If, however, you need to remedy the distortion, you can do so through Paint Shop Pro's

Adjust menu. There are three options available:

- Barrel: Looks pushed out from the center
- Fisheye: May look circular, as if it were wrapped around a sphere
- Pincushion: Looks pushed in at the center.

For the corrections to work properly, the axis of the camera lens must coincide with the center of your image. This means that you should apply any lens-distortion corrections before cropping.

FIGURE 19
Examples of barrel and pincushion distortion

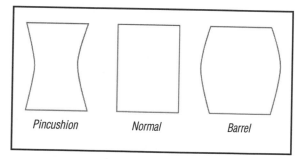

Pincushion   Normal   Barrel

Quieting Noise

In hearing the term noise, you think of something you hear with your ears, not something you see with your eyes. Image noise appears as tiny spots or grain, and is usually the result of taking the picture with the camera at high speeds but with longer-than-normal exposure. Fortunately, most of today's digital camera's offer a noise-reduction feature. However, they don't allow for much control. A good noise-reduction tool should remove distracting, unwanted noise but retain a natural, low level of noise. Paint Shop Pro to the rescue!

Digitally speaking, there are several types of noise. Before you can determine which command or feature to use, you must determine the type of the noise you want to eliminate. If the noise is consistent throughout the image, One Step Noise Removal is the best tool for the job. If the noise is isolated, the Digital Camera Noise Remover (DCNR) tool offers much more control. DCNR allows you to sample specific areas of your image. However, for JPEG artifacting or moiré patterns, you should use their respective tools in the Adjust > Add/Remove Noise menu. Figure 20 shows the before and after of an image that contained a large amount of noise throughout the entire picture; the baby's face is the most noticeable part of the correction.

Using Smart Photo Fix

By this point, you might be feeling a bit overwhelmed at all of the ways you can correct a digital image in Paint Shop Pro. Rest assured—another command will wash away your anxiety. This may be a great place to start if you are new to image-correction software or just don't have the time to learn all the ins and outs about photo editing. Smart Photo Fix takes an overall assessment of your photo. It judges it on its **highlights** (brightest areas), **shadows** (darkest areas) and **midtones** (areas between highlights and shadows), and makes suggested corrections in the Smart Photo Fix dialog box, as shown in Figure 21. You have the option to click OK and accept the suggestions or to play around with the various sliders, such as Saturation, Focus, and Highlights. You can make the same corrections to an image and bypass the Smart Photo Fix dialog box by simply clicking Adjust, then clicking One Step Photo Fix.

FIGURE 20
DCNR applied

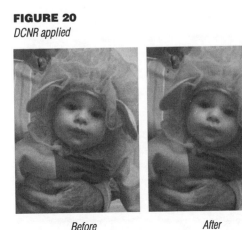

Before   *After*

FIGURE 21
The Smart Photo Fix dialog box makes suggestions

Click to see suggested settings

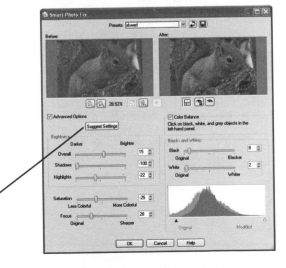

Correct barrel distortion

1. Open **PSP7-8.PSPImage**, then save it as **Barrel**.

2. Click **Adjust**, then click **Barrel Distortion Correction**.

3. Enter **40** for Strength.

4. Paint Shop Pro applies the correction, as shown in Figure 22.

5. Click **OK**, then close the image.

You applied the Barrel Distortion Correction command using the guidelines in the image for straightening.

FIGURE 22

The Barrel Distortion Correction dialog box

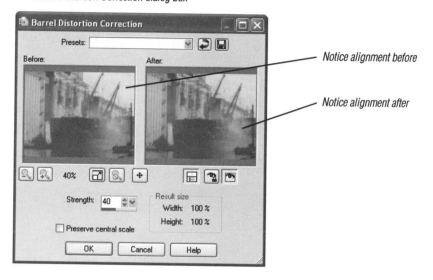

Notice alignment before

Notice alignment after

FIGURE 23

Correct Pincushion Distortion

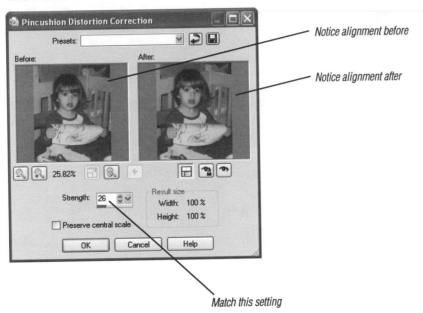

Notice alignment before

Notice alignment after

Match this setting

1. Open **PSP7-8a.PSPImage**, then save it as **Pin**.

2. Click **Adjust**, then click **Pincushion Distortion**.

   The Pincushion Distortion dialog box appears, as shown in Figure 23.

3. Enter **26** for Strength.

   Paint Shop Pro applies the correction.

4. Click **OK**, then save your image.

You used the back of the chair as a guide to correct pincushion distortion.

Quiet noise

1. Open **PSP7-9.PSPImage**, then save it as **Baby Lion**.

2. Click **Adjust**, then click **One Step Noise Removal**.

   Paint Shop Pro applies the command and the noise is replaced with a smoother texture, as shown in Figure 24.

3. Save your image.

You applied the One Step Noise Removal command to remove unwanted noise, clearing up the image.

FIGURE 24

Before and after applying One Step Noise Removal

FIGURE 25
Quickly fix color cast with Smart Photo Fix

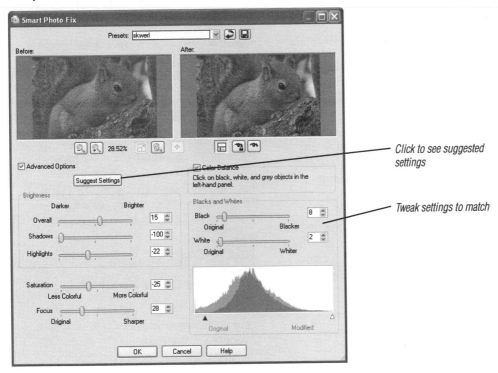

Click to see suggested settings

Tweak settings to match

1. Open **PSP7-10a.PSPImage**, then save it as **Smartfix**.

2. Click **Adjust**, then click **Smart Photo Fix**.

    The Smart Photo Fix dialog box appears, as shown in Figure 25.

3. Click **Suggest Settings**.

    Smart Photo Fix suggests settings and displays the proposed "after" image.

4. Using the settings shown in Figure 25 as a guide, tweak the settings to match (if necessary).

    Changes apply and the image displays with new settings in the Preview window.

5. Click **OK**.

    The Smart Photo Fix dialog box closes and the affects are applied to your image.

6. Save your image.

You used Smart Photo Fix to quickly fix a yellow-ish color cast problem in an image.

IMPROVE AND
ENHANCE PHOTOS

What You'll Do

In this lesson, you'll learn how to enhance photos by improving lighting and color, and you'll learn how to create an adjustment layer.

Understanding Color

Earlier in this chapter, you read about quick fixes for specific problems, such as scratches or color imbalance. Probably not all of your images will require such major surgery. A picture may just need to be lightened or one of its colors need slight adjustment. You don't have to understand all of the gory details about how color works to use it for corrections or eye-catching effects. It's possible to use trial and error to achieve your desired results. However, just as you don't need to be a chef to know that oil and water don't mix, it's good to know a little bit about each ingredient before you start mixing things.

Artificial color systems—computers, scanners, monitors and other peripherals—attempt to model the colors that the human eye perceives. The colors within the definition of each model are referred to as its **color space**. Of the three most common models, the one based on the hue/saturation/lightness (HSL) of colors is the most natural and easiest for the human eye to perceive, since it has a continuous range of colors that vary in brightness or richness. You use this type of model when you adjust colors with the Hue/Saturation dialog boxes. Figure 26 shows the Hue/Saturation/Lightness dialog box. The color ring represents the colors in the image, where the outer ring represents the original values and the inner ring represents the adjusted values. By selecting an option from the Edit drop-down list, you can edit the master color ring, or you can choose a specific color range to adjust.

Improving Color Balance

Paint Shop Pro offers two Color Balance control options, one of which is located in at Adjust > Color Balance. The second one, and the better of the two, is hidden in your customization menu. If necessary, review Chapters 1 and 2 on how to access these commands; then place an icon on your toolbar for easy access, as shown in Figure 27.

FIGURE 26

Hue/Saturation/Lightness dialog box

FIGURE 27

Adjust Color Balance dialog box

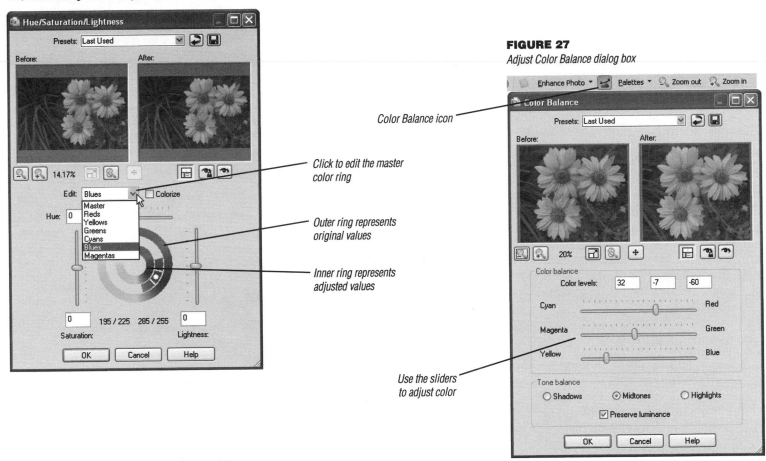

Color Balance icon

Click to edit the master color ring

Outer ring represents original values

Inner ring represents adjusted values

Use the sliders to adjust color

Paint Shop Pro allows you to set color balance separately for shadows, midtones, and highlights. What you are interested in at this point is the color sliders. These let you adjust the amounts of a particular color from –100 to 100 percent. You can either add one color or subtract its two component colors. For example, moving the Cyan/Red slider to +20 (toward red) has the same effect as moving the Magenta/Green and Yellow/Blue sliders both to the –20 position (left).

Figure 28 shows an image with a very distinctive red color cast. You can remove the red tone by sliding the Cyan/Red slider control toward cyan, which is the opposite, or complementary, color of red. Because Paint Shop Pro lets you preview results before applying them, it's just a matter of removing enough red (adding cyan) until the picture looks right. In this case, changing the slider to remove red (add cyan) at a setting of –35 was sufficient. In most cases, that is all you need to get the job done.

Sharpening Dull Images

Dullness can be the result of applying image correction commands, such as removing noise, or of moving the camera during its capture. Dull images need to be sharpened. Can you ever completely recover all of the lost detail? No, not really. But through sharpening, you can make it appear as though you have. Paint Shop Pro offers a number of tools to sharpen your

images, including Sharpen, Sharpen More, Unsharp Mask, and the new High Pass. All are under Adjust > Sharpen. These all work basically on the same principle: increasing the contrast of edges.

Clarify, under Adjust > Brightness/Contrast, works best for images that are slightly out of focus or foggy. Try the Sharpen or Sharpen More command on a dull image. If you want more control, try the Unsharp Mask or the new High Pass

FIGURE 28
Remove red to add cyan

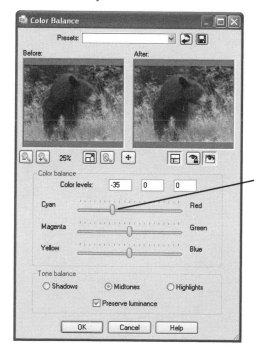

Sharpen command. For best results, sharpening should be the last thing you do to an image.

Creating Adjustment Layers

If you know you are going to edit an image, you may want to create a backup file first, so that you can always go back to your original. Or, if you just want to see how an image looks without permanently changing it, consider jumping into adjustment layers. Adjustment layers, built into the Layers palette, allow you to tweak settings such as brightness and contrast. The image itself is not altered in any way. Changes you make in the adjustment layer affect all layers below it, or you can apply a change to just one layer and below, avoiding the others.

Move the slider to the left

FIGURE 29

Improve color in the Hue/Saturation/Lightness dialog box

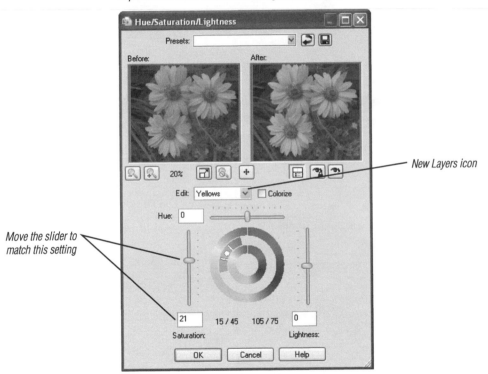

New Layers icon

Move the slider to
match this setting

1. Open **PSP7-11.PSPImage**, then save it as **Saturate**.

2. Click **Adjust**, **Hue/Saturation**, then click **Hue/Saturation/Lightness**.

   The HSL dialog box appears.

3. Click the **Edit arrow**, then click **Yellows**.

4. Move the **Saturation slider** to 21.

   Paint Shop Pro adds saturation and the new settings display in the After window, as shown in Figure 29.

5. Click **OK**.

6. Close your image.

You used the Hue/Saturation/Lightness command to further saturate your image with yellow, improving the overall color.

Improve color balance

1. Open **PSP9-12.PSPImage**, then save it as **Balance2**.

2. Click the **Color Balance icon** 🖌️.

   The Color Balance dialog box appears.

3. Move the **Cyan/Red slider** to the left.

   The red cast disappears and your image looks more natural, as shown in the After window in Figure 30.

4. Click **OK**.

5. Close your image.

You used Color Balance to remove a red cast from your image, giving it a more natural, realistic look.

FIGURE 30

Color Balance removes red and adds cyan

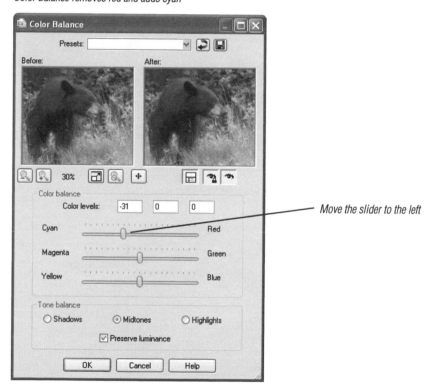

Move the slider to the left

FIGURE 31

Match the settings to sharpen image

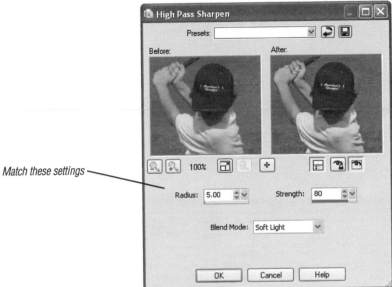

Match these settings ——

FIGURE 32

The sharpened image is clearer

1. Open **PSP7-7.PSPImage**, then save it as **Sharpen**.

2. Click **Image**, then click **Resize**.

3. Enter **600** pixels for Width, mark the **Maintain ratio checkbox**, then set Resample Using to **Smart Size**.

4. Click **OK**.

   The Resize dialog box closes. Your images resizes and blurs slightly.

5. Click **Adjust**, **Sharpness**, then click **High Pass Sharpen**.

   The High Pass Sharpen dialog box appears, as shown in Figure 31.

6. Enter **5** for Radius, **80** for Strength, then set Blend Mode to **Soft Light**.

7. Click **OK**.

   Your image is clearer, as shown in Figure 32.

8. Save your image.

You reduced an image, which caused blur. You then used the High Pass Sharpen filter to bring back some of the details lost during the resizing.

Create an adjustment layer

1. Open **Adjustments.PSPImage**, then save it as **Layer**.
2. Click **Layers**, then click **New Adjustment Layer**.
3. Click the **Layer Visibility icon** 👁.

   You see the layer with the changes.
4. Click the **Layer Visibility icon** 👁.

   You see the layer without the changes.

You created an adjustment layer to you can see changes without saving over the original image.

FIGURE 33
An adjustment layer lets you keep the original image

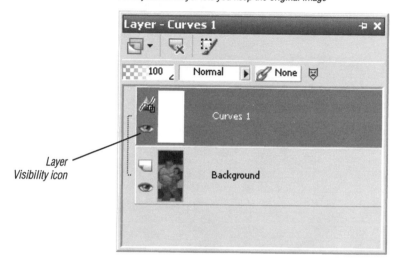

Layer
Visibility icon

CHAPTER SUMMARY

This chapter reviewed the definition of color depth, as well as how to calibrate and profile your monitor for better image display. You removed red eye, scratches, unwanted objects, noise, and distortion. You also enhanced photos with lighting and color, and created an adjustment layer.

What You Have Learned

- How to calibrate and profile your monitor.
- How to removed red eye with the Red Eye tool and the Red Eye Removal command.
- How to remove scratches, unwanted objects, noise, and distortion.
- How to enhance lighting and color.
- How to use the Smart Photo Fix feature.
- How to create an adjustment layer.

Key Terms

adjustment layer Lets you tweak settings without changing an image itself

calibrating Fine-tuning a monitor's settings

color depth Number of shades; also known as bit depth

color space Colors within the definition of each artificial color system (computer, printer, monitor)

glint The tiny white part of your eye inside the pupil

highlights Brightest areas in an image

HSL Hue/saturation/lightness

midtones Areas between highlights and shadows in an image

noise Tiny spots, or grain, on an image

proprietary Made by a specific manufacturer

retouching Repairing part of an image

shadows Darkest areas in an image

8

PRINTING
WITH EASE

1. Learn printer basics.

2. Master resolution.

3. Choose printer, paper, and ink.

4. Simplify with print layouts.

chapter 8 PRINTING WITH EASE

Diving into Prints

Sooner or later you'll want to print images so you can share them with friends or frame them for display. You can put a digital sketch on plain paper or put a photograph on specialty paper. Paint Shop Pro has the tools that help you print efficiently—and with professional results—everything from single images via the Print dialog box, to multiple images via the Print Lay Out dialog box. Use any of the built-in templates, which offer preset layouts, to create image sets. An image set lets you place multiple images on a page, and they can be all the same or different. For example, you may have one 5 × 7" image and four wallet-size images of a single image, or two 5 × 7" images, each one different. Paint Shop Pro offers a wide variety of templates, and you can save custom templates.

Managing Color and Size

You get things just so in your image. The color looks right onscreen, but when you print it out, your ruby-throated humming-bird looks more like he's wearing pink. To ensure that the colors you see on your computer monitor consistently match prints, Paint Shop Pro provides a Color Management feature that allows you to set the correct color space for the task at hand. Preparing your image is just as important as using the correct color working space, a formula that tells your programs how to display color or what range of colors your image can display. Color space is not to be confused with the color palette, which specifies the number of colors but not the color spectrum.

Choosing Your Equipment

Finally, you have to select the correct printer and medium for the job. Printers range from multipurpose, designed to handle everything from text to photographs, to specialized, designed for lab-quality photographs. Paper varies widely too, ranging from what you see in most offices and homes, to high-quality glossy and matte photo papers.

Tools You'll Use

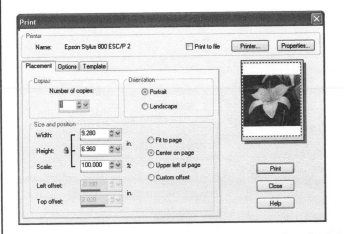

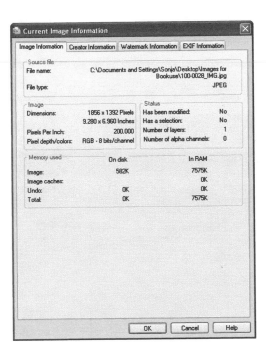

LEARN
PRINTER BASICS

What You'll Do

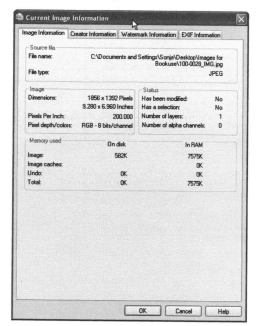

 In this lesson, you'll explore some of printing's basic principles, including image information and color profiles.

Viewing Image Information

Every image that your computer stores has information that isn't visible onscreen. You may need to know an image's resolution or size. Do you want to add watermarks or shooting parameters to a photograph that has EXIF data? Choose the Image menu to access the Current Image Information dialog box. The dialog box, shown in Figure 1, gives you the current image's information divided into four tabs.

The first tab, Image Information, is broken into several areas:

- The Source file area displays the source file, including the complete filename, location, and file format. Location can be one of the following: your hard drive, a removable drive, a CD, a DVD, or a digital camera. File format is discussed in detail in Chapter 1, "Getting Started with Paint Shop Pro X."
- The Image area gives the image dimensions (physical size for printing at the current resolution), pixels per inch, and the pixel/color depth. Color

depth is the number of shades the image is capable of displaying.
- The Status area tells you if the image has been edited, if a selection is in the image, the number of layers, and if there is any data saved to the alpha channel.
- The Memory used area tells you what the file's size is.

In the Creator Information tab, you can add personal information to store with the image if the chosen file format supports it. The Watermark Information tab displays information about the image's creator or copyright holder. Chapter 4 tells you how to place a watermark on images. The EXIF Information tab is next. Most digital cameras use EXIF, or Exchangeable Image File Format, to store additional information like date, time, exposure, aperture, and focal length. The EXIF Information tab contains data recorded by a digital camera and gives information on camera settings, time taken, and shooting parameters and conditions.

FIGURE 1
The Image Information dialog box displays data on four tabs

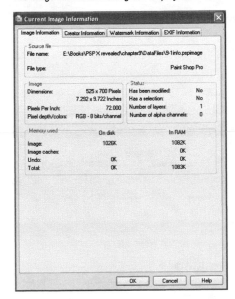

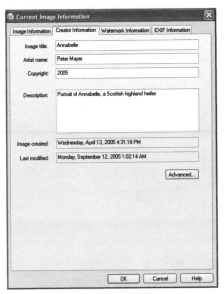

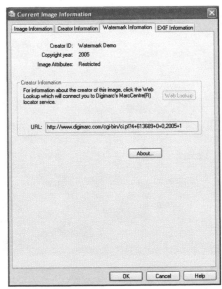

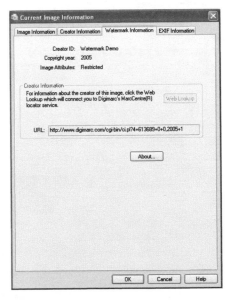

QUICKTIP You can also access image information in the PSP Browser by clicking the Image Information icon. The data appears in the Browser's left pane.

Understanding Color Management

In a nutshell, **color management** is a way of matching colors from your input device (such as your digital camera or scanner) to your computer monitor, then to the printed image. Matching colors ensures that what you see on the monitor matches your print output, avoiding surprises. Monitor calibration and profiling are the first steps to good color management. This chapter talks about the basic aspects of managing color. The Color Management dialog box shown in Figure 2 lets you specify the color space, monitor and printer profiles, and the intended output.

You can specify your color working space by using the Color Working Space dialog box found at File > Color Management. There you also can choose an **ICC profile**, telling Paint Shop Pro how to display colors and in what range of the color spectrum. Your system should include many profiles. In the Printer Profile area, choose from color profiles that came with your printer; in the Rendering Intent area, choose how you want PSP to handle color matching.

FIGURE 2

Note the color profile in the Color Management dialog box

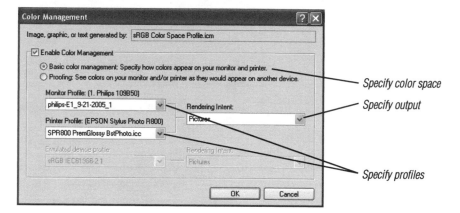

Specify color space

Specify output

Specify profiles

Rendering intent

Pictures: Best for photographic images. All the colors are scaled to fit into the selected gamut.

Proof: Best for logos and graphics that need only a few of the colors matched accurately.

Graphics: Best for graphs and charts where vividness is more important then accurate color matching.

Match: Best for soft proofing to a color space. Soft proofing means seeing onscreen what your photograph's colors will look like when printed on a particular printer/paper.

RGB stands for red, green, blue color channels. sRGB is the standard color profile for the web, but you can use it for printing. Many photographers and graphic artists prefer Adobe RGB, because it has a wider color gamut, displaying a wider variety of colors in the spectrum. In Figure 3 you can see a 3D rendering of the sRGB (solid) and Adobe RGB (wire frame). However, most monitors won't show a difference; the majority display only sRGB. **CMYK**—short for cyan, magenta, yellow, and black—is an option most professional print shops use.

QUICKTIP At the time of this writing, color management isn't working accurately. A **patch**, or update, is expected. Check for patches at Help > Check. If you experience color inconsistencies or your display colors don't look right, try disabling color management in the Color Management dialog box.

FIGURE 3

sRGB color space fits inside the Adobe RGB and has a smaller gamut

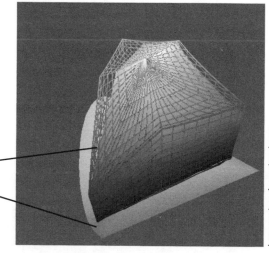

Adobe RGB

sRGB

Image courtesy of www.chromix.com

FIGURE 4

The Current Image Information dialog box

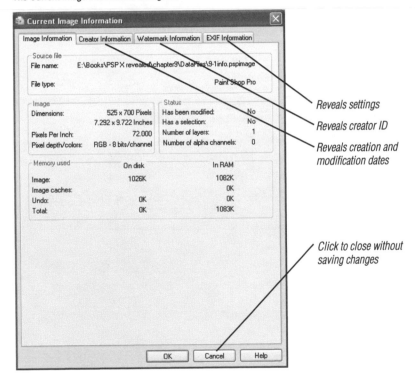

Reveals settings

Reveals creator ID

Reveals creation and modification dates

Click to close without saving changes

1. Open image **PSP8-1.PSPImage**, then click the **Image Information icon** ⓘ.

   TIP Image data is also available through Image > Image Information.

   The Current Image Information dialog box appears, as shown in Figure 4.

2. Click the **Image Information tab** (if necessary).

   The Image Information tab appears.

3. Click the **Creator Information tab**.

   The Creator tab reveals the image's creation date and the date of its most recent modification.

4. Click the **Watermark Information tab**.

   You know a watermark is present because you see the creator's ID, the copyright year, attributes, and the URL that leads to more information.

5. Click the **EXIF Information tab**.

   Settings that were recorded with the image appear: shooting parameters, time, and date.

You accessed the Image Information dialog box to discover many image properties. Now you know who created the image and can find out more about it.

Understand color management

1. Click **File**, **Color Management**, then click **Color Management**.

   The Color Management dialog box opens, as shown in Figure 5.

2. Take note of the color profile chosen in the Image, graphic, or text generated by box.

   You know how Paint Shop Pro will display colors.

3. Check the **Enable Color Management checkbox**, then select **Basic color management** (if necessary).

   This ensures that what you see on your monitor matches printer output.

4. Take note of the Monitor Profile setting.

   The monitor profile should be the same as Windows display properties.

5. Click the **Monitor Profile arrow**, then choose a **profile**.

6. Click the **Printer Profile arrow**, then choose the **profile** that matches your paper.

7. Click the **Rendering Intent arrow**.

   Choose from Pictures, Proof, Graphics, and Match.

8. Click **OK**.

   The dialog box closes and your settings are saved.

You explored the Color Management dialog box setup and enabled color management.

FIGURE 5

The Color Management dialog box reveals monitor and printer profiles

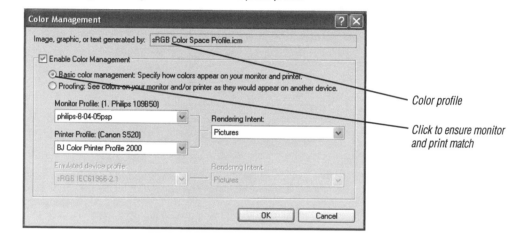

Color profile

Click to ensure monitor and print match

MASTER RESOLUTION

What You'll Do

In this lesson, you'll discover the difference between dpi and ppi and the difference between resizing and resampling.

Understanding Resolution

Images come in many sizes and resolutions. If your 72-dpi camera takes an 800 × 600-pixel image, the printed size would be just about letter size: 11.11 × 8.33". Of course, the print quality may not be high, since the resolution is set low (at 72 ppi) and the pixel density (at 800 × 600 pixels) is great. To reproduce with high quality, you need to understand the roles that image resolution and printer output resolution play. The terms **dpi** (dots per inch) and **ppi** (pixels per inch) are sometimes used interchangeably, but they are not the same thing.

Resolution (ppi) defines the pixel density. An 800 × 600-pixel image will always be 800 × 600 pixels, regardless of resolution. At 72 ppi, it will print 11" wide. If you set the resolution at 1,600 ppi, the image would print ½" wide, but would still be 800 × 600 pixels.

- dpi is the number of ink droplets an ink jet printer can place on an inch of paper. The printer's output quality settings affect dpi, whose rating is based on the maximum output. Lesson 3 offers a closer look at printer quality.
- ppi defines how many pixels make up a square inch of image. A pixel is the smallest part of an image, and if viewed close up looks like a colored square.

QUICKTIP Depending on your preference, resolution can be specified in pixels per centimeter (PPC) in the Preference dialog box. Depending on where you live, your printer's resolution may be defined by dots per centimeter (DPC).

Here's an example of how resolution affects output: If your resolution is set to 75 ppi, that means there are 75 pixels running horizontally and 75 pixels running vertically, making a total of 5,625 pixels. If you double your resolution to 150 ppi, you will have four times as many pixels per square inch. The result? A much clearer printed image.

Resizing Versus Resampling

Often you have to resize an image because the current resolution doesn't provide the size print you want. You may want to print a wallet-size photo from a picture that's sized to print as an 8 × 10". You resize when you change resolution to affect the print size. Resizing does not alter the pixel or file size. Resampling affects your image's physical size, but it does not affect the resolution. In Table 1 you can see what the resampling options do and for what type of image each is suitable. Both resizing and resampling can be done in the Resize dialog box (found in the Image menu) or by clicking the Resize icon on the toolbar. The Resize dialog box provides the original dimensions and lets you change pixel dimensions, resolution, and width and height. You can see the Paint Shop Pro Resize dialog box in Figure 6.

FIGURE 6

The Resize dialog box lets you view and change dimensions

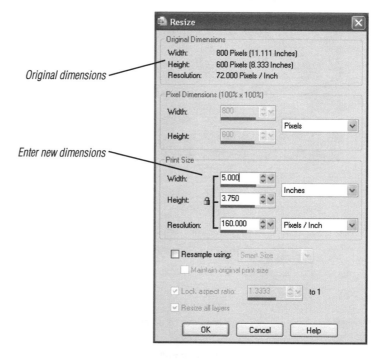

Original dimensions

Enter new dimensions

TABLE 1 Resample Options

Element	What it does
Smart Size	PSP selects the best method from the available options.
Bicubic	Best for enlarging images. Minimizes the jaggedness that can accrue by enlarging images. Works well with photographs or complex images.
Bilinear	Evaluates the nearest two pixels to determine how the newly created pixel will look.
Pixel Resize	Duplicates or removes pixels as needed. Best for simple images, one-color images, and line art.
Weighted Average	Evaluates the color value of the neighboring pixels to create new pixels. Best for reducing photographs.

FIGURE 7
View the images at 100%

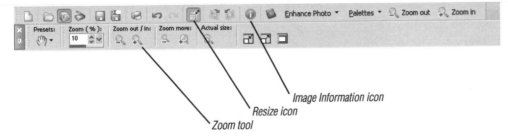

Image Information icon
Resize icon
Zoom tool

1. Open **PSP-8-3.PSPImage** and **PSP-8-4.PSPImage**.

2. Click and drag the **title bar** of one image, then the other, arranging them side by side.

3. Select the **Zoom tool** , then choose **100%** for both images.

4. Click **PSP-8-3.PSPImage**, then click the **Image Information icon** , as shown in Figure 7.

    The Image Information dialog box appears.

5. Click the **Image Information tab** (if necessary), then note the settings.

    You see the pixel size, resolution, and printed size in inches.

6. Click **Cancel**.

    The Image Information dialog box closes.

7. Click **PSP-8-4.PSPImage**, then click the **Image Information icon** .

    The Image Information dialog box appears.

8. Click the **Image Information tab** (if necessary), then note the settings.

    You see the pixel size, resolution, and printed size in inches.

9. Click **Cancel**.

    The Image Information dialog box closes without saving any changes.

You compared data in the Image Information dialog box and discovered that resolution greatly affects print size.

Resize an image

1. Open **PSP-8-5.PSPImage**, then save it as **Resize**.

2. Click the **Resize icon**.

   The Resize dialog box appears.

3. Review the settings and information in the Resize dialog box, as shown in Figure 8.

4. Uncheck the **Resample using checkbox**.

   A number of options are disabled.

5. Enter **5** for Width in the Print Size section.

   The resolution increases from 72 ppi to 160 ppi, as shown in Figure 9.

6. Click **OK**.

   The Resize dialog box closes.

7. Save your image.

You resized an image without affecting its dimensions, increasing print quality but making the print size smaller.

FIGURE 8
Resizing doesn't change dimensions

FIGURE 9
Resolution increases

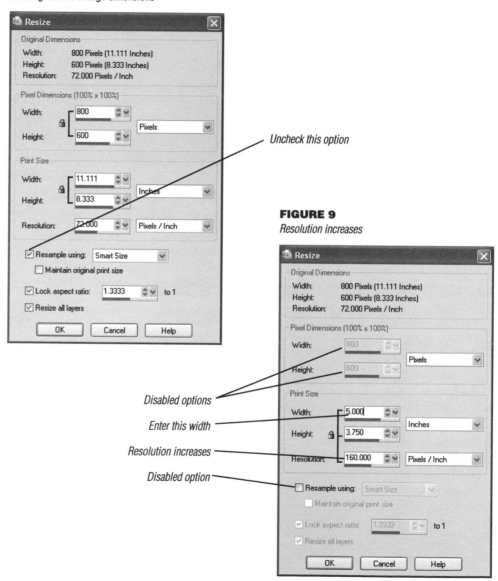

Uncheck this option

Disabled options

Enter this width

Resolution increases

Disabled option

FIGURE 10

Enlarge and make sharing easy with resampling

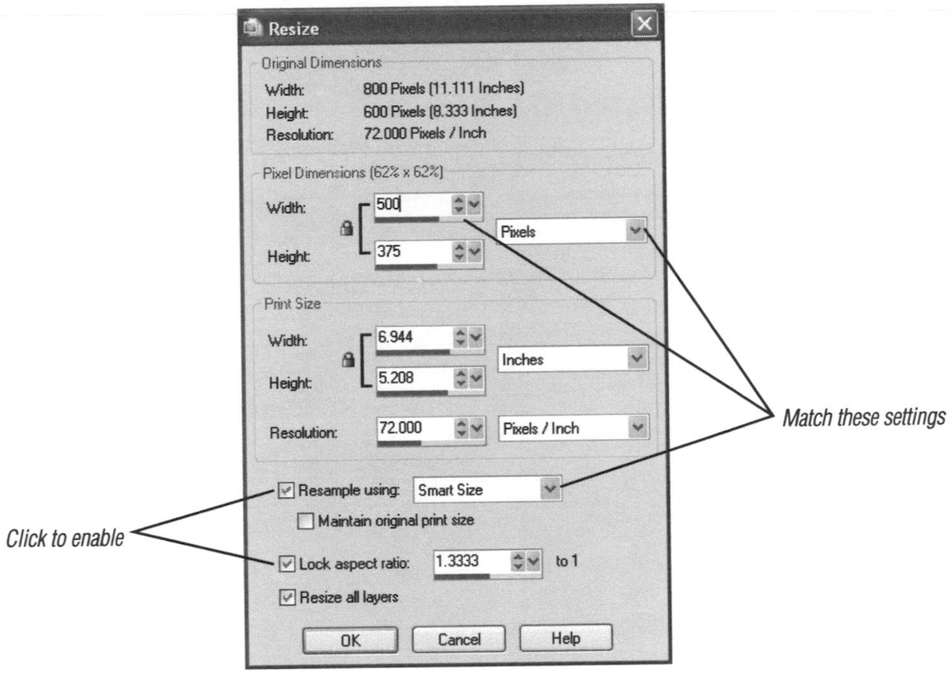

Click to enable

Match these settings

Resample an image

1. Open **PSP-8-5.PSPImage**, then save it as **Resample**.

2. Click the **Resize icon** 🔳.

   The Resize dialog box appears.

3. Check the **Resample using checkbox**, then choose **Smart Size** in the drop-down menu (if necessary).

   Resampling is enabled, as shown in Figure 10.

4. Check the **Lock aspect ratio checkbox**, then set Width to **500 pixels**.

5. Click **OK**.

   The Resize dialog box closes and the settings are applied to the image.

6. Save your image.

You reduced an image's dimensions using resampling, making it easy to share files. You locked the aspect ratio, so when the width changed, the height automatically changed.

Enlarge an image with resampling

1. Open **PSP-8-5.PSPImage**, then save it as **Upsample**.

2. Click the **Resize icon** 🖼️.

   The Resize dialog box appears.

3. Check the **Resample using checkbox** (if necessary).

4. Select **Bicubic** from the drop-down menu.

5. Enter **300** Pixels/Inch for Resolution.

6. Enter **8** inches for Width, as shown in Figure 11.

7. Click **OK**.

   The Resize dialog box closes and the image enlarges by 300%.

8. Save your image.

You used the Bicubic option to change resolution, ensuring a high-quality print from an image that would have been too small otherwise.

FIGURE 11

Resampling makes the image larger and of higher quality

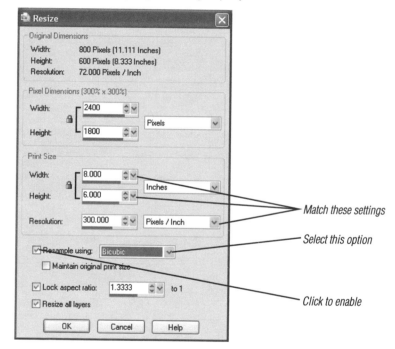

CHOOSE PRINTER,
PAPER, AND INK

What You'll Do

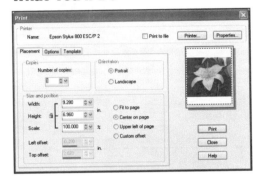

 In this lesson, you'll learn which kind of printer and paper best suit your needs. Then you'll learn how to navigate the Print dialog box and create a contact sheet.

Choosing a Printer

Ink jet or laser: What is your best option? Both are very good printers, but each excels at something different. Ink jet is probably the most popular printer because it's inexpensive and can handle a variety of jobs. This printer ejects tiny droplets of wet ink on paper and is well suited for photographic images. When printing text, however, it can get fuzzy. Ink jet printers come in two flavors:

- All purpose: Optimized to fill printing needs from text to photos.
- Photo: Optimized for lab-quality prints. Their more-advanced settings make photo printing easier and higher quality. Can hold as many as 8 cartridges at a time, increasing color accuracy.

Laser printers are designed for high-volume printing. In other words, if you are going to run lots of copies, laser might be a good option for you. Laser printers use a toner cartridge (similar to that in copy machines); static electricity deposits the toner powder on the paper. These printers really shine when producing sharp text and graphics, but are not as suitable for photographic images. They're also not as versatile as ink jet printers. If you're still not sure, check the comparison in Table 2.

Selecting Ink and Paper

Not all papers and inks are created equal. Two basic ink types exist: dye based and pigment based. Dye-based ink is composed of liquid dye that's very similar to food coloring. Pigment-based ink is composed of colored powder dissolved in media. Pigment-based ink is more expensive, but produces prints that are more resistant to fading.

TABLE 2 Ink Jet Versus Laser Printers

Ink Jet	Laser
<$100	>$700
Slow	Fast
Uses a single-color or multicolor ink cartridge. Between $12–$35.	Uses toner cartridge. As much as $250 each.
Letter-size full-color print cost: $.30*	$.08
Excels at photographic images	Excels at text and graphic presentation
Large variety of specialty papers and media available	No specialty or photographic papers available

*Depending on paper and printer. All prices are approximate and may vary.

QUICKTIP That not all papers and inks are created equal is especially true when shopping for ink jet supplies. An ink jet printer takes everything from plain to special photo papers, and different types of inks, too.

Ink jet paper starts with the regular, all-purpose paper you use for everyday printing. For photographs, purchase special photo paper in glossy and matte finishes. You can also choose from a variety of special media, which Table 3 tells you about.

TABLE 3 Special Printer Media

Medium	Purpose	Cost
CD labels	Creating your own CD labels	$
Ink jet printable CD/DVD	Labels printed directly on disc	$$$
Iron-on transfers	Iron-ons for shirts	$$
Transparencies	Transparent images for portfolios and presentations	$$
Glossy photo paper	Glossy, photo lab-quality images	$$
Matte photo paper	Photograpic images for framing	$$
Cotton rag paper	Gallery-grade prints	$$$$

$ = inexpensive, $$ = moderately expensive, $$$ = very expensive, $$$$ = most expensive.

Using the Print Dialog Box

The easiest way to print an image in Paint Shop Pro is directly from the main dialog box. Simply open your image, make corrections if necessary, and click the Print icon — the Print dialog box appears. There you can select the printer you want to use and access its properties to make further adjustments. The Properties button lets you select paper and quality settings, which are crucial to getting the best print. If you have more than one printer installed on your system, select among them by clicking the Printer button. Access the printer properties by clicking the Properties button. In the printer properties dialog box, shown in Figure 12, select your quality, paper type and size, print options, and orientation. Your printer properties dialog box's appearance depends on your printer.

The Paint Shop Pro Print dialog box has three tabs. The Placement tab offers choices for number of copies, orientation, scaling, and position. The Options tab lets you decide whether you want to print in color, greyscale (black and white), or CMYK separations (every color channel separately). You can also add background color, print the negative, and add marks such as cropping, registration, and image name. Select from existing layouts on the Template tab, which is covered in the next objective.

FIGURE 12

Your printer properties dialog box may vary

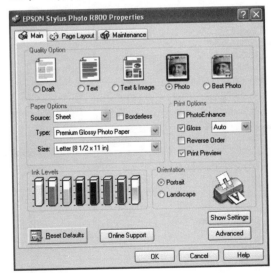

Printing a Contact Sheet

You may need to reference a printout of all the images on your computer. With Paint Shop Pro you can easily print a **contact sheet** of all (or some of) the images in a folder; Figure 13 shows a printed contact sheet. The Browser, which is explained further in Chapter 1, "Getting Started with Paint Shop Pro X," has a Print dialog box similar to the regular Print dialog box. In it you can select your printer, choose orienta-tion, and indicate a number of copies. In addition, you can specify that only thumb-nails be printed, that image names be added, and where on the page the image be placed. If you click the Modify contact sheet button, the Custom Contact Sheet dialog box opens and lets you choose between Autofit and Manual. Autofit decides the best layout for you, but Manual requires you to specify the number of rows and columns, the **pitch** (the space between the pictures), and the cell size.

FIGURE 13

Browser contact sheet

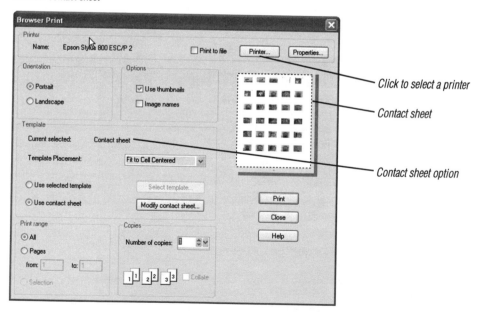

Click to select a printer

Contact sheet

Contact sheet option

FIGURE 14

Choose from several options in the Print dialog box

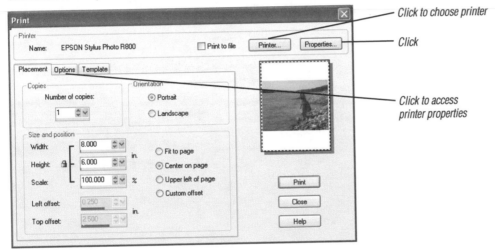

Click to choose printer

Click

Click to access
printer properties

1. Open **PSP-8-6.JPG**.

2. Click **Image**, **Image Information**, then check the size in pixels, resolution, and print.

   You determine that the image is 1,600 × 1,200 pixels, has a set resolution of 200 ppi, and prints as an 8 × 6".

3. Click **Close**; click **File**, then **Print**.

   The Print dialog box opens, as shown in Figure 14.

4. Click the **Printer button**, then choose the **printer** you want to use.

5. Click the **Properties button**; click the **Placement tab** (if necessary), then review the settings.

6. Click the **Options tab**.

   The printer's properties dialog box opens.

7. Select **Photo** for Quality; in Paper Options select the paper source, type, and size.

8. Select **Portrait** for Orientation.

   > TIP Consult the manufacturer manual for your printer's recommended settings. Step 7 uses the Epson R 800 photo printer.

9. Click **Print**.

   The dialog box closes and your image prints.

You used the Print dialog box, accessed the printer properties, and changed the settings to optimize your final print.

Print a contact sheet

1. Click **View**, **Palettes**, then click **Browser** (if necessary).

2. Select a folder that has the images you want on a contact sheet.

   > TIP If you don't want to print all the images in a folder, press the Ctrl key while clicking the images you want to print.

3. Click the **Print Contact Sheet icon** 📇.

   The Browser Print dialog box opens, as shown in Figure 15.

4. Select your **printer**.

5. For Orientation select **Portrait**, mark the **Use thumbnails checkbox**, then select **Use contact sheet**.

6. For Print range select **All**, then for Number of copies select **1**.

   Your settings should match those shown in Figure 15.

7. Click **Print**.

   The dialog box closes and the contact sheet prints.

You printed a contact sheet from the Browser, so you can keep a printed archive of images.

FIGURE 15

The Browser offers a printer

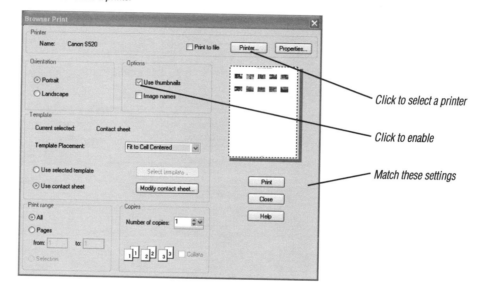

Click to select a printer

Click to enable

Match these settings

SIMPLIFY WITH
PRINT LAYOUTS

What You'll Do

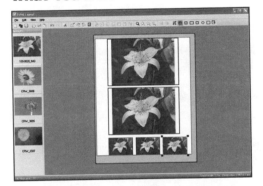

 In this lesson, you'll use the Print Layout dialog box, learn to print multiple images and templates, and learn how to create templates.

Using the Print Layout Dialog Box

You can access the Print Layout dialog box from the File menu. Images that are open in PSP or selected in the Browser appear on the right side in the Image tab. You also can open images from within the Print Layout dialog box, which is shown in Figure 16. From the Images tab, you can drag and drop your images on the page to be printed. Once your image is on the page, the Print Layout dialog box has all the tools to help you position and evaluate your layout. Options include rotating, positioning, resizing, and zooming. When you work with templates, additional tools optimize your workflow.

QUICKTIP When using the Print Layout dialog box, the image should be prepared to print. Access the image information from within Print Layout in the Edit menu. Also, set up your printer options the same way you would if you were printing from Paint Shop Pro's Print option.

Printing Multiple Images

Printing more than one image on a sheet of paper can be more cost efficient than using smaller photo paper cut to size. Paint Shop Pro makes it easy to arrange this. After you made your image selection either in the Browser or opened the images in Paint Shop Pro you can go into the Print Layout dialog box and simply drop and drag the images onto the workspace. Tools that help you arrange the images are accessible in the toolbar. An auto-arrange option positions the images automatically for the best layout.

FIGURE 16

Open images from the Print Layout dialog box

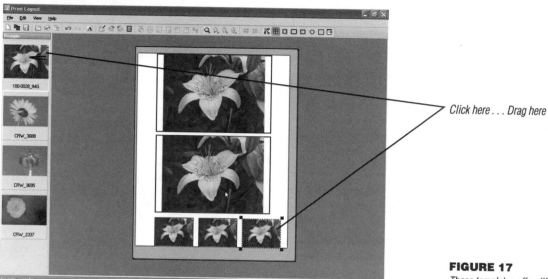

Click here . . . Drag here

FIGURE 17

These templates offer different layouts

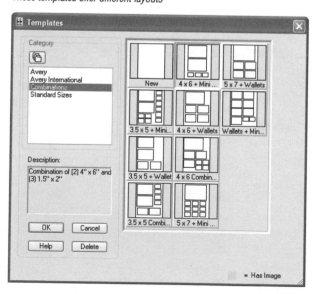

Using, Creating, and Saving Templates

Templates offer settings so you don't have to spend a lot of time tweaking things when you want to print special things. If you intend to print business cards or design labels, use the included templates, which are shown in Figure 17. The templates make printing on special papers such as precut business cards a snap.

You might come up with a layout that you would like to use again. For example, maybe you create scrapbook page layouts.

Instead of having to re-create the layout and arrange images again, save your layout as a template. You can save the template with or without images. The advantage of saving your template with images is that when printing the layout, you just load the template in the Print Layout dialog box.

FIGURE 18

Fine-tune images locations in the Print Layout dialog box

Center icon

Print icon

Click here . . . Drag here

1. Click **File**, then click **Print Layout**.

   The Print Layout dialog box appears, as shown in Figure 18.

2. Click **Open**, then open **PSP8-12.PSPImage**.

3. Click and drag the **image** onto your working space.

4. Click the **Center icon** [⊡].

5. Click the **Print icon** [⊘].

   The Print dialog box appears and your image prints.

6. Click the **Close Print Layout icon** [⊡].

   The Print Layout dialog box closes.

You used the Print Layout dialog box to print a single image.

Print multiple images

1. Open **PSP-8-6.PSPImage** and
   PSP-8-7.PSPImage.

2. Click **File**, then click **Print Layout**.

3. Click and drag each **image** to your working
   space.

4. Click the **Auto Arrange icon** 🖼.

   The images are automatically arranged on
   the workspace, as shown in Figure 19.

5. Check your printer settings by clicking the
   Print Setup icon 🖼.

6. Click **Print**.

7. Save your file.

*You printed multiple images on one sheet of paper,
saving time and resources.*

FIGURE 19
The auto-arranged images

Auto Arrange icon

Click here...Drag here

Click here...Drag here

FIGURE 20

Choose from these templates

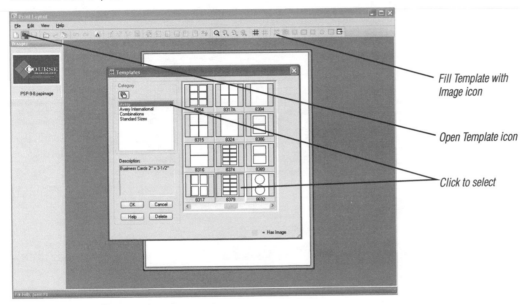

Fill Template with
Image icon

Open Template icon

Click to select

1. Click **View**, **Palettes**, then click **Browser** (if necessary).
2. Browse to **PSP-8-8.PSPImage**, right-click the **image**, and then select **Print Layout**.
3. Click the **Open Template icon** [icon].

   The Templates dialog box opens, as shown in Figure 20.
4. Click the **Avery category**, then select **8379**.

   Business Cards 2" × 3-1/2" appears in the Description box.
5. Click **OK**.

   > TIP The number on the templates corresponds to the Avery product number. Be sure to use the correct product for the selected template.
6. Click the **image** on the left side to select it.
7. Click the **Fill Template with Image icon** [icon].

   Every cell in the template is filled with the image.
8. Click **Print**.
9. Save your file.

You used a template and filled all the cells with the same image, saving time.

Save templates

1. Open **PSP8-9.PSPImage**, then open **PSP8-10.PSPImage**, then open **PSP8-11.PSPImage**.

2. Click **File**, then click **Print Layout**.

   The Print Layout dialog box displays the three images.

3. Click, then drag each **image** into the workspace, as shown in Figure 21.

4. Click **File**, then click **Save Template**.

   The Save dialog box opens, as shown in Figure 22.

5. Enter a name and description, then click **OK**.

   The dialog box closes and the new template saves.

6. Click **File**, then click **Close Print Layout**.

   The Print Layout dialog box closes and returns to the Paint Shop Pro interface.

You arranged images, then created and saved your own template for future use.

FIGURE 21
Drag images into the layout

Click here . . . Drag here

FIGURE 22
Enter details in the Save dialog box

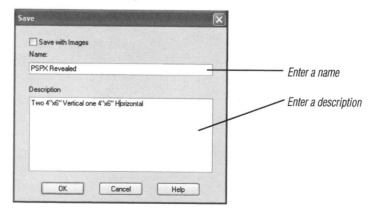

Enter a name

Enter a description

CHAPTER SUMMARY

This chapter familiarized you with color management, the Print dialog box, and the Print Layout dialog box. You also discovered the differences between ink jet and laser printers and how to decide which one you need. You learned that there are many special printing media and that they vary by performance and price. You also learned how to use a template and to create a contact sheet.

What You Have Learned:

- How to set up color management.
- How to choose printer, paper, and ink.
- How to print contact sheets.
- How to use the Print Layout function.
- How to use templates.

Key Terms

color depth Number of shades.

color management A way of matching colors from your input device to your computer monitor, then to the printed image.

color palette Specifies the number of colors but not the color spectrum.

color space A formula that determines how color displays and what color range your image can display.

contact sheet A single-page printout of many (or all) of the images in a folder.

dpi Dots per inch.

ICC profile Instructions that determine how and in what spectrum range colors are displayed.

image set Multiple images on a page.

image source A file's complete name, including location and format.

ppi Pixels per inch.

resample Affects an image's physical size, but it does not affect the resolution.

resize Changes resolution, affecting print size, but it does not alter the pixel or file size.

templates Preset layouts.

appendix A

As of the writing of this book, Paint Shop Pro X supports the following cameras, which in turn support RAW file format.

This list will be expanded in Paint Shop Pro X updates. Go to Help > Check for Updates to check for and download updates. As an alternate option, you may want to consider using RawShooter Essentials by Pixmantec if your camera is currently unsupported.

RawShooter Essentials comes with Paint Shop Pro X and can convert RAW files into TIFF files for editing in Paint Shop Pro X. You can also download RawShooter Essentials from the Free Trials page on www.corel.com. Note that RawShooter Essentials is supported by Pixmantec. See the Support menu at www.pixmantec.com for more information on Pixmantec support.

Canon	Fuji	Kodak	Konica Minolta	Nikon	Olympus	Pentax
EOS-1D Mark II	FinePix F700	DCS720X	DiMAGE 5	Coolpix 8800	C-5050	*ist D
10D	S5000Z	DCS760C	DiMAGE 7	D1H	C-5060	
20D	S7000Z	DCS760M	DiMAGE 7Hi	D1X	C-8080	
Rebel			DiMAGE 7i	D2H	E-1	
Rebel XT/350D			DiMAGE A1	D50	E-10	
300D			DiMAGE A2	D70	E-20	
Kiss				D100		
EOS Kiss Digital N						
D30						
D60						
PowerShot G3						
S30						
S40						
S50						
S60						
Pro1						

GLOSSARY

1-bit image An image that contains a maximum of two colors.

4-bit image An image that contains a maximum of 16 colors.

8-bit image An image that contains a maximum of 256 colors.

15-bit image An image that contains a maximum of 32,768 colors.

16-bit image An image that contains a maximum of 65,536 colors.

24-bit image An image that contains a maximum of 16,777,216 colors.

48-bit image An image that contains a maximum of 281,474,976,710,656 colors.

additive primary colors The red, green, and blue hues used alone, or in combination, to create other colors.

adjustment layer A layer that applies adjustments to the layer below it.

Airbrush tool The Paint Shop Pro tool that digitally sprays a fine mist of paint.

anti-alias The smoothing and blending of pixel edges to eliminate jagged edges on curved and slanted lines.

artifact Unwanted noise added to an image, usually by digital cameras, scanners, or high compression. *See* noise.

aspect ratio The ratio of width to height.

attribute Items that determine the appearance of text, such as font, bolding, underlining, italics, or size.

automatic rollups Floating palettes that appear as a mouse hovers over them, and disappear when the mouse moves away.

AutoSave A feature that periodically saves a version of your document.

background In graphics, the canvas on which graphics display.

background color The canvas color on which graphics display.

background layer The bottom layer automatically created in many images.

Backlighting filter A Paint Shop Pro filter that darkens the bright, overexposed areas of a photo.

batch processing A technique for applying the same photo-editing action to multiple images at the same time.

bevel A three-dimensional-looking edge on an object.

bit The smallest unit of digital information that a computer handles.

bitmapped image An image composed of small squares that are arranged in columns and rows. Each has a specific color and location. *See* pixel.

black The color formed by the absence of reflected or transmitted light.

blend To combine two layers or areas of an image. Often used to create a more realistic transition between image areas, as when retouching or compositing in image editing.

blur An effect that reduces areas of high contrast and softens the appearance of an image. Achieved by reducing the contrast between pixels that form the edges of any element within the photo.

BMP Abbreviation for bitmapped. File format.

brightness The amount of light or white color in an image. Usually represented by a percentage of 0, which is black, to 100, which is white.

Browser palette A Paint Shop Pro feature that allows you to preview multiple small images. Also known as simply Browser. *See* thumbnail.

Burn tool A Paint Shop Pro brush tool used to make areas darker.

calibration Correcting for the color differences in printer or monitor output when compared to the original image.

Camera RAW A file format that allows manipulation of unprocessed images captured by digital cameras.

canvas The area on which an image is displayed.

canvas size The size of the area within an image window.

cast An undesirable tinge of color in an image.

chromatic aberration An image defect, often seen as colored fringing around the edges of an object. Common in digital images. *See* fringing.

Clone tool A tool used to duplicate a portion of an image.

CMYK Abbreviation for cyan/magenta/yellow/black, which are the four standard ink colors used in printing.

color depth The number of bits of color information available for each pixel.

color model Any system for representing colors as ordered sets of numbers. Paint Shop Pro uses the most common color models, which are RGB, CMYK, and HSB.

Color palette Contains a selection of available colors and displays the current foreground and background colors.

Color Replacer tool A Paint Shop Pro tool that simplifies changing all of a selected color to another hue.

color swatch Small box of color, pattern, or texture located in the Materials palette that is used to select fill colors, patterns, and so on.

color picker Palette used to select colors to be used with most tools.

color wheel The circular color area from which you can create a custom color.

colorize An effect that converts an image or selection to a uniform hue and saturation while retaining its lightness.

composite In photography, an image composed of two or more parts of an image, taken either from a single photo or multiple photos.

composition The arrangement of the main subject, other objects in a scene, and/or the foreground and background.

compression A process applied to saved images, reducing file size. Some compression schemes, such as JPEG, discard image information.

contiguous Sharing an edge or boundary; touching. Connecting without a break.

Contract command Shrinks a selection by a specific number of pixels.

contrast The difference between the light and dark areas of an image.

crop To remove part of an image outside a selection.

DCNR Abbreviation for digital camera noise reducer. A tool that removes digital camera noise.

default The program's original settings, out of the box.

defloat To combine a floating selection into a layer. *See* merge.

deformation To change an image's appearance by moving data from one area to another.

density The ability of an object to stop or absorb light. The less light reflected or transmitted by an object, the higher its density.

depth-of-field The distance between the nearest and farthest objects in focus as seen by a camera lens. Depth-of-field determines how much of an image is in sharp focus, and what parts, such as the background, are out of focus.

desaturate To reduce the purity or vividness of a color, making it appear washed out or diluted.

diffusion The random distribution of grey tones, producing a fuzzy effect.

digital camera A camera that takes pictures and stores them in its memory or on a disk.

digital image An image made from tiny dots called pixels to form an image or photo.

docking To attach, or stick, a palette to any edge of your workspace.

distortion A change in the shape of an image.

dithering When a computer monitor substitutes a color and cannot display a similar color.

Dodge tool A Paint Shop Pro brush tool used to make areas lighter.

dpi Abbreviation for dots per inch. Related to the resolution of a printed image, is a unit that measures the number of dots that fit horizontally and vertically into a one-inch measure.

Dropper tool A Paint Shop Pro tool used to sample color from one part of an image, for painting, drawing, or filling elsewhere in the same or another image in the workspace.

effect A graphics function that modifies an image.

emboss An effect that causes the foreground of an image to appear raised from the background.

EXIF Abbreviation for Exchangeable Image File Format. A standard used by most digital cameras to record additional information such as shooting parameters, time, date, and rotation.

export The process of saving a file into a different format.

exposure In photography, the amount of light allowed to reach the film or sensor, determined by the intensity of the light, the amount admitted by the lens, and the shutter speed.

feather The process of fading an area on all edges of a selection. Measured in pixels.

file associations A method of determining which files open automatically.

file format The structure of a file that defines the way it is stored. Includes BMP, JPG, PNG, TIFF, GIF, JPEG, and PSP.

fill flash A Paint Shop Pro filter that allows you to lighten the darker, underexposed areas of a photo.

FireWire A fast, serial interface used by scanners, digital cameras, printers, and other devices. Also known as IEEE-1394.

flat An image with low contrast.

flatten Merging multiple layers into a single layer.

Flip command Reverses an image vertically.

Float command Temporarily separates a selection from an image or layer.

focus To adjust the lens to produce a sharp image.

foreground color The primary color for the painting and drawing tools.

format The shape and size of an image or text. Also, the method that a browser uses to display an image.

fringing The outer portions of an object or photo, usually with a ragged edge.

f-stop A camera lens aperture setting that corresponds to an f-number, which helps determine both exposure and depth-of-field.

Gamma A term given to the brightness values in an image. A numerical way of representing the contrast of an image.

Gamma correction A correction to the display contrast between an image and the monitor.

Gaussian blur A method of diffusing an image by calculating which pixels to blur, rather than blurring all pixels. Produces a random look.

GIF Abbreviation for a Graphic Interchange Format. File format whose images support transparency, but only 8-bit (256) color. Commonly used with Web graphics.

gradient fill A fill created by the gradual blending of different colors.

greyscale image An image that uses up to 256 shades of grey.

grid An equally spaced series of vertical and horizontal lines that help align objects.

handles Control points on vector objects that are used to edit the object.

hardness Determines the solidity of the brush tip.

high contrast A wide range of density in a print, negative, or other image. *See* density.

highlight The lightest part of an image.

histogram A graphical representation showing the distribution of color and light in an image.

History palette A Paint Shop Pro palette that tracks the changes you've made to an image during the current session.

HSL Abbreviation for hue/saturation/lightness. A method of defining colors in an image.

HTML Abbreviation for Hypertext Markup Language. A programming language that creates Web pages.

hue A color.

image window The window surrounding your image or canvas.

interpolation A technique used to create new pixels or to remove pixels when resizing or changing an image's resolution.

invert In image editing, to change an image into its negative: Black becomes white, white becomes black, dark grey becomes light grey, and so forth. Colors are also changed to the complementary color: Green becomes magenta, blue becomes yellow, and red becomes cyan.

jaggies Staircasing effect of lines that are not perfectly horizontal or vertical, caused by pixels that are too large to represent the line accurately.

JPEG Abbreviation for Joint Photographic Experts Group. *See* JPG.

JPG Abbreviation for Joint Photographic Experts Group. A file format that supports 24-bit (16,777,216) color, but not transparency. *See* lossy.

kerning The distance between text characters.

landscape The orientation of a page in which the longest dimension is horizontal. Also known as wide orientation. *See* portrait.

layer A level of an image that can be edited independently from the rest of the image.

layer stack The order in which the layers are arranged in the Layers palette.

Layers palette A Paint Shop Pro palette that lists each layer in the current image.

leading The distance between lines of text.

Levels A feature used to apply changes to image contrast and brightness.

logo A name or symbol that many businesses and organization use for easy recognition.

lossless compression An image-compression scheme that preserves all image detail. When the image is decompressed, it is identical to the original version. Includes TIFF, RAW, and so on.

lossy compression An image-compression scheme that creates smaller files by discarding information, which can affect quality

luminance A physical measurement of the brightness information in an image. Luminance is determined by the amount of grey.

Magic Wand tool A Paint Shop Pro selection tool that works by selecting content rather than defining edges.

mask A feature that allows some portion of an image to be hidden.

marquee A selection area. Also known as marching ants.

material A texture, pattern, color, or any combination of the three, used in the Materials palette to paint and/or fill.

Materials palette A Paint Shop Pro palette that contains the color swatches, textures, and patterns used in painting with the Brush tools or filling with the Flood Fill tool.

matte A non-glossy finish on a surface. Also denotes the surface surrounding a framed picture, between the picture itself and the frame; usually made from colored card. Also known as mat.

midtones Parts of an image with tones of an intermediate value. Paint Shop Pro allows you to manipulate midtones independently from highlights and shadows.

mirror An exact copy of an image placed in reverse of the copied image.

moiré An objectionable pattern in an image, usually generated by scanning newsprint or magazines.

monochrome Having a single color, plus white such as greyscale.

negative *See* invert.

negative image A photographic image in reverse, where light areas are dark and dark areas are light.

neutral color In image editing's RGB mode, a color in which red, green, and blue are present in equal amounts, producing a grey.

node A control point on a vector object.

noise A grainy appearance in an image.

object A single element in an image.

opacity The density of a color or layer.

overexposure A condition in which too much light reaches the film or sensor, producing a dense negative or a very bright/light print, slide, or digital image.

overview window Displays entire image when zooming in to a small area.

palette A collection of tools providing quick access to selected Paint Shop Pro elements.

panning Moving the camera so the object stays in the same position in the view finder.

panorama A broad view usually created from combining together several photographs.

path The guiding line for a vector object.

perspective The interpretation of how far the foreground and background appear to be separated from each other.

picture tubes Pictures you paint with.

pixel The smallest element in an image.

plug-in An outside, or third-party, filter that can be accessed from within Paint Shop Pro.

PNG Abbreviation for Portable Network Graphics. A file format designed for Web graphics. Supports both transparency and 24-bit (16,777,216) color.

portrait The orientation of a page in which the longest dimension is vertical, also called tall orientation. *See* landscape.

posterize Effect that replaces areas of continuous color tone with single colors.

ppi Abbreviation for pixels per inch. The number of pixels that can be displayed per inch, often used to refer to pixel resolution from a scanned image or on a monitor.

preferences The area in which each user maintains customized settings for Paint Shop Pro.

print preview The feature that allows you to view an image prior to printing it on paper.

PSP Abbreviation for Paint Shop Pro.

raster image A bitmapped image made up of pixels.

rasterize To convert a vector image to raster.

RAW An image file format offered by many digital cameras that includes all the unprocessed information captured by camera.

red eye A photographic effect that frequently occurs in photographs of humans and animals, giving a shiny or red appearance to eyes.

resample To change the size or resolution of an image. Resampling down discards pixel information; resampling

up adds pixel information through interpolation.

resize The ability to make an image or object larger or smaller.

resolution The number of pixels per inch (ppi); determines the size of an image when it's printed.

retouch To edit an image, most often to remove flaws or to create a new effect.

RGB Abbreviation for red/green/blue, the three primary colors that compose most images.

rotate To turn an image or object.

saturation The measure of an image's color strength.

scale To change the size of a piece of an image.

scanner A hardware device used to translate pictures and text into digital language that a computer can interpret.

script A file that holds recorded steps and is used to automate those steps.

selection The outline that appears around an area to be modified. *See* marquee.

sensor array The grid-like arrangement of the red, green, and blue-sensitive elements of a digital camera's solid state capture device.

shadow The darkest area of an image. Sometimes applied as an effect.

sharpen An effect that works by boosting contrast between adjacent pixels that form an edge.

skew A deformation that tilts an image along its horizontal or vertical axis.

SmartMedia A type of memory card storage for digital cameras and other computer devices.

smoothing To blur the boundaries between edges of an image, often to reduce a rough or jagged appearance.

soft focus A Paint Shop Pro feature that creates soft outlines.

soft proofing The ability to view, onscreen, what your image colors will look like when printed on a particular printer and or type of paper.

status bar The space at the bottom of an application window that displays help and image details.

stroke An outline of text.

telephoto A lens or lens setting that magnifies an image.

text banner Animations often seen on Web pages, usually at the top, that have text moving around.

threshold A predefined level that determines whether a pixel will be represented as black or white.

thumbnail A miniature version of an image.

TIFF Abbreviation for Tagged Image File Format. A file format that scanners commonly use.

tint A color with white added to it.

title bar The space at the top of an application window that has icons, the application name, and the active image's filename and format.

toggle To switch an item back and forth from one state to another. Frequently used to turn the display of layers on and off.

tolerance The range of color or tonal values selected with Paint Shop Pro tools.

toolbar Similar to a palette, a collection of frequently used tools that manage files and perform common menu functions.

tool options palette Displays options for the currently selected tool.

Tools palette Contains Paint Shop Pro's image-editing tools.

transparency An area that lacks color. Indicated in Paint Shop Pro by a checkerboard.

tripod A three-legged supporting stand used to hold the camera steady.

TWAIN A common computer interface among scanners, digital cameras, and computers.

underexposure A condition in which too little light reaches the film or sensor, producing a thin negative, a dark slide, a muddy-looking print, or a dark digital image.

undo The ability to reverse actions.

unsharp masking The process of increasing contrast between adjacent pixels in an image and boosting sharpness.

USB Abbreviation for Universal Service Bus. A high-speed serial communication method commonly used to connect digital cameras and other devices to a computer.

vector image An object that uses mathematics to create images. Can be edited, moved, and resized easily.

vignette Typically, a picture or portrait whose border fades into the surrounding color at its edges.

warp The process of distorting digital images.

watermark Information embedded to mark an image with copyright and author information.

Web browser A software program designed specifically to view Web pages on the Internet. Examples include Internet Explorer, Netscape Navigator, and Opera.

white The color formed by combining all the colors of light or by removing all colors.

white balance The adjustment of a digital camera to the color temperature of the light source.

white point In image editing, the lightest pixel in the image's highlight.

window *See* image window.

workspace The portion of the Paint Shop Pro window where you work on your image and contains all the palettes, toolbars, and any open images.

zoom The process of viewing an image in a larger or smaller magnification.

INDEX